BOOKS BY

Eda J. LeShan

————————————

THE CONSPIRACY AGAINST CHILDHOOD *1967*

HOW TO SURVIVE PARENTHOOD *1965*

THE
CONSPIRACY
AGAINST
CHILDHOOD

Eda J. LeShan

THE
CONSPIRACY
AGAINST
CHILDHOOD

ATHENEUM   NEW YORK

1968

For My Parents—who understood when I
said, "Let me be how I grow."

In Appreciation

The writing of a book depends on so many treasured riches in personal experiences and relationships that any attempt to list such times, places and people becomes a hopeless task. But some expression of thanks must be made to those most directly involved: to my daughter, Wendy, for having enough courage to protect her own childhood against parental forgetfulness and for keeping me on my toes; to my parents, Jean and Max Grossman, my grateful thanks not only for serving as conscientious first readers and for correcting my grammar, but also for contributing so much from the richness of their own experience; to Ruby Hogans, who calmly and comfortingly kept my house in order while listening to me pace the floor and swear when nothing was coming out of the typewriter; to Mae Jaffe, who serves ostensibly as my secretary but who incidentally offers enough moral support and patient encouragement to keep us both going through twenty revisions; and to Lawrence LeShan, whose part in this book goes far beyond any possible verbal expression of thanks, my partner in work and in life, who gives meaning to both beyond measure.

EDA J. LeSHAN

New York, 1967

Contents

1 The Conspiracy to Eliminate Childhood   3

2 The Computerized Baby: Or How to Teach Two-Year-Olds to Fail   43

3 From the Cradle to the Grade: This Montessori Madness   70

4 Getting into the Nursery School of Your Choice   90

5 Child's Play   111

6 The Healthy Aspects of Under-Achievement   135

7 Any Dope Can Have a High I.Q.   165

8 Are They Dropping Out or Are They Dropping In?   197

9 Life Is a Banquet: The Real Meaning of Human Excellence   237

10 Everybody's Children: The Stench of Social Neglect   278

11 "Let Me Be How I Grow": The Sacredness of Childhood   324

READING LIST   355

INDEX   357

THE
CONSPIRACY
AGAINST
CHILDHOOD

The Conspiracy to Eliminate Childhood

NEVER before in history, nowhere else in the world, has so much time, attention, energy and money been spent on the raising of children as here and now in the United States. Collectively, as a nation, we spend billions of dollars every year on services to children. Individually, as parents, we spend our adult lives more concerned with the welfare of our own children than with any other matter.

There are more child specialists—teachers, psychologists, psychiatrists, social workers, pediatricians, pediatric nurses, guidance counselors, school administrators, recreation leaders and parent educators—devoting their professional lives to the welfare of our children than in any other country in the world. Thousands of husbands and fathers spend as much as three hours a day commuting to their jobs for no other reason than to provide their children with suburban schools and play space, while equal numbers of wives and mothers find themselves cut off from the world of adults as they frenetically chauffeur their young from one "important experience" to another, providing them with ballet lessons, music lessons, art lessons, Scout meetings, Little League practice, parties, magic shows, puppet shows, visits to museums and zoos, trips to beaches, picnics and historical landmarks, sailing and swimming lessons, tennis and dancing instruction, plays for children, library story hours and the latest Walt Disney film. Our children own more toys, musical instruments, cars, boats, clothes, tape recorders, radios, phonographs, records, books, bicycles, skis, surf boards, swings, slides and sand boxes, TV sets, typewriters, sewing machines, chemistry sets and games than any children who have ever lived, anywhere in the world.

And yet, despite all this and much more—would *you* want to be a child today? Not *me!* It is my belief that this is a *terrible* time to be a child—and if this is so, despite the child-centeredness of our lives, then surely we must be doing *something* wrong!

The rate of child suicide mounts each year; an increasing number of children under the age of sixteen suffer from diseases associated with tension, such as ulcers, colitis, migraine, falling hair and asthma; some of our most indulged and privileged adolescents take drugs, steal, become involved in sex orgies; increasing numbers of American children are failing in their schoolwork. No matter how quickly psychiatric facilities are provided, they are unable to handle the demands for services for children and their families. Increasing numbers of parents each year find themselves feeling more and more helpless and hopeless about the behavior and attitudes they see developing in their children, for, despite all we do to try to make our children happy, more and more of them seem "shook up" and angry at us. *What* is going on?

Is it possible that, in spite of our obvious concern, we may be giving our children the wrong things? Is it possible that, despite professing our love for our children, we really have some quite negative feelings toward them? What is it that we want and expect from our children? What needs of ours do we ask them to satisfy? What is there about the world we live in that may interfere with the best of intentions and the soundest of goals?

Dr. James L. Hymes, Professor of Education and Chairman of the Childhood Education Department at the University of Maryland, speaking at a conference of The Play Schools Association, reported that in his work he thought he was hearing "sounds" of concern for children; he hears concern about science, math, testing, homework, TV teaching; he hears anxiety about drop-outs, school failure, college entrance, and job training in an automated world. He said:

> I must confess that I am not sure I am hearing right . . . for after a second, more careful look, I think I would have to say that almost no one seems to be thinking about children. . . . We are thinking about what these children will some day become. . . . We really like children best only when they stop being children and become like us—adults. We don't like the noise youngsters make. . . . We can't put up with their energy and we can't stand their messiness . . . what they want to know is often not at all what we want to teach them. . . . Adults can't be bothered with what is childhood's best way of learning—

through first-hand experience and through their own personal exploration. We seem more and more determined to get children who will sit, who will be quiet, who will produce . . . conform . . . give up childhood and become little adults.

It appears that in all our efforts to provide "advantages" we have actually produced the busiest, most competitive, highly pressured and over-organized generation of youngsters in our history—and possibly the unhappiest. We seem hell-bent on eliminating much of childhood.

The Play Schools Association published a booklet in 1963 which read in part:

> Being a child isn't what it used to be. Huck Finn is a delinquent, Tom Sawyer isn't working up to capacity, and Heidi is in foster care. Jim Hawkins is too young to be a cabin boy, and whoever would let Alice just sit there, doing nothing at all but dream through a summer afternoon? . . . Today's child often walks a tightrope between neglect and pressure. He gets too much stimulation or none at all. He may have forgotten how to play . . . parents worry whether children will excel before they have left kindergarten.

In the September 1961 issue of *Childhood Education,* Winifred E. Bain, in an article entitled "With Life So Long, Why Shorten Childhood?" wrote:

> It is well known . . . that life expectancy is longer than ever before in history. . . . Despite this vista of longevity, there is rife among many who "really want the best" for children the tendency to curtail the period of childhood, not by denial of vitamins and tender

loving care, but by haste toward getting them into adult patterns. By the age of seven, children are supposed to be fully ready to blast off into life space whereas by seventy-seven or even eighty-seven they will still be in orbit. . . . Adults have shorter work weeks, shorter working days, more . . . hobbies, more outdoor recreation than in previous times. . . . At the same time it is thought children must be put through their paces or they will not pass to the next grade or they will not match the achievements of children in other countries or, in the long look ahead, they will not be ready for the competition involved in serious, strenuous times to come.

It seems to me that our impatience with and intolerance of the growing years of childhood reflect a climate of feeling that is violently anti-child. For a variety of complex reasons this is a time in which it is increasingly difficult for each of us to truly nurture our young—and they know it. Many of us have a deep and profound sense of failure; we feel we are being swept along in a flood of forces over which we seem to have no control.

During the years when I was growing up, there was a climate of fresh hope and idealism, a passionate faith in human possibilities. The revolution in our psychological insights and the impact of the progressive-education movement were creating a new respect for childhood. The growing years were vitally important, we were discovering, and there were ways in which we could help children grow well. As we learned more and more about the significance of childhood experiences, we wanted to protect and nurture the unique qualities of each growing person. Learning could be fun; children could be taught the rules of civilized living without fear of punishment; by helping children understand their feelings, we could protect them from the painful and crippling neuroses we were learning so much about. There was an air of warm protectiveness toward children as well as a sense of great confidence that we would be able to guide children in such a way that they would become compassionate, responsible citizens, capable of a deeper humanity, fulfilling themselves more creatively.

I have been studying child development, teaching, and working with children, parents and teachers for about twenty-five years. During most of this time I have felt excited and optimistic; it seemed to me that we were making real progress in finding new and better ways to raise our children, to help them grow toward a healthier and more creative adulthood than had ever been possible before. In the past five or ten years I have gradually found myself becoming uncertain and frightened; I have had the uneasy and disturbing feeling that we have been losing ground we had been gaining.

I know there is always the danger of romanticizing the past. When I was a little girl, we had a painting in our living room of a fair-haired young boy lying in a green pasture, gazing at the clear blue sky while dreamily chewing on a piece of grass. I still recall the lovely sense of peace and quiet that the picture evoked, and I know that it is all too easy to create other images of the same kind: Ye Olde Family Farm with the little children at play, the charming deference and innocence of the children in *Life with Father* or *Ah, Wilderness*, Marmee and her *Little Women*, Tom Sawyer and his non-union painters. To look back from the 1960's to almost any other time in our history is to do so with some degree of nostalgia and some tendency to see what one wishes to see: wide-open spaces, an easygoing and relaxed way of life, simple goodness and joy in simple pleasures—the bucolic life in all its glorious illusions!

But I do not think I have let myself judge a child's world today by such a yardstick. There are other equally vivid memories and images: the childhood that Charles Dickens recorded for us, or the knowledge one has of past plagues, famines and wars; the ignorance that led to unspeakable cruelties; the hardships almost beyond our comprehension in many periods of human history. What can be so bad about childhood today by comparison with the burning of fifteen-year-old "witches" or of children of ten working sixteen hours a day, six days a week, in factories and coal mines? If there are those among us who despair about childhood today, it is not because we long for something in the past, but rather that we had hoped for so much in our own time. As a parent and as an educator I would like to share with other parents and educators my deep concern, my sense of disillusion, my uneasiness about our children.

There is too frequently today a tense and frantic quality in our relationships with our children. We seem often to have forgotten how to be, or afraid of acting like, parents— afraid of guiding and controlling our children's behavior in order for them to become increasingly responsible human beings with a sense of dignity and purpose in life. We do things for them that they should be doing for themselves, such as driving them to school when they ought to walk or apologizing to Grandma about how busy they are when they should have written a thank-you note for the birthday present. On the other hand, we make them do things for which they are totally unready, such as learning numbers and letters at two and a half.

We push hard for a kind of pseudo-maturity on the one hand, and on the other we seem often to be drowning our children in material comforts. We respond to every "I want" with an alacrity that is dear to the hearts of advertisers and manufacturers. We buy the rainbow-colored cereal treat that promises some miraculous new toy in every package, even though we know that the cereal may not be to the child's taste and may never be eaten and that the promised toy will break in a day. We buy the expensive tape recorder that our teen-ager is "desperate" to have, knowing full well that the same pleas preceded the purchase of the guitar, the sewing machine and the typewriter that now lie broken and gathering dust at the bottom of the closet. Our indulgence about possessions is matched only by our permissiveness about behavior; though we do not really consider it appropriate for twelve-year-olds to be catapulted into an unnatural social sophistication, we give in when a daughter screams that *everybody* is going to a dance; we cannot really believe for one moment that our son will benefit from being permitted to dress like a derelict at Dad's birthday party, but after a somewhat feeble and tentative objection, we give in. All too often our children say what they please, dress as they please and seem to have more freedom than adults; we permit them to be rude, thoughtless and irresponsible and to express anger in ways that would appall us among any group of adults. On the other hand, especially in the area of learning, we can be far more demanding of our children than of ourselves. We come home at the end of a day's work, take off our shoes, have a drink and spend the evening talking, reading or watching TV; our children arrive home after a six- to eight-hour day at school and put in four more hours on homework.

An example of the way in which we give on the one hand and demand on the other was brought home to me vividly in talking with the mother of a fifteen-year-old boy. Steve has been to Europe, he has gone to expensive camps and schools, he has a hi-fi set that is worth over $1,000 and next year his parents have promised him a car for his birthday. He gets a weekly allowance of $10 and complains that this isn't enough for his week-end dates at discothèques, movies and coffeehouses. Having given him the freedom to come and go over week ends and to stay out as late as he pleases on Saturday nights, his parents were recently shocked and dismayed to discover that some of his week-end forays had involved experimenting with the use of marijuana. The only area in his life over which his family has exerted severe and continuing pressure has been in relation to his school grades. He does quite well in some subjects, but he is having great difficulty with math and science. He is tutored two evenings a week, and he will be going to summer school; he knows that he is a terrible disappointment to his parents, who want him to go to an Ivy League college. He has come to think of himself as stupid, and he jokingly commented at dinner one night, "If I work hard, I should graduate from high school in about three hundred years!" His younger brother, an A student, is the darling of the family, and Steve, despite all the privileges and comforts of his life, is becoming more and more hopeless about his future. He has everything he does not need and little of what he needs most—self-esteem and confidence in his ability to grow and learn.

We seem to have two entirely separate sets of criteria for judging children and adults. We are far more tolerant of our friends, relatives and co-workers when it comes to an appreciation of their worth as individuals. As adults, we admire each other for whatever narrow range of talents each of us may have—but we are quite insistent that our children should excel in everything. We watch a comedian perform, and we roar with laughter; the fact that he left school after third grade does not lessen our admiration—it seems entirely irrelevant. We admire the self-made businessman who started out as a messenger boy and now, owning his own factory, has amassed a sizable fortune in ladies' coats and suits; the fact that he has not read a book in years does not bother us at all ("Did you *see* that *swimming pool?*") We find ourselves deeply moved and inspired by a poem, a story, a painting or a symphony, and it never occurs to us to wonder if the creative artist who has provided this pleasure ever passed a course in geometry. Any evidence of similarly special inclinations, of narrow interests or talents on the part of our children keeps us awake nights; we seem to have the idea that children and adults are two separate species. We like grown-ups who are shy, and we also like people who are gay at parties; we respect some adults who work wonderfully in groups and others who are veritable recluses; we enjoy remarkable athletes who have never seen or read a Shakespeare play, and we admire intellectuals who never walk a block if they can avoid it. In our adult world we accept and enjoy differences—but when we see exactly the same human qualities in our children, we are unnerved. Let any child of ours prefer sitting alone and listening to classical music to playing ball with the neighborhood kids, let any child of ours get 20 per cent in a math test and 95 per cent in an English exam—and we run frantically for the nearest guidance counselor.

There is no area in which our discontent, our impatience with growth shows up more clearly than in our attitudes toward learning. In one suburban school system the superintendent of schools requested all teachers to ask the children, "What would your parents do if they could change you in some way?" The large majority answered, "Make me smarter." Only one child said, "They like me the way I am."

At a dinner party my husband sat next to a woman who said that her eleven-year-old son was not at all interested in his schoolwork and was just "getting by." She asked my husband what she could do about the situation, and when my husband asked, "What *is* he interested in?" she replied, "His great passion is baseball—but that isn't going to get him into college!" When my husband tried to reassure her that very few eleven-year-olds were normally interested in college, she confessed, "Just the same, every night I go into his room after he's asleep and I whisper, 'I want to be a lawyer, I want to be a lawyer'; it's sort of a homemade 'sleep-suggestion' program." The conversation came to an abrupt conclusion when her dinner partner replied, "Well, that's a pretty good way to make sure he'll want to be a truck driver!"

College hysteria is a disease that has reached epidemic proportions in this country. Early spring has become a disaster season among families of high-school seniors waiting to hear from admissions offices; and when the inevitable disappointments come, one would think that the world had come to an end. One evening when I called a friend, she said, "I'm utterly exhausted. I've been working on Charles' future plans." I had no idea what she meant until she explained that her son, a high-school junior, wanted to apply to two small liberal-arts colleges in the midwest and that she had spent the whole evening arguing with him. "But those colleges sound fine to me," I said naively, "I should think Charles could be happy and do well at either one of them— what's bothering you?" "What's bothering me has nothing to do with being sensible," she answered tartly, "I want him to go to Harvard, *that's* what."

I was shocked when I met a father who told me that he did not have any pictures of his children in his wallet but that he *did* carry their report cards around with him! We are in such a rush to educate our children that department stores are now selling special pillowcases and towels for children that say PLEASE TEACH ME TO READ—and then provide imprinted letters, numbers, words and clocks for telling time. A book that suggested that we start reading readiness at ten months sold 75,000 copies in a short time. Another book that promised to *Give Your Child a Superior Mind* gave careful instructions which would help a child read 150 words a minute, add, subtract, multiply and divide, understand fractions and simple algebra, all before the age of five. All a parent had to do was "make lessons a rigid part of the child's daily schedule, starting at 30 months of age."

A million-dollar project was announced in one school system, involving the use of typewriters that can speak, read aloud, show pictures, take dictation and play games. Each machine costs $30,000 and will be used to help teach reading, writing and other subjects to children from four to ten years of age. A recent headline in a magazine asked, "Is Your Baby Reading Good Books?" Research centers all over the United States are operating laboratories to study ways for accelerating academic learning. In an article in

The New York Times Magazine ("Two Year Olds Are Very Smart," September 6, 1964), Ronald Gross reports: "Professor Robert Karplus, a bespectacled University of California physicist . . . is showing that second-and-third-graders can engage in original inquiry concerning "physical systems, equilibrium, interaction and simple relativity.' "

An experimental school in Washington, D.C., is teaching reading, literature, composition, speech, spelling, grammar, penmanship, principles of geometry, science, geography and history in kindergarten. Martin Tolchin, in an article entitled "Children Under Pressure" in *The New York Times Magazine* (June 18, 1961), reported:

> The heat is on. The mad scramble for fame and fortune begins long before kindergarten. The youngster who has failed to distinguish himself by junior high school is just about out of the running. . . . In this high pressure atmosphere it is understandable that many parents have a gnawing sense of insecurity about how their youngsters "measure up." . . . Specialists who work with children are beginning to see the effects of all this parental anxiety. School principals and counselors report mounting tensions in children. In at least one school system tranquilizers are said to be part of the daily diet of a high percentage of the kindergarten class.

A mother wrote me recently:

> I am really frightened by what I see happening to my children. We live in a middle class area with high pressure parents who are pushing their children unmerci-

fully. Any child who isn't reading "two years above grade level" feels like a moron. Last year a high school girl died of colitis. She was an honor student, but nothing she did was ever enough. Because she was talented her parents made her feel that she could never let up for a single minute. I have a friend whose 14-year-old has begun to lose all her hair. The doctor says it's tension, so they took her out of the advanced class. Her hair stopped falling out, but now she gets nauseous every morning before school—she's ashamed to admit that she couldn't take the pace, in front of the other kids. And that isn't the only kind of pressure. A junior high school in our neighborhood just announced that all the 7th graders going to the school dances had to go in couples—the girls with escorts, no one coming stag. In other words, the school itself is insisting on a dating pattern for 12 and 13-year-olds. I don't know where it will end. My brilliant son does nothing but work, my normally intelligent daughters who do average work are convinced that they are feeble-minded.

What we see developing is an attempt to view childhood, growing and learning in what we consider to be the terms of modern science. We live in an era in which science and technology represent a new religion, a road to salvation. It is quite natural that we should be impressed by our technological progress. It has provided us with benefits in many areas of life; it has solved problems of human survival—if we wanted to, we now know enough to provide food, clothing and shelter for all the people who populate our planet. Science has increased our life span, prevented and cured hundreds of diseases, given us material comforts undreamed of a century ago. It is pretty impressive to realize that scientific research has produced the telephone, radio, TV, the automobile, the automatic dishwasher and washing machine, airplanes, rockets, atomic power, movies, artificial hearts, X-ray and ten thousand other miracles, all in less than a hundred years. But our current problem is that, because we are so giddy with the successes of modern technology, we have tried to apply it to areas in which it serves no useful purpose. Unfortunately technology and scientific research have fostered a new way of looking at human beings. We find ourselves in a world of engineers; of technically and scientifically trained people who view the human brain simply as a machine and who seek to design our environment, invent machinery for educating our young, and extract from us all a rigid, antiseptic view of human life and growth.

The following news item appeared in *Today's Child*, November 1966;

JERSEY CITY, N.J.—School children join the TGIF Club (Thank God It's Friday) too young and it often turns out to be a lifetime membership, Dr. Jeanette Veatch, prof. of English at Jersey City State Teachers College, told a conference on elementary school teaching at State Univ. of Iowa. One reason children learn early to meet Monday mornings with regret and Friday afternoons with rejoicing is that teachers and administrators place too much reliance on machines and equipment in the classroom, she said, stating that 75% of government allocations to schools is spent on visual aids, tape recorders and shelves of workbooks. "Teaching is a human act and comes from humans, not ma-

chines," says Dr. Veatch. "Humans learn best from
other humans." Workbooks help teachers kill time, she
observed, but also kill children's joy of learning.

The tragedy of the scientific revolution seems to me to be
that we may lose more than we have gained. In our worthy
struggle to know, to understand our own nature, we have
used methods and procedures that are entirely inappropriate in human affairs and that have alienated us from our
own humanity.

An exaggerated scientific view of life encourages a splitting of thinking and feeling; it invites us to separate facts
from values and seduces us into believing that the human
mind is merely a fancy complicated computer. We begin to
see vast possibilities for exploiting the human mind, and of
course, the place to start is in the education of our children.

The arguments for a computer approach to education are
dangerously convincing. Scientific experimentation has convinced many educators and psychologists that children *do*
have capacities for learning that have not been tapped. It is
possible to teach many children a great deal more than we
have in the past during the first few years of school, and at
first glance such a procedure seems efficient and sensible.
We are constantly told that our children will grow up in a
world where the amount of knowledge and information
available and necessary to them is increasing by geometric
progression; if we are to provide all this within the growing
years, we will have to increase the rate of learning.

As a people who have always admired machines and efficiency, we are easily persuaded to the point of view that we
can be more efficient in educating our young if we will use
the technological know-how now available, such as teach-

ing machines. The theory seems pretty good—until you try to relate all this to children.

In his book *How Children Fail* (Pitman Pub. Co.), John Holt reports that more and more children are failing in school.

> They fail because they are afraid. . . . They are afraid, above all else, of failing, of disappointing or displeasing the many anxious adults around them, whose limitless hopes and expectations for them hang over their heads like a cloud. . . . Schools give every encouragement to *producers,* the kids whose idea is to get the "right answers" by any and all means. . . . These schools are often very discouraging places for *thinkers.* . . . The expectation and fear of failure, if strong enough, may lead children to act and think in a special way . . . like an animal fleeing danger—go like the wind, don't look back, remember where that danger was, and stay away from it.

Rather than encouraging a love of learning, we seem to be making many of our children more and more terrified of school. What impresses me so much is that it was not always thus—at least not in the milieu in which I grew up and which I thought at the time was the "wave of the future." This was the progressive-education movement, and it *did* have a significant impact on American education for quite a few years; it is in rapid decline at the present time—and it seems to me that this fact demonstrates quite clearly our changing attitudes toward childhood.

A high-school teacher recently asked a group of his students what it was about a noisy, crowded discothèque that they liked so much. They responded by saying that it was a place where they could be "themselves" and where they could "forget about school." This struck me because I attended one of the pioneer experimental schools—one of the schools that was related to the philosophy exemplified by John Dewey and other educators of the early 1900's, who developed the strange notion that school might be the place where children *could* be "themselves," where learning might be fun!

The progressive-education movement had some bugs in it, of course; no new idea is perfect—if it has worth, it must be developed and refined over a long period of time. While it is true that some of the ideas of progressive educators were taken over by public education in general, we never really gave the movement a chance; by the time we had realized that children needed somewhat more and stricter external controls and were not able to handle quite as much free choice as they were first given, by the time we had realized that *some* drill in skills must go along with "learning projects"—it was almost all over. There were some unhappy and unsuccessful children in progressive schools, there were some children who got into trouble; there were some poor teachers and administrators, there were some serious errors in judgment. But with it all, the majority of educators knew they had struck gold; children looked forward to coming to school and hated to leave; rare and wonderful talents were discovered and nurtured; the encouragement to express oneself and be oneself was bringing rich rewards in creativity. And what is most fascinating of all —children *were learning*.

However, despite the evidence that progressive education was effective, there were enough weaknesses in it to permit devastating attacks. In addition, the process required teachers' training and dedication that were difficult and demanding. Actually, the public schools did take over many of the ideas and practices of the earlier experimental schools, but never since has there been that degree of wholehearted, child-centered, child-loving quality in classroom teaching—and because it nurtured me so well, I feel the loss deeply. There was a sense of trust between teacher and student that was precious indeed. Irrespective of the subject matter, the way a child learned, we then believed, was by being exposed to a learned and learning mind, a person who could encourage the quest for knowledge, a person who could infect a child with his own love of ideas.

Most of the original experimental private schools have now become college-preparatory schools. In view of the tremendous numbers of applications and with the increasing parental panic about getting children into "good colleges," entrance requirements have become increasingly selective. Slowly but surely the character of these schools has shifted from eagerness to give special opportunities to *all* kinds of children, with *all* kinds of strengths and weaknesses to adequacy to handle only the student with superior over-all intellectual ability. There are still some private schools across the country that continue to promote progressive educational techniques, but they are few. There are still some public-school systems that show the influence of the earlier years of experimentation, but these are being bombarded by new problems of population explosion, the special needs of large numbers of culturally or socially deprived children, and by increasing pressures for college-directed education. With more and more rigid and inflexible educational goals for children, it is sad but true that very few of our children can be provided with the kind of school experience I had.

Progressive education—in fact, education in general—was greatly concerned with moral values in times past; the goal was not to teach mere facts, but to help young people to become concerned and responsible citizens. If you look through some of the statements of educational goals written by boards of education in the past, you will find that on almost every list the first items had to do with the moral education of the young—helping a child to live well in the world with other people. A special commission of The National Education Association in 1918 prepared a statement of goals called "Purposes of the School." It listed these items, in this order:

1. Provide child with a sense of ethics, ethical behavior in human relationships.
2. Teach child responsibility for his own health; independence in self care.
3. Help child towards sensitivity to the responsibilities of citizenship.
4. Mastery of skills, teaching fundamental processes, the three R's.
5. Learn to use leisure time well.
6. Encourage worthy human relationships, ability to function within family group.
7. It is appropriate to teach children to make a living.

In 1960 the Educational Policies Committee of The National Education Association, with John Fischer (the President of Teachers College, Columbia University) as Chairman, produced the following document to supersede the 1918 version. This one was succinct and to the point:

The central purpose of the schools is to develop the rational powers of man. The basic subjects for thinking and reasoning: English, Math, Science and History.

So much for the frills of an ethical life!

In the progressive school that I attended a great deal of time was spent in study and discussion of social issues and moral values. Great emphasis was placed on our learning to work with others—to use our individual talents in such a way that we could enrich each other's experiences. We felt that it was just as important to learn to appreciate and respect each other, to live sensitively and compassionately and to take responsibility for our own behavior as it was to learn the multiplication tables or to memorize the capitals of each state.

It is one of the great and confusing ironies of life that although the moral education of children becomes increasingly important as society becomes more complex, as change becomes more and more rapid and as the family finds it more and more difficult to serve as the interpreter of change and uncertainty, that we seem to be doing less and less of this kind of teaching. In a more stable society it is not as difficult for parents to hand down unchanging values to their children. In small, cohesive, homogenous communities, where little change occurred from generation to generation, it was not too difficult to educate children about their place in society, what they could expect, what would be expected of them, what was considered right and wrong. Now we find ourselves in a time of enormously rapid transition. There are no stable values, no clear and consistent attitudes about what is good or bad, right or wrong. There is less and less communication between generations. There is so much freedom and so much confusion—old institutions such as the church are themselves in such turmoil that neither child nor adult can really find answers for the dilemmas of life. And it is just at such a time that the schools, the institutions of education, focus on the teaching of skills, seeming to imply that values will have to take care of themselves.

Where today's children need more help than any children ever did before in coming to terms with all the free choices they must make, when social standards and moral issues are in a state of upheaval and change, it would seem logical that schools would find it necessary to spend more time than ever before on helping young people examine and come to terms with serious social issues; instead we find ourselves curtailing these matters, viewing them as unnecessary frills. At a time when marriage, family life and parenthood seem most threatened by increasing divorce rates, uncertainty and instability, rather than increasing the opportunities for children and young people to get some guidance and direction in facing their own futures as men and women and citizens of a complex and frightening world, we are instead focusing increasing amounts of our time and attention on academic skills. The basic rationale of our current approach to education is that society is dependent on technology, on scientific know-how. Because so much of modern life is devoted to the development and use of machines, and because so much of our progress in space research and other fields involving future expansion and development is based on the physical sciences, we have arrived at the conclusion that the only way we can survive is by expanding our knowledge in math, engineering and physics.

The truth of the matter is that we cannot survive unless people know more about social interaction, sociology, ethics and civics and learn to respect different ways of thinking and behaving.

What we need more crucially than ever before is basic education in learning to live with ourselves and others. Most fields of science have become so highly specialized that we cannot possibly all be trained to understand them; in one lifetime we can learn only a small part of the available knowledge. But what we all *must* learn, if we are to survive, is how we can use our increasing technological knowledge for the good of mankind rather than for its destruction.

Symbolic of the current inclination to turn away from the complex challenges of modern life is the fact that in Harlem, a veritable laboratory of the current social issues that face our society, the prize-winning design for a modern elementary school building was one that had no windows at all! It had air conditioning, teaching machines, special tutors, all the latest advances in technological equipment and know-how—but no new or imaginative resources for helping the children face the massive and overwhelming problems of the neighborhood. Turned inward on its windowless self, it could "see no evil, speak no evil, hear no evil."

There are literally thousands of high schools in all our big cities, housing 3,000 to 5,000 young people, in which every student is exposed to intimate first-hand knowledge of homosexuality and lesbianism, out-of-wedlock pregnancies, the use of heroin and marijuana, violence and crime, family disintegration, racial prejudice, school failure and school drop-outs, truancy, and cheating—yet almost none of these schools has a dynamic or meaningful program for helping the students deal with these realities of their daily lives. There are few, if any, opportunities for discussion of these issues, there are no courses of study to help the students deal with these forces in their lives, there is no opportunity for learning about the self or learning to live in a world in which one is faced with unbelievably difficult human problems. We concern ourselves instead with devising "academic tracks," rules and regulations for handling disciplinary problems, and somehow or other finding new and better ways of cramming facts into reluctant and preoccupied heads. In the face of such pressures, when much of the curriculum should be scrapped and teaching methods should be changed, where there should be small discussion groups and personnel equipped for conducting classes in human relations, we are instead providing more teaching machines. We just go right on as if nothing at all had happened, talking about how to teach children to learn more facts faster.

There is surely no internal domestic problem in the United States more pressing and serious than that of integration. The New York *Post* of October 14, 1957, carried a news item about a Norwegian-born reporter living in Missouri who arranged a discussion among Negro and white children involved in the Little Rock, Arkansas, school-integration crisis. One of the white girls who attended this discussion had just a short time before thrown her arms around Governor Orville Faubus, thanking him for trying to stop the integration of her high school. The discussion with the reporter lasted about two hours, both Negro and white youngsters expressing the most candid attitudes and feelings, opinions and fears. The white students talked about their fears of intermarriage, of too many Negroes coming into the school all at once and taking it over. The Negroes said that high schools were not supposed to be marriage bureaus; they expressed their feelings about being led into school by soldiers, of their real and terrible fears of being physically attacked by white mobs. By the end of the discussion both Negro and white participants agreed that they had never in their lives been confronted in this way by the real feelings of each group, that the confrontation made a difference and that they wished such discussions could take place within the school. I do not remember the name of the reporter—he or she had the makings of a great teacher—but the point is that this approach is a rarity to-day; it is a classic example of how we attempt to leave the moral and social issues outside the classroom and suggests that this kind of concern and action has far more to do with the strength of a democratic society than do high test scores.

Our preoccupation with scholastic achievement at the expense of moral values is easy to substantiate by hundreds of examples of delinquent and anti-social behavior on the part of some of our most intellectually gifted students. Typical of these was the report in *The New York Times* of May 29, 1966, of a shocking situation in a southern city. It seems that about ten children (affluent, with an average I.Q. of 150, considered to be at the genius level) had formed a gang and called themselves "The Brain Trust." They had stolen chemical ingredients, mostly from the high-school science laboratory, to manufacture plastic bombs, LSD and dynamite. They had been responsible for about seventy burglaries, and they were reported to have had some fantastic schemes, including blowing up a bank. The sons of highly respected citizens—teachers, newspaper edi-

tors and successful businessmen—they were attending a na-
tionally known experimental high school, ungraded, with
an eleven-month school year. Its over 4,000 carefully selected students from elementary school through junior college were encouraged to advance at their own rate. The
boys involved were by and large "loners"—they did not
socialize with many other students, and all considered themselves part of an intellectual elite. Bored, they decided to
test themselves, to see what they could get away with. One
boy was quoted as saying that the group did not have any
moral principles, that they were stealing for no other reason
than a "thrill and a challenge." Some of the stolen chemicals
were used by two of the boys in experiments to gain West-
inghouse college scholarships. A boy who manufactured a
nerve gas said, "We made various uses of these compounds
which appealed to our sensationalism." When asked why
they committed these acts, one boy said that he did not
really know—they had not taken themselves very seriously.
One boy with a $10,000 bank account who was involved in
the burglaries and who was making hand grenades, planned
to study nuclear chemistry in college the following year,
and he had already studied at Columbia University in a
summer program for gifted students under the sponsorship
of the National Science Foundation.

Our most serious international problem has to do with
the control of nuclear weapons. If ever a citizenry with a
sense of moral responsibility in the use of our scientific
knowledge was needed, it is surely right now; and yet,
while we are willing to teach our most brilliant youngsters
the facts of science that can be used for our destruction, we
seem unconcerned about the kinds of human beings whom
we allow to acquire this knowledge. What is so frightening

is that, unlike laboratory rats which researchers can throw away if an experiment fails, we are dealing with children who must grow up and live in this world, with themselves and with others—and if our experimentation is one-sided, blindly and arrogantly over-confident in the power of technological knowledge, the destruction may be beyond our comprehension.

A de-humanizing society must take the consequences of what it does. Computer-like men are more likely to pull the wrong switches and blow up the human race than the kind of human being who is taught to think and to feel, to make his own judgments and to live in a framework of moral and ethical concern for himself and his fellow men. Such well-rounded human beings can only reach the maturity of arriving at responsible purposes when they are allowed to grow slowly and well in *every* aspect of life—understanding their feelings and emotional needs, sensing that *all* of life is an adventure, not merely a collection of factual information, but also an experience of warmth and love and a concern for all people everywhere. A genuine sense of self grows slowly, over many years of living. Intellectual development alone cannot provide the basic sense that it is good to be alive and human.

We are making a fetish, a cult, of mental gymnastics—mind all by itself, not in association with other human qualities. It is a dangerous game. Everything we know about human development and experience tells us that we are in serious trouble when we separate intellect from such emotional and social attributes as a capacity for warmth and compassion, imagination, a capacity for reflection, creativity, humor and relatedness to others. The use of teaching machines; the status value given to objective examinations;

team teaching in elementary schools, which places emphasis on the subject rather than on the young child's relationship with a teaching *person;* research on teaching two-year-olds to read; the return to an over-valuation of certain specific subjects as crucial to learning in preference to the exploration of ideas—all symbolize a depersonalizing of children and seeming indifference to many important aspects of personality growth and development.

It is no accident that the number of school failures is increasing. It is no accident that some of our most able college students are becoming hedonistic, disillusioned, oriented toward escape, toward the immediate gratification of every infantile wish or impulse. These most erudite young people who *do* get into the colleges of their choice, who do *brilliantly* on exams, who seem to represent our cultural ideal in every respect, are often promiscuous, are eager to experiment with the use of dangerous drugs, and are frequently incapable of making mature judgments about their personal lives and their vocational plans.

The change in our attitudes toward learning is more than simply a symptom of a mechanistic view of life and growth. Other social forces have also played a part. At the same time that we have seen such a widespread and sweeping faith in science and technology we have also seen a disillusionment with earlier beliefs. The current impact of the mechanistic view of man could never have been so overwhelming, unless an earlier view of life had not been profoundly challenged.

Psychology and education are not the only areas in which an earlier idealistic fervor has been replaced by discontent and disappointment. In a much more general sense the Age of Innocence is dead. From the seventeenth to the twentieth century there was a growing faith in human progress and in the perfectibility of man. Two awful world wars, and the appalling twentieth-century evidence of the depths of inhumanity to which we are far from immune despite all our knowledge and all our faith in the potential of "rational man," have left us deeply disillusioned.

In reviewing *Justice in Jerusalem* by Gideon Hausner in *The New York Times Book Review* (May 29, 1966), Mrs. Barbara Tuchman, author of *The Proud Tower*, wrote:

"[w]hat we are confronting here is the soul of man in the 20th century. "The Terrible Twentieth," it was called by Winston Churchill. Until it opened, the idea of progress had been the most firmly held conviction of the 19th century. Man believed himself both improvable and improving. Then, twice in 25 years, or in the space of one generation, came the . . . plunge into world war, accompanied the second time by the Germans' . . . killing—pursued with fanatic zeal for more than five years amidst the simultaneous demands of foreign war—of six million people. . . . For sheer size and deliberate intent, this episode of man's inhumanity to man was unprecedented . . . in vitiating our idea of human progress, the experience inflicted a moral damage upon mankind. It scarred man's image of himself horribly . . . a moral barrier like the sound barrier was broken through, with the result that man, at this moment in history, may no longer believe in his capacity to be good or in the social pattern that once contained him. Disillusioned and without certainty or sense of direction, he appears afflicted and fascinated by self-disgust. . . .

If we have suffered from the events of human history, we also suffer from the effects of the machine on modern life. Machines have given us factories and cities; industrialization and urbanization have crowded us together so that we live too close to each other; science and technology have made us healthier and more long-lived, resulting in a population explosion, which adds to our sense of being too crowded on this planet. We have become increasingly separated from the earth as we destroy our forests and live on concrete. The automobile endangers our lives on the streets and spews forth waste products that poison the air we breathe. In our cities we live in the midst of factories that pollute our air and our water. We are surrounded by the sounds of a mechanized world, and the noise is often beyond endurance.

Every generation of parents has had to try to protect its children from various kinds of hazards—plague or volcanic eruptions or famine or flood and fire. We like to think that our world is in some ways less dangerous to the physical well-being of our children, and perhaps it is—but the inconveniences and hazards are many, though different. Perhaps one of our problems in child raising, is that we have been led to believe that we were creating a fine world for our children to grow up in—that science and technology were only going to benefit us—and that we believed it. Science and technology have given us many benefits, but they have also created new problems. We pay a price for indoor plumbing, antibiotics and electricity. It is *not* so easy or so safe to raise children today; the physical environment simply offers us new and different problems.

Machines send us letters, talk to us, keep records of us. They make us wonder if we are real, whether we own them or they own us. We often feel that we are becoming digits in some giant computer system. Typical of the hundreds of experiences that give us this feeling was the time several years ago when my daughter forgot to return a book to the library of the school she attended, in which there were almost 4,000 children and in which most classes had fifty or more students. I received a mimeographed notice which read in part:

> If the book is not returned, we must make a notation of this on the PERMANENT RECORD CARD and we shall not be able to send any favorable recommendation for your daughter to any future business employer when she applies for a CIVIL SERVICE job, or when she applies to a business school or college.

My daughter was fourteen at the time, and somehow it seemed a little early to wipe out her entire future because of a lost book! The impersonal, mechanized communication, with its portent of doom, is something that our children live with every day of their lives, and what is most frightening of all is that they are learning to live with this so well! One mother told me that at her daughter's high school all report cards are now processed by a computer. All sorts of information is fed into the machine, including such data as the child's I.Q., past test scores, current grade averages and so on; after all this information has been properly "digested" by the machine, a statement appears on the report card, such as "You must try harder" or "Keep up the good work." Innocently, this mother asked, "Does the guidance counselor add these messages to the report card?" Betty could not have been more contemptuous and patronizing when she answered, "Honestly, Mother, sometimes I wonder about you. Don't be silly—the *machine* sends the messages."

Technology has made possible a world of over-abundance and affluence and has changed the world for our children. We do not give them only what they need; industry has discovered what impulsive, insatiable creatures children are, and in an economy able to provide all the basic necessities of life and forced to encourage people to buy other things as well, children are the greatest economic market. Since they are bombarded, we are bombarded, and our children find themselves surrounded by things, with no real demands made on their own inventiveness or ingenuity; they do not have to use their imaginations, they do not have to entertain themselves, they are bored half to death with everything they have. Affluence provides them with pleasures they are not ready for and things they do not need. When I commented to a group of teen-agers that I was surprised at their lack of interest in all the interesting and exciting things going on in New York, they told me that they had been taken to plays, movies and museums since they were old enough to walk; they were blasé and bored—but, interestingly enough, there were two things they enjoyed doing: rowing on the lake and going to the zoo, both unsophisticated, natural, childlike activities.

Machines have changed the nature and meaning of work. It used to be that a man measured his worth by how hard and how long he worked. Machines have given us a leisure undreamed of by past generations, and we are unprepared for it. We have our roots so deep in a belief in hard work that we are uneasy about leisure and early retirement. It is no longer true that the best provider works the hardest; it is no longer true that the harder we work, the richer we will be.

And one of the strangest aspects of this changing nature of work is that it finds many of us working fewer hours than our children do! Work in its old sense may well occupy less than half of our children's time when they grow up, but we still feel that our children should study long hours—even though we really have no idea where they are going so fast, or what they will do with themselves when they get there.

Machines have given us mobility, and mobility is hard on children; it was easier to grow up in one place, knowing the people around your neighborhood, living where most of your relatives also lived. Today, as thousands of families move from one part of the country to another, we have become more and more rootless, our children frequently facing new schools, new friends, new neighborhoods. They are less likely to have much contact with aunts, uncles, cousins and grandparents. What is most startling of all is that our lives have changed so much that we no longer even need family groups for economic survival. The ties of economic inter-dependency that once held a farm family together, no matter what, no longer exist, so that we are raising children who must face the fact that families do not always stay together. The impact of this on the experiences of childhood and the nature of parenthood is tremendous. Industrialization has made children unnecessary to us in an economic sense. As long as we were an agricultural society, as long as we had to produce for ourselves all that we needed, children were an economic necessity. In less than 100 years we have gone from the fact that a family's very survival depended on raising strong, healthy children—who could work along with adults in providing the food, clothing and shelter that meant the difference between life and death—to the modern-day parent who expects his child to be a financial burden often until the age of twenty-five or thirty. Children nowadays are an investment of gigantic proportions on which there are no financial returns. Of course many psychological and social needs have always been satisfied by marriage and parenthood, but now these are the *only* reasons for getting married and having children; coming as this change did at the same time that insights into human personality and development were emerging, a perfectly natural development has taken place. There would be, we assumed, new and deeper emotional satisfactions in having children; not only would they be an expression of our need for giving and receiving love and affection, providing a sense of our immortality, a fulfillment of a loving marriage —even beyond all this, as parents, we would have the added gratification of being the first parents in history to raise our children rationally and scientifically, based on our new insights. However, the psychiatric revolution, while changing us immeasurably—and for the better—did not provide this new reward for parenthood. We are beset by more doubts and misgivings, more confusions and uncertainties, than ever before. Our children have gone right on having all the aches and pains of growth, in spite of our hopes that we could learn enough to make our children always happy, always loving, free of pain and frustration.

We have placed an enormous new burden on our children. I suppose it was hard enough to come into a world that expected you to chop wood, husk corn, dig wells, plant seeds, feed animals and build houses—but that was nothing to what we demand of children today; we want them to *love* us, all the time, every day. We want our children to be happy, to learn quickly, be studious and athletic, independent and yet respectful, well-adjusted and interesting. We want our children to show the world by their behavior and attitudes that we have been the world's most wonderful, insightful, loving parents. We have been taught to believe that we can be successful parents if we try hard enough, and when, despite very good efforts, we somehow do not change nice normal little rascals into pseudo-human robots, we feel defeated, frightened and angry. Children have problems, no matter how smart we are; growing up is difficult— it always has been, it always will be; children must inevitably experience discomfort, unhappiness, frustration, disappointment, fears and tensions. One father said, "My wife and I were absolutely sure that we knew exactly how to raise children. With love, understanding and patience, our kids were going to be so happy, charming, talented and responsible that they would be the envy of every family on the block! So now we have three nuts: one is so shy he trembles when his own grandmother comes to visit; another one is doing lousy work in school, although everybody tells us he's a genius; and the third one has been having nightmares every night for three months. Believe me, we don't feel so smart anymore!" It is not particularly pleasurable to live with children if they make us feel that we are failing as parents.

As I meet and talk with parents, I have the impression that pushing children to grow up quickly reflects something about our feelings about ourselves in addition to reflecting all the complex social forces I have mentioned.

Too many parents hope for some illusive fulfillment through their children. Living without significance in their own lives, they hope that their children's successes will give them some status or prestige. We feel caught up in patterns of living and doing that seem to make no sense at all; and out of our frustration, our discontent, our lack of a sense of identity and of meaningfulness in our own lives we some-how hope that our children will provide us with some vicar-ious satisfactions and pleasures. An example of this situation was presented by a young suburban mother who became very upset when I tried to explain why we refused to teach reading and writing in the nursery school. After much dis-cussion she smiled ruefully and said, "But if I can't have a genius son, what *can* I have?" As we went on talking, she began to describe a life of unquiet desperation—a much-too-early marriage, a growing feeling of never having had an opportunity to find out what she herself might be or be-come. She finally said, "I'm too lazy to go back to school, I'm too rich to make the effort to work—I guess I'll just spend the next twenty years having babies and ruining them by being an over-ambitious mother!"

The rapidity of social change has left us spinning dizzily. We are constantly exposed to such a range of ideas and be-havior that we are no longer so clear or so sure about who we are and what we believe. One of the most serious human problems in modern society is a sense of loss of identity. We keep busy, but we do not know why we do what we do; we have no roots, and we do not know where we are going.

A psychiatrist, Dr. Allen Wheelis, in his book *The Quest for Identity* (W. W. Norton, 1958) wrote:

> In some measure we have lost the sense of continuity with the past and future. More and more quickly the past becomes outdated, and if we look back two or three generations the character and values of our fore-bears become as strange to us as their beards and high collars. . . . As we have lost touch with the past, so

we have lost touch with the future. We know that we are in motion but do not know where we are going and hence cannot predict the values of our children. . . . Modern man cannot recapture an identity out of the past; his old identity was not lost, but outgrown. Identity is not, therefore, to be found; it is to be created and achieved. . . . Identity is a coherent sense of self. It depends upon the awareness that one's endeavors and one's life make sense, that they are meaningful in the context in which life is lived. . . . It is a sense of wholeness, of integration, of knowing what is right and what is wrong and being able to choose.

It is this sense of uncertainty about ourselves and our unease and discomfort with the world we live in that we have communicated to our children.

To sum up, it is my belief that we are trying to eliminate childhood, and *that* is what is so terrible about being a child today. Whatever agonies children have ever lived through before, it was never so clearly childhood itself that was felt to be the enemy. And the saddest part of the current inclination to wipe out childhood is that the one thing that every field associated with child development has agreed on over the past fifty years is that you are in terrible trouble if you skip any necessary part of childhood; children cannot grow up whole and strong unless their psychological, physical, intellectual and social needs are met at each stage of growth. An anti-child social climate robs our children of what is most natural and human in themselves, and dooms us all to a terrible impoverishment of the spirit.

When I mentioned the subject of this book in a letter to a

friend who works in the Children's Bureau in Washington, she wrote back, "It's a marvelous idea. . . . Today's child of the affluent society has every miraculous opportunity that *technocracy* can invent, the only thing that is lacking is humanity." This may well have been the poignant message in the childish scrawl on a subway wall, "Chicken Little Was Right!"

I am convinced that as we attempt to eliminate childhood, we will destroy ourselves as well as our children. Any society that looks with suspicion, impatience or hostility on childhood has within it a deep and awful sickness that infects adult and child alike. The young and growing child is our deepest expression of hope; the most profound qualities of human sensitivity and morality flow from the nurturing of childhood—a sense of meaning and purpose in life. Birth and growth reflect the theme of life, the miraculous mysteries of renewal, of hope and faith in the possibilities of life, a sense of awe and wonder at nature's marvels. Our young are our own new beginnings, a testament to our trust in the future. The innocence, the delight, the wonder, the vitality, the openness to life, of childhood, are necessary to us. Without them we lose touch with what is young and tender and creative within ourselves. When we lose our patience with childhood, and our joy in it, we lose touch with our inner selves, with our own growing and becoming. When we become alienated from childhood, we are also alienated from the deep wellsprings of feeling within ourselves. If it is true that we have lost touch with childhood—if we fear it or despise it—then we have been terribly diminished; we live a death-in-life.

I have certainly painted a gloomy picture. But I would not have concerned myself if I did not also feel a fundamental optimism—a confident belief that we *can* do something about it. We hoped for too much, and we feel the loss of our illusions deeply, but if that were the end of the story, there would be no point in writing a book in defense of childhood. For me this is simply a new beginning. For what lay behind our faith in the future, however naive we may have been, was a deep and abiding faith in the marvelous resources in human beings, and in this I remain unalterably starry-eyed.

I think it is natural, when one sees many problems, to concentrate on them rather than to enumerate all the positive and satisfying aspects of a situation. I am well aware of the dedication and wisdom of thousands of educators and parents who are doing everything possible to help children grow well; I am aware of the tremendous complexity of our problems and the enormity of our responsibilities. It is very easy to be critical, and a whole lot harder to come up with constructive suggestions. My goal is simply to describe to the best of my ability the climate of life in which our children live and to hope that, as we can delineate the problems, all of us, together, calling on all our resources and talents, will be able to initiate new programs, develop new approaches, find new ways of responding to the challenges that confront us.

The chapters that follow are not in any way an attempt to analyze the problems objectively or scientifically. Far from considering myself an objective scientist, I see myself as a parent, speaking informally—and I hope, passionately—to other parents about many of the things that worry and frighten me. While my thinking is, of course, colored by my training and my work experiences in psychology and education, I want to speak simply as a human being to other human beings, expressing what I see and feel. Wherever possible I will try to substantiate my opinions with what I consider to be sound facts and information. But I do not want any reader to view what I say as the words of an "expert" telling others what to do. I would only hope for an authenticity derived from the never-ending internal struggle to find my own humanity.

TWO

The Computerized Baby:
Or How to Teach Two-Year-Olds
to Fail

SITTING on a bench in Central Park one day, I saw a young mother tickling her baby's stomach as the baby lay in her carriage, kicking her feet, waving her arms and gurgling ecstatically in the kind of *total* pleasure with life and with the world that seems to be the unique province of babyhood. The mother was making those special very personal kinds of meaningless cooing sounds that infants and mothers understand perfectly. As I watched, I thought to myself that this was one of the most touching and civilized and universal scenes one can be witness to. With the cars speeding by, poisoning the air with their exhausts, with horns honking and a nearby steam shovel screeching its triumphant way to creating a newer and uglier and more monstrous steel and glass "rat maze" for people to live in, this

43

moment, this intimate participation in the sounds of life, seemed infinitely precious. My reverie came to an abrupt end when another mother, sharing our bench, leaned over and said disapprovingly, "You know, it's really a very serious mistake to make nonsense sounds to a baby. It interferes with good patterns for speech development."

If I were not essentially a law-abiding and peace-loving creature, I think I might have committed my first murder. A chill ran through me, and I felt haunted by a sense of impending doom. That lovely moment, so tender and human, was shattered, and I was back in a world that seems to have less and less tolerance for such communications between mothers and children.

I am sure I would not have reacted so strongly to such an incident ten or fifteen years ago; there have always been foolish busybodies telling other people exactly how to raise their children, and every generation of mothers has had to put up with nuttier and sillier admonitions than this one. As I thought about the incident, I realized that I was reacting sharply because it was so typical of the mood of our times—a mood that seems to have little patience with life and with growth.

On another occasion my husband and I were having dinner in a restaurant that had high walls separating the booths, so that the diners at the next table were not visible. We heard an irate mother threatening, "Now stop acting like a baby or we'll never take you out again!" When this admonition was followed by a loud howl, we peeked around the corner of our booth, to behold a little boy who could not have been more than a year old, sitting in a high chair!

If you cannot be a baby at the age of one, when *can* you

be? Despite all the superficial comforts we supply to babies, despite all our pediatric expertise, our tempting baby foods, the unbelievable and almost indecent number of baby toys, the charming and attractive baby furniture and clothes that are so much part of our affluent society, I have become increasingly convinced that the times we live in are frighteningly and violently anti-baby.

In a culture that seeks ever new and better ways to view man as a machine, it is easy to understand a growing antipathy, a suspicion of, and impatience with, babyhood. If ever there is a time in the course of human growth when one is constantly reminded of the miracle of the uniqueness, unpredictability and mystery of personality development, it is in the nursery years. The newborn infant presents himself to the world with so many possibilities for what he may be and become that it staggers the imagination. If he bears any real resemblance to what our modern world conceives of as a machine, it is only in the digestive department of input and output! Moreover, babies are so new, so poignantly vulnerable—and so cute—that it takes us some time to get them oriented to the demands of our modern world. And until we are able to turn them into the more acceptable learning machines that we are now trying to create among three- and four-year-olds, babies tend to lie about and remind us too often and too much of nature.

I think my own awareness of the ways in which scientific technology was beginning to affect the lives of infants began some years ago, when I first heard of "The Skinner Box." This glass enclosure, similar to a large incubator, was invented by Dr. B. F. Skinner, a professor of psychology at Harvard University. His idea was that during the first few months of life babies should spend a large proportion of time in this air-conditioned and sound-proofed box. The naked baby lay on a kind of rolling platform; when he eliminated, the soiled pad was simply rolled out of the box. Dr. Skinner reported that the germ-free and temperature-controlled atmosphere made it possible for the baby to move more freely and easily, unhampered by clothes or blankets. He reported that "Skinner Box babies" cried much less than other babies, slept more regularly (sleeping patterns could be controlled by changing the temperature in the box) and gained weight more rapidly. Parents were allowed to take the babies out of the box for short periods of time, but I remember that those among my contemporaries who were most enchanted with this approach to baby care ten or fifteen years ago were also inclined to think that kissing, hugging or fondling babies was sentimental nonsense, endured by the poor baby to satisfy the needs of hopelessly old-fashioned parents.

This mechanistic approach to child care suggests that by keeping the child in a controlled atmosphere, he can be made into a more predictable machine. We have become increasingly impatient with life and growth as we find it in nature. If we can make tomatoes grow faster and bigger by the use of chemicals, then surely we ought to be able to cut out the waste of time and effort involved in taking care of young babies. If we think of the human mind as a machine and nothing more, then it is appropriate to start operating this machine as soon as possible. The purpose of our having developed other kinds of machines has been to save time and energy, and so we bring the same expectation to our behavior with children once we conceive of them in this way.

We are in the process of creating an environment that makes it quite clear to children by the time they are two years old that time is not to be wasted. If a machine is well built, one doesn't have to sit around and wait for it to grow up! Once we make these subtle and insidious assumptions about human life, it naturally follows that those qualities or dimensions of human experience that are unknown and un-named in the world of machines lose their significance. What was once called "the soul," or in more recent years has been somewhat clumsily defined in terms of personality, feelings and emotion, becomes waste product. We find our-selves becoming suspicious and intolerant of such sissy no-tions as affection and love. If our goal is to computerize our lives, we must distill what is coldly intellectual and objec-tive and get rid of anything that makes us warm and soft, muddled or disorderly, idiotically cooing and gurgling for no reason at all except that it gives us and the object of our deplorable weakness so much pleasure.

There is an interesting and ironic twist in the application of technological thinking to infant care. We seem to be most concerned with the brain as a machine for producing intellectual performance rather than for streamlining body processes. Probably this approach is due to the fact that many years ago, before we got around to being so intrigued with intellectual potential, we had already tried conditioning bodily functions, and are now aware of the disastrous re-sults. Way back in John B. Watson's day we tried regulat-ing digestive processes by conditioning babies to eat, sleep and eliminate at regular intervals. While some babies re-sponded well, many more did not, and we learned that many children who were "toilet trained" at six months were mak-ing a mess of things at the age of three—both physically and psychologically. We failed so completely in trying to mech-anize bodily functions too early that nowadays one rarely hears the notion that those two-year-olds whom we are so eager to teach reading and writing must also go to the bathroom and relinquish the bottle! We seem content to allow nature to take care of those areas of growth because we are conscious of having been outwitted long ago in our quest for physical regimentation.

Evidence of this kind of division in our goals is beginning to appear. Starting about ten years ago, a number of research studies were initiated which involved very careful observations of children from birth onward. These longitudinal studies were planned to follow the growth of individual children into adulthood. The researchers report that, to their surprise, they found very few infants and toddlers with severe eating, sleeping or toilet-training problems. They concluded that this finding was the result of the generally permissive and tolerant approach to growth accepted by parents in these areas. However, as these children reach school age, the researchers are finding what they feel to be an inordinately high number of school problems and failures. It seems logical to conclude that now that we are so hell-bent on demanding mental gymnastics, we are likely to find more and more problems developing in this area of growth. One can only hope that it will not take us quite so long to come to our senses about the wisdom of nature in the area of intellectual development as it did in relation to bodily functioning—but there is plenty of evidence to suggest that several generations of babies may be sacrificed on the altar of the new god, conditioned intelligence.

An example of this dichotomy in our thinking is demonstrated by the report of a friend who told me that her next-door neighbor had been working diligently to teach her nineteen-month-old child to learn words and numbers through the use of a kit which she had bought for this purpose, euphemistically called "A Learning Game for Tiny

Tots." When her reluctant son seemed to get restless and bored with these efforts to improve his chances for obtaining a Phi Beta Kappa key, Mama gave him a pacifier to suck on while she continued with the lesson plans.

There is no need to search very hard or long to find ample evidence of the new mood about infants and toddlers. A beautiful example of the impatience with growth is exemplified by the advertisement of a large insurance company which appeared in many newspapers and magazines. A handsome young father holds his newborn son on his lap. The baby has adorable chubby fingers curled in his father's big hand and soft downy fuzz on his head, and he is doing his best to focus his wobbly eyes on Daddy's face as he snuggles comfortably, the perfect picture of baby bliss. The caption under the picture reads, "Thomas, I want to talk to you about college!" Insurance companies are not likely to spend millions of dollars on such an ad unless they have had some clear indication that the approach is likely to produce very genuine interest in the purchase of college annuities. There are some old-fashioned relics of a bygone time like myself who still protest when high-school freshmen are made to feel that life in their immediate present is of no significance at all except as a preparation for future College Boards; but that kind of living-for-the-future seems relatively innocent and naive in the face of such evidence as this advertisement of our impatience with the present.

Another advertisement that I have saved for my file on Nightmares and Horrors is one that I received from a famous bookstore. The headline on this flyer reads, "Your Baby Can Read!" It goes on to state:

Teach your baby to read the revolutionary new "Toddler Reading Technique." . . . If your baby is two

years old he CAN read—and you can teach him in only
ten minutes a day! Tiny tots have photographic memories. Their minds can photograph a particular thing
and it's immediately stored in their memory files
forever.

If that last comment isn't mind-viewed-as-a-machine, I
don't know what is. It is the description of a computer that
never forgets as long as someone puts in the right question.

An advertisement that has appeared in *The New York
Times Magazine* week after week, month after month, and
may still be appearing all over the country, has a similar
theme: "Now! Even your two year old child can learn to
READ! New research studies prove the child that starts ahead,
stays ahead." The same theme has been covered in almost all
popular magazines in the past few years. One women's magazine, for example, published an article entitled "You Can
Teach Your Baby to Read." The facts are really very
simple, we were told; tiny children want to read, can read
and should read. In fact, "In research centers, babies as
young as ten months are reading. In thousands of homes
across America, forward-thinking parents are giving their
2, 3 and 4 year olds the gift beyond price; the world of the
printed word!"

In another women's magazine there appeared an article
entitled "Train Your Baby to Be a Genius." An article by
Ronald Gross in *The New York Times Magazine*, Sunday,
September 6, 1964, entitled "Two-Year-Olds Are Very
Smart," reported: "A Rutgers psychologist, Omar Khayyam Moore, has shown conclusively that children from the
age of 2 can be taught to read . . . through their own curiosity and drive."

Related to all such pronouncements was the publication of a book, *How to Teach Your Baby to Read*, by Glen Doman (Random House, 1964). Based on the Doman-Delacato Reading Development Program developed at the Institute for Achievement of Human Potential in Philadelphia, this book, which has become a best-seller, states:

> The human brain is unique in that it is the only container of which it can be said that the more you put into it, the more it will hold. Between nine months and four years, the ability to absorb information is unparalleled, and the desire to do so is higher than it will ever be again.

The impact of these attempts to accelerate learning might have sifted down to the layman more slowly in other times, but the explosion in print has given them an apparent validity and importance before it has been possible to discover the long-range effects of these new approaches. It has become almost impossible to pick up a magazine or newspaper without reading a report on some new and astounding "breakthrough" in teaching two-year-olds to read and write, three-year-olds to understand geometry and four-year-olds to speak at least two languages.

I believe that these approaches to learning in young children reflect a sick and distorted point of view; that in a few years these promises and goals will have been discarded as wholeheartedly as the earlier attempts to accelerate and regulate the eating habits and toilet training of infants and toddlers. I think we will soon see that great damage has been done to children through this forced intellectual feeding and that our children will be paying a price for this pseudo-scientific approach to learning. There will be more school failures, more resistance to learning, an increase in severe emotional disorders which will reflect our hysterical and ill-conceived impatience with growth and our intolerance of the normal, gradual, individual ways in which children grow and learn.

For many years careful and sensitive observers of young children have been attempting to guide parents on how to encourage the full use of a child's potential. Sound guidance in the education of young children has been practiced for years—but it has not been of the kind that makes headlines; it is not flashy or sensational. The times in which we live have distorted our vision; children have not changed; what we have known in the past few decades about their needs has not really changed. It is just that we are so caught up in this wave of technological double-talk that we have lost our sense of balance and good judgment. It is a matter of great urgency that parents take a good look at what they are being encouraged to think and do, and fight back in order to protect the welfare of their children.

There is no reliable evidence that children who can read words at two are better readers by the time they are in the sixth grade. There is no reliable evidence that children who learn to read in kindergarten do any better later on than children who are not good readers until third or fourth grade. Furthermore, there is no evidence that children who were considered poor readers until fifth or sixth grade are necessarily poor scholars, or that early reading skills have any correlation whatsoever with whether or not they may be brilliant intellectuals in adulthood.

There is also no valid reason to assume that young children learn faster, better or more, or that they are more highly motivated, during the early years of life. They may learn to *imitate* or *memorize*, but these are not to be confused with the learning. Learning is not just the accumulation of odd facts; it is developing the capacity to think, to direct one's natural curiosity in order to find answers to meaningful questions; it is the development of thoughts and ideas that make it possible to become increasingly mature in making decisions. There is, and has always been, plenty of clear and irrefutable evidence that some of the most profound and significant kinds of learning do not take place until we have reached middle or old age. Meaningful learning which involves discrimination of ideas, relating knowledge to meaningful situations, goes on all through our lives, and the more experience we have, the more mature we become, the more deeply meaningful our learning is. As for motivation, we had all the evidence we could possibly need, years and years before the manipulators took over, that when an adult consciously knows what he wants to do with his life, when he has found work that he loves, he can learn anything he needs to know to enrich or advance his knowledge.

As for the written word's being a "priceless possession" at the age of two or three, it is not necessary for us to look for scientific data to view this belief as complete nonsense; all we have to do is think about our own life experiences. Just recently I reread a book that I had not looked at since I was about sixteen years old—*Crime and Punishment* by Dostoevsky. This rediscovery was one of those exciting adventures that leave one breathless with an inner sense of joy and fulfillment. As a middle-aged woman, with all the years of living and learning that are now behind me, I could see priceless dimensions in this book that were totally incomprehensible to me as a teen-ager. The subtle nuances, the richness, the depth of insight I now saw provided me with a learning experience which affected me in such a profound way, that it added new color and dimension to my understanding of myself, of others, of the world in which I live. *Now* words are priceless; woven into the web of experience and maturity, they provide exquisite excitement.

All of us have had such experiences; we reread a poem that we memorized in high school and have not thought of in twenty years. Or we pick up a book on history or philosophy that bored us half to death even ten years ago—and suddenly we are "ready"; something that has happened to us in growing or living makes the experience so thrilling that we eagerly seek for more of the same. Some of the most profoundly thoughtful people I know, with the greatest thirst for knowledge, are people who as adults, and on their own, have discovered whole new worlds of intellectual challenge twenty, thirty, forty years after leaving school. As parents, we must clearly define for ourselves the difference between learning facts and learning to think. Good teachers know this, but what they know is not spectacular or easy to define, it offers no simple panaceas, and so at this moment in history too many people have stopped listening to them.

One of the claims of the new wave of experts is that by the time a normal child is six years of age he has already absorbed a fantastic amount of information—"perhaps more than he will learn the rest of his life." Even if we could accept this theory (which I don't), what would it really tell us? The crazy part of it would be that if he *has* learned all these facts, he has not done it by rote or by being taught in a consciously planned program. He learned in a highly individualistic way, picking up what was important to him, what he was curious about, what he was motivated to find out. He did not learn facts in any special order; sometimes big ideas came first, sometimes little pieces of information. Early learning is done without self-consciousness in a random selection based on each child's own needs and the methods most satisfactory to him.

Glen Doman, in *How to Teach Your Baby to Read*, says: "There has never been, in the history of man, an adult scientist who has been half so curious as is any child between the ages of eighteen months and four years." Plato, Leonardo da Vinci, Sigmund Freud and Albert Einstein might be among those who would care to differ with this notion; but aside from that issue, these new experts on learning are treading on dangerous soil when they begin to talk about scientists. The true scientist, like the normal baby, works on hunches, on trial and error, following wherever his curiosity leads him. It is a quality of *freedom from circumscribed or unchanging "facts"* which has been the source of almost every important scientific discovery. The accidental observation of freely thoughtful men with a penchant for creative hunches and indefatigable curiosity has provided us with everything from electricity to penicillin and rockets to the moon. If programmed learning of facts had been the order of the day, we might never have heard of Edison, Sir Isaac Newton or Sir Alexander Fleming.

What about these supposedly brilliant babies who cooperate so politely with adult insanities and *do* learn to typewrite or read and repeat whatever facts we pour into their heads? Are they really learning? I asked a highly respected scientist about this, and he replied, "Anyone can teach a laboratory rat to press a bar in order to get food, when the word 'press' is lit up on a panel. (We are so smart now, we've got pigeons doing it!) Anyone can teach a child to read in the same conditioned-response manner. However, this method is useless to teach the rat to decide if rats should be taught to press bars in the first place—and it is equally useless as a method for teaching children to evaluate the difference between reading *Mein Kampf* and the Declaration of Independence."

The emphasis on accelerated learning in infancy must of necessity be related to the accumulation of facts, since reasoning and evaluating depend on a degree of maturity and experience in living which is simply not available to such a young child. By putting this kind of special value on the accumulation of facts, it naturally follows that the child will accept the assumption we are making by feeding him facts, that facts are what are needed in order to understand the world in which we live. Certain kinds of facts, such as that touching a hot stove hurts, are essential, of course, but since we live in a rapidly changing world, relevant facts keep changing too, so that it would seem that one important feature of any learning experience would be the flexibility to change and to seek out new facts in new situations. This is another way in which the whole structure of this new philosophy collapses like the house of cards it is—for flexibility is something we develop primarily through our *feelings*, and one finds little or no awareness of, or concern for, the emotional aspects of child growth in all these training programs.

Nor does one find any acknowledgment in these reports about improving the intellectual levels of children, of a fact that educators and psychologists have observed for many years, that naturally gifted children, those who have always been able to absorb facts in the ways that are now so admired, those natural geniuses who have been born from time to time, were not infrequently emotionally disturbed, unable to relate to others, isolated, lonely and lost in every other area of their lives except in the accumulation of facts. I remember that when I was a little girl my family knew the parents of one of these "geniuses." At the age of three he could do algebraic formulas. Walking down the street, he could immediately memorize the license plates of every car that passed and could also tell the year and make of each car. At ten he could memorize entire books. He did not have a single friend, he was unable to function in the world of reality in almost any sphere, and at eighteen was hospitalized after a suicide attempt. A therapist who works with young adults told me recently that he has seen many brilliant young people in their early twenties who are unable to deal effectively with work and with human relationships and who had been graduated from college by the age of twenty, or earlier, been elected to Phi Beta Kappa, had done outstanding work in different fields in graduate school—but were severely handicapped and totally unable to function in terms of job or marriage. It would seem that children who are born with the capacity to absorb information very rapidly do not *necessarily* represent an image that we ought to strive for in all children. The brilliant child may become a fulfilled and productive adult, but there are enough hazards in the situation to suggest that we are hardly in a position to encourage using the infant genius as a model and a goal for all children.

There are literally thousands of specialists in child development who have never for one moment been taken in by the new mystique. But their voices are too quietly reasonable, and they offer more complex and less glamorous and dramatic ways of helping the young child to grow well and fully. The dangerous part of this noisier new wave of experts is that they are so vocal, so fanatically certain, and they make the process sound so easy. Many of the careful and thoughtful books on child care and education tend to sit on the bookshelves while parents grab for the latest panacea which will guarantee Little Willie's ultimate acceptance at Harvard or Yale. The only solution for children is for their parents to come out of this hypnotic haze and look at the facts.

First of all, you cannot teach a ten-month-old to read—you can just make him imitate what you read. It is like saying that you are teaching a child to speak at ten months just because he says "Bye Bye" when you say "Bye Bye." All he is doing is showing that he wants to be friendly and have you smile at him. Those who promise that you can teach your toddler to read are simply capitalizing on the fact that babies are natural mimics and out of their friendliness, joy in living and natural curiosity are willing to follow you in any number of foolish antics, just for the fun of it. Saying letters or numbers over and over, for that matter, if it is just for fun, may be no better or worse than crooning a lullaby. The difference is that when a mother sings, her only expectation is that her baby will enjoy it, and maybe even fall asleep. When she starts in with the letters and numbers, she wants a lot more in the way of performance—and if she does not get it, she begins to think her child is slightly retarded, and he gets the message that in some mysterious way he is failing to measure up to her expectations. What rears its horrible head in that child's playpen is the idea of *failure*. It looms like a black cloud over the baby's head, and if he gets enough of this feeling that he is a careless and incompetent thinker, the whole idea of learning may become unpleasant, frightening, confusing and to be avoided at all costs. What kills the natural intelligence and curiosity of a baby is his growing awareness that life is not full of fun but full of threats and promises, punishments and rewards. Babies who in an earlier time were toilet trained too early often became constipated; babies who are forced to learn facts too early are just as prone to constipation of the thought processes.

Probably the most remarkable event in a child's life between the ages of one and three is that he learns to speak a language; in fact, he learns to speak that langauge at least as well if not a whole lot better than his parents could have learned a foreign language during the same two-year period. How does he do it? Are there "flannel boards" and "drill cards" and "teaching machines" for this? Not at all— at least not yet, thank heaven—and yet we take this miracle completely for granted without ever really observing how it comes about.

Babies begin to learn to speak because they are surrounded by speaking people. They recognize speech as communication—a way in which human beings reach out to each other for understanding, acceptance and affection. At first it is the sounds themselves which convey this message—simply the pleasure of hearing a human voice. *The New Yorker* recently published the following item: "A reader reports the greatest device for keeping tots quiet since the invention of the pacifier. She dials WE 6-1212, hands the phone to her two-year-old, and goes happily about her business while he carries on what appears to be a stimulating conversation with the girl giving the weather report." In the beginning, speech is only the pleasure in feeling in touch with others, and this satisfying experience provides the motivation to begin by free trial and error to make communicating sense with sounds. In talking about language development in an article in *Parents' Magazine* (September 1966) John Holt writes, "Parents and teachers should remember that every child learns in his own way. . . . From babyhood on, each child makes his own path through the wilderness of speech. . . . Some children begin with nouns, others with adjectives, others with verbs." In another article, in *Redbook* (November 1965), he makes the point that if we taught children to speak the way we are now trying to teach them to read, they would never learn how.

> Even the most expert teaching tends to *slow down* the learning of young children. . . . What are the differences between our teaching and a young child's learning? We break down what we want to teach into parts arranged in what is a logical order *to us*. Then we break down those parts into steps, making the first steps small and simple. . . . But anyone who has watched an infant or young child knows that this is not at all how he learns. He does not take one thing at a time and get it down pat before going on to the next. Instead he tries a great many different things, and gradually gets better at all of them. In learning to talk . . . he does not learn to pronounce one word perfectly before trying another. He says many words, all of them badly, and by practice gradually improves them all.

Mr. Holt goes on to say that in continuing to observe the way children absorb language it becomes clear that they do not follow a rigid plan or a clearly defined pattern. They explore in many directions all at once, and in doing this, learn a language without apparent effort and almost no instruction. Because the results are so remarkable, experts have tended to believe that this language aptitude is some special and transitory condition of the central nervous system—a mysterious knack that will eventually wear off. In making this judgment, they miss the point completely.

The reason the young child learns so well and so fast is that *his* way of learning is his own best way. When he is allowed this freedom to explore the world of language, he pursues his own interest and curiosity, and that is what makes him go so much faster than we could lead him. He sees more, he picks out the information he needs and leaves the rest until he is ready. He comes at things from many directions and is therefore more likely to see the way they fit together and relate to one another. A child learns because he wants to make sense. He learns not to please others, but to please himself. When he is pleasing himself he goes at top speed into the unknown, not worrying for a second about being wrong. When he starts learning to please us, mistakes become crimes to be avoided or covered up at all costs. This fear of failure can cripple his progress. Mr. Holt says:

Some children become interested in talking very early, work on it, get good at it. Other children find other things more interesting, explore the world in other ways and work on talking at a later time. . . . The story is told of Thomas Carlyle that he did not speak a word until he was over three. Then one day, hearing his baby brother wailing in the crib, he asked his parents, "What ails wee Jock?"

Despite all the current hullabaloo, a child who is surrounded by written language, who enjoys being read to and
who sees the people around him enjoying this experience,
will learn to read in his own good time, without having to
feel harassed or pushed or frightened. He will eventually, if
he has pleasurable experiences with reading, read well.
When reading is presented to him as a gradually expanding
adventure that can provide him with many satisfactions, he
can learn to read with almost no instruction at all. Millions
of people have done just that, in the course of history. Any
normal, healthy child growing in an atmosphere of approval, in which there is also challenge and opportunity for
exploration, will want to make sense out of the world he
finds himself in; he will want to fit things together, he will
want to correct his errors—he will want to grow and to
learn. Unless we permit children the freedom to explore
and to make corrections on their own, they will get the idea
that nothing should be attempted unless it can be known
ahead of time that it will be right—and the only way to be
sure is to ask a grown-up. Only a small percentage of child
experts are concerned with teaching babies to read. The
majority continue to believe that so long as we provide our
children with an exciting and interesting and accepting environment, we do not have to worry about reading. A child
who learns to read when he wants to, because he wants to,
does so better and faster than by any method we could invent.

The problem is not one of being for or against a standard
of excellence in thought, for or against the fullest enjoyment of learning, of intellectual development. It is rather
the question of how to help babies grow up in life so that
they can become *persons*, not computers; can become

warm, feeling adults, gleeful to be alive, free to love and be loved and to find work that uses them and entrances them —that adds to a sense of aliveness, a joy in discovery and in *being. It simply does not matter* if a baby learns to read. He is too young to enjoy reading or to gain anything from it. He has other more important business just exploring the first feelings and sensations of being alive.

There is an important distinction between a mechanistic and arbitrary demand for specific kinds of training and performance and the wish to encourage a child to grow as fully and deeply as he can. It is perfectly true that we *can* stunt intellectual growth in babyhood—by keeping crawlers in cages we call playpens too much of the time, by punishing them for feeling, touching, tasting, by letting them know that we are anxious and frightened and annoyed by their explorations, by teaching them to be unnecessarily fearful, afraid to move away from the safety and security of our arms. No one in his right mind would suggest that we interfere with growth and learning or that little children should not be encouraged to test, experiment, explore in an environment that is rich in challenging, stimulating resources.

But when we try to decide just how quickly growth and learning are to take place, and what specific forms it must take, we are playing a dangerous game. A baby's mind is a confusion of fantasies and feelings, vague awarenesses and unfinished perceptions. Despite being so new in the world, he manages with remarkable speed and accuracy to figure out so many things about the world around him; somehow he instinctively senses things, without conscious knowledge or direct information. Babies know when they are loved or rejected, when they create feelings of joy or disappointment. They want someone to hold them, to feel close and warm; they feel safe when they are rocked or stroked. During the first two years of life, without any interference on our part—except that we go on living naturally and normally—they begin to learn some of the most profound and important things they will ever have to learn: how to give and receive love; whom to trust and distrust; how to recognize dangers and how to let others know when help is needed; how to explore the hazards and possibilities, the ecstatic pleasures, of life with eyes, nose, fingers, mouth and feet; how, above all, to begin to sense, vaguely and diffusely, what it is to be oneself. They learn not to trust blindly, to accept frustration, to endure it as the sometimes necessary price for love and approval; they are learning to relinquish the tyranny of wanting what they want when they want it in order to have the pleasures and satisfactions of being with others; they are learning ways to test the self for errors in observation and judgment, to know hard from soft, hot from cold, yes from no, anger from joy.

Any parent who may be feeling vaguely guilty because Junior's only interest in Webster's dictionary is to suck on the cover or tear out the pages would do well to contemplate the number of things that children have learned and are capable of doing by the time they are about two and a half. They are developing patterns for eating, sleeping and eliminating; they can resist sleep for social obligations, wait to be fed, and "hold it in" from the back yard to the toilet. They have already experienced the problems and consequences of jealousy, rage, fatigue, frustration, fear, illness, physical discomfort and pain. They have learned ways of getting attention and of giving it up. They have learned to eat literally hundreds of different-tasting foods, they can recognize almost as many different sounds and smells. They are learning acceptable patterns of eating, whether or not they are always willing to follow them. They recognize more and more people and know what most of them are like and what they do. They are fluent enough in what for them was once a foreign language in that they have quite an extensive vocabulary and can connect hundreds of objects with names. Despite a normal inclination to resist the idea, they are well aware of what is expected of them in terms of times to sleep, take naps, wear clothes, take baths and brush their teeth. They are adept at communicating their own feelings to others and have developed sensitive perceptions in understanding what others communicate to them through gestures and facial expressions as well as through words. They recognize different textures and may even know some colors. They have learned to tolerate and endure separation from parents and have made other deep and important love relationships. They know hundreds of things that give them pleasure, and an equal number that do not. They have learned the important art of giving in to higher authority some of the time, as well as how to assert their independent opinions and feelings when they feel strongly inclined to do so. They have learned scores of ways to find out about things. They have learned to control even quite strong impulses for the pleasure of social approval.

A two-year-old is a wondrous thing to behold even though he cannot read a word! He can contradict his mother and obstinately fight to be a person in his own right. He has probably figured out which toys float and sink in the bathtub. He has strong preferences in food, toys, activities, clothes and people. He can be regal, bossy, compliant, selfish, brave, scared, curious, thoughtful and noisy. He knows what he likes and what he doesn't like, and he makes it quite clear that he wants to have a good deal to say about this! He recognizes favorite stories and songs, he can build with blocks, paint, play with clay, possibly do simple puzzles, string beads, paste, climb, run, hop, swing and, perhaps most exciting and wonderful of all, he is *beginning to imagine*. He can be a policeman, a farmer, a bus driver, a doctor and a storekeeper, as well as a Mommie, Daddy, baby or big brother. He has experienced feelings of love, affection, jealousy, compassion, hatred, fear and wonder. He is beginning to understand which things are alive and which are not. He has made friends with both animate, and inanimate objects. He has learned ingenious ways for taking things apart, he can pour and spill, pile and push. He has found his own special ways of handling the normal anxieties of life, by holding a special blanket, hugging a teddy bear or asking for help and comfort. And, for a long and truly significant life in the world, he is beginning to learn one of the most important talents required for what one hopes will be an increasingly civilized world—*empathy for others*.

When you think about this long-winded list of attributes (which could have been a lot longer if I were not exerting remarkable self-control), you will, I think, be forced to the logical conclusion that *this isn't bad at all* for just being alive in the world for approximately *twenty-four months!* Isn't this enough? Where are we going in such a hurry that we dare to demand more of our toddlers? In a life that may last eighty or more years, is there no time to let our babies explore the world and themselves in their own way and in their own good time? If we turn our little children into performing intellectual seals, what will we have accomplished? To become fully and deeply mature in adulthood we need time; this is probably one of the most important and necessary aspects of growth. Does it make the slightest difference whether or not Michelangelo or Edna St. Vincent Millay could read or write at two or three? What has happened to our sense of values about what is really important in life?

One of the most important signs of increasing mental health and a sense of well-being in patients who are receiving psychiatric treatment is when they begin to care about what is young and tender and vulnerable within themselves, when they stop despising the baby and the child within themselves, who—or so they felt—somehow never measured up to what was expected. It is a strange irony that just when we are beginning to understand that a central goal of psychotherapy must be to help those who have been wounded in life to rediscover their feelings, their instincts, the fresh and young and awakening part of themselves, we are at the same time living in a society that seems bent on making young children feel dissatisfied with their own growth, unacceptable and unlovable unless they dance to our tune.

A world that does not allow or even encourage mothers to coo idiot syllables of love to their babies is a world that is rejecting what is most human and civilized. Heaven knows that all is not sweetness and light in the care of infants; there are the sleepless nights, the dirty diapers, the tyranny of a screaming baby who can at times seem to be taking over all of one's life and vitality, the not infrequent moments when we get fed up with the normal demands of being parents. In this perspective, moments of exquisite pleasure are doubly precious, and anyone who tries to rob parents and children of such moments ought to be shot!

But the issue goes deeper than that; a world which negates these natural and human moments is doomed. For once we are robbed, at the very beginning of life, of what is most human in ourselves and our children, we are deformed; however brilliantly we may someday be able to understand atomic physics or to invent a new and better computer, we will be out of touch with our inner selves; and when that occurs, there can be no genuine creativity in science or art, engineering or poetry.

Babies are necessary to grown-ups. A new baby is like the beginning of all things—wonder, hope, a dream of possibilities. In a world that is cutting down its trees to build highways, losing its earth to concrete, cutting off its openness to sky and air with skyscrapers, polluting its waters, crowding its mountains and valleys with factories, replacing its teachers with machines—in such a world babies are almost the only remaining link with nature, with the natural world of living things from which we spring.

In the general fiasco of the New York World's Fair of 1964-65, one shining gem shone through all the technological tinsel. That was a film produced for the Johnson's Wax Pavilion by Francis Thompson, Inc., entitled *To Be Alive!* On three large screens we were allowed to see what makes us human, what makes us feel most alive and at home in the world—the simplest kinds of pleasures: watching a child on a swing, looking at a leaf floating in a pool, eating and drinking with those we love, walking in a wood in springtime, observing the dancing shadows and lights, breathing in deeply the scent of new-mown hay. The film's artistry was in looking at the human race when it is being most itself, in touch with the wonders of feeling and growing, cherishing the cycles of nature, the charm of young animals, the poignant and inspiring human cycles of birth and marriage and death. It demonstrated with sharp accuracy that, despite all our science and technology, to be human is to *feel*, to experience directly and personally the wonders of earth—a starlit night, a sunset, a morning coming up over the sea.

Young children help to give *us* perspective, caught as we are in our noisy, dirty, crowded cities, manipulated and controlled by things and machines. They help us to go on knowing what we are and what we may become. To hold a young warm life in one's arms is to find one's own inner being and to be refreshed. When we burden our babies with our arbitrary demands and expectations, based on nothing more than the questionable goals of a particular era in history, we teach them to fail; we offer discouragement and self-hatred as a substitute for the wonder and excitement of a time of life in which they have all the equipment they need for exploration and discovery of the joys in living.

If we keep going in the direction we seem to be headed at present, the next step will undoubtedly be intra-uterine teaching machines! After all, why should we let those kids just lie around for nine months, doing nothing but growing?

THREE

From the Cradle to the Grade:
This Montessori Madness

You can walk into almost any bookstore these days expecting to see at least one shelf of books about Dr. Maria Montessori; it is almost impossible to spend an evening with a group of friends who have young children without discussing a Montessori nursery school. And if, like me, you find this new wave of interest in an old-time educator quite unsettling, you may feel haunted as I am by number rods, geometrical forms and counting beads.

Why should there be such renewed interest in the first woman to become a physician in Italy at the turn of the century? Why should her ideas about the education of young children suddenly find such favor? It seems to me that The Montessori Method as it is being formulated today is simply another expression of our impatience with childhood, and our mechanistic concept of learning and growth.

Dr. Montessori was a bright, able, kind woman who, in

the early 1900's, found herself very much disturbed about the neglected and poverty-stricken pre-school youngsters in the slums of Rome. For her day, she had extremely foresighted and modern ideas about little children; she introduced what at that time were revolutionary ideas, such as that furniture for children should be their own size; that children were interested in exploring their immediate environment and becoming more competent to handle everyday activities with greater independence and freedom. Many of the toys she designed, which seem old-fashioned and narrow in concept to me today, were imaginative and original at the time when she was trying to introduce meaningful learning experiences to pre-school children.

Since the time in which Dr. Montessori worked, vital changes have taken place in education and psychology, to say nothing of human history in general. Freud was beginning his work at about the same time; his observations about the psychological meaning of a young child's play were not yet generally known. Dr. Montessori could not have the benefits of all that we have learned from psychoanalytic theory and psychiatric research. She could not have read the fascinating reports of Anna Freud and Susan Isaacs about their play experiences with children in England during the Second World War, which provided us with so much data on the way children handle their psychological problems through play activity. She could not enrich her own observations by evaluating them in relation to the results of the work of such contemporaries as John Dewey, William Heard Kilpatrick, Caroline Pratt, Felix Adler, Harold Rugg, Elizabeth Irwin and many others who were also developing new approaches to education. She could not relate her thinking to the important theories of Jean Piaget

or see all of these contributions in the perspective of life
today.

We know so much more about children than anyone
could have known in her lifetime, and our children are so
different. They eat better food, and when they are ill they
are treated with antibiotics—so they are stronger and bigger and more active than children have ever been before.
We live in a world in which people understand so much
more about feelings, about what goes on inside a child's
mind, about anxiety, fears, anger, imagination and a host of
other emotional and social adjustments. The children Dr.
Montessori dealt with had never heard of the radio or of
TV, the airplane or space travel, the two terrible world
wars or the death camps, or the ideological struggles of
communism, fascism and democracy. People could not talk
to each other on the telephone; there were few cars and
movies. What she contributed was fine for the times, and
some of it was ingenious and creative enough to bear the
passage of time and to still be usefully adapted to the modern world. But when any group of people finds it necessary
to choose one idol from the distant past in a world that has
changed more in the last half-century than in the preceding
five or six centuries, I am drawn to the conclusion that the
adulation is not wisdom but blind faith—a mystical religious revival. Because Maria Montessori was herself a creative thinker, I cannot believe that she would be at all happy
about what is being done in her name. The passionate fervor of today's Montessori proponents, their single-minded
dependence on a narrow formulation and program despite
all that has been learned about children and education since
Dr. Montessori was alive, does not represent an objective or
thoughtful pooling of all the resources at our disposal, but

rather an intense and irrational clinging to a symbol that is being interpreted in terms of the special pressures of our times. It means to think rigidly and inflexibly, to regiment children and to avoid facing the tough challenges and problems of helping children to grow in a complex and changing world. What many parents are being led to regard as a new scientific approach to childhood education is really a mystical faith in a heroine who would probably be horrified if she could hear what values and purposes her disciples have attached to the developing mystique. I have tried to learn as much as I could about the new Montessori movement. I have read books by its proponents, gone to lectures by Montessori teachers, talked with many colleagues and received detailed reports of their visits to Montessori schools, listened to the reports of parents about their own children's experiences, both good and bad, and visited a Montessori school myself. I know that Montessori teachers and schools vary greatly in professional skills and point of view. I also know from personal experience that good teaching is always good, no matter what school of thought it may derive from, and bad teaching is always bad, even if it springs from ideas that I accept and promote myself. But whatever the variations and nuances in individual settings and among its enthusiasts, it seems to me that there are some fundamental assumptions, practices and goals that stand out in sharp and consistent focus.

There is a tendency to push children into standardized patterns of achievement. It is an approach that covers up the exuberance and energy of young children, it represses their vitality, their obstreperousness, it makes them nicely manageable. It makes them look like miniature grown-ups, so that we can comfortably forget that they are not. It narrows the range of what a child may do because the equipment is to be used in certain circumscribed ways. And while the advocates protest that they are opening up new vistas and teaching new skills, they are really encouraging conformity and the narrowing of experience.

In attempting to support my own view, let me start with my direct observations of one school. The children ranged in age from two and a half to five. As they came in, I noticed that they were dressed in a way that is no longer customary for nursery-school children. The little girls wore dresses, the boys either long- or short-legged suits with jackets. As they came into the classroom, a teacher shook hands with each child; many of the children curtsied or bowed. The older children, four to almost six years of age, sat at tables waiting for instructions; in another room the two-and-a-half- to three-and-a-half-year-olds wandered around aimlessly, waiting for the teachers to officially open the morning session. No mothers or fathers were allowed beyond the door. The rooms were extremely quiet—the teachers all seemed to be the "whispery" type, and the children seemed to move almost silently from place to place; there was no gleeful shouting, no boisterousness, no running or playing, no display of the kind of vitality and energy that I have been accustomed to seeing in nursery-school youngsters.

The equipment in the playroom seemed meager and limited; in the past sixty years all sorts of marvelous play equipment has been created to help children express their feelings, explore their world, encourage creative dramatic play and help them to develop mastery over themselves and their environment. But there were no big construction blocks, no dolls or dollhouse equipment, no puppets, no animals, no boats, trains, cars or trucks, no evidence of crayons, paints or clay. All I could see were materials designed by Dr. Montessori some fifty or more years ago—equipment for washing up and for learning to tie laces, bells for distinguishing musical tones, long strings of beads for counting, number rods and letters, geometric forms, stencils, puzzles, small pieces of paper to write on, pencils and an assortment of special objects used by the teachers and children for special kinds of "concept formation."

This was a general visitor's day, and many of the other observers were obviously entranced by some of the goings-on, such as a little girl's using a flannel board on which she was "organizing" objects into categories. For example, next to a hat she placed a dress ("things we wear") and next to a picture of a tree she placed a flower ("things that grow"). There was general glee that we were watching "conceptualization" take place! What drove me nearly wild was that in twenty-five years of watching nursery-age children play freely and spontaneously in a flexible environment full of all kinds of resources, I had seen the same kind of brilliant deductions going on incessantly in play that was so light and quick and individualized that it was almost impossible to notice when and where this kind of learning was going on.

Another example of what seems to me the unrealistic hope that we have found some mysterious and magical answer to the complexities of learning was the reaction of many observers to a teacher who was sitting on the floor with four children. She had a box of shells, and on the floor was a chart with colored pictures of different geometric shapes. She was helping the children place each variety of shell on the corresponding shape. Several visiting teachers sitting near me were entranced. "What a marvelous idea," they were exclaiming. Now, anyone who has ever worked for any length of time with young children knows that children do this sort of thing all by themselves and that in any environment that provides objects of various sizes and shapes they will make such associations constantly, in such an easy and unselfconscious way that nobody marvels at what they are learning.

The other visitors also seemed delighted by the quiet in the classrooms. No one shouted—in fact, there was very little verbal communication, and what there was was in undertones and whispers. I wanted to yell, "What is so great about *silence?*" Assuredly, most adults enjoy and value it— but is it really natural in children? Do we find it at all times among children playing freely without adult restraints? Do children usually mind noise, does it distract them as it does us? The silence, the lack of animated conversation—and the pleasure this seemed to evoke in other observers—reinforced my conviction that in a time of great turbulence and uncertainty "The Montessori Method" provides adults with some nice, comfortable, secure answers to some complex, uncomfortable and anxiety-producing questions about life in today's world.

Toward the middle of the morning two little boys who were getting pretty bored with the circumscribed tasks available to them began carrying a tray of some "building units" to the floor. These resemble building blocks, but they are built in specific size units to teach number concepts. The two renegades started to build, as children do with ordinary blocks; I heard them discussing how they would build a garage. As soon as the teacher observed the unorthodox way in which they were using these units, she quietly asked them to put the materials away or to use them in an orderly pattern for studying tens and hundreds. It seemed to me that there was *less* genuine and significant learning going on than in most of the good nursery schools where I had taught or observed. It seemed to me that much of what I saw was meaningless busy-work. A number of children spent most of the morning just sitting at tables idly leafing through books. The limitations of the environment were not encouraging the kind of free and vital explorations that Montessori proponents talk about so much.

I had the eerie sensation all morning that I had gotten into a "time machine" and had traveled back to 1910 or thereabouts, and that I was seeing what would have been considered a wonderful and childlike world for that time in history. I was not seeing any evidence of the richness of our knowledge about children from that day to this—nothing that gave me the feeling that here was a place where teachers could bring together the myriad ideas, experiences and knowledge now available to us. Visitors to other Montessori schools report that some schools do use a wider variety of materials, but they tend to be used in more formal, stereotyped ways than in a free-play program.

When I was in college studying early childhood education, our professors tried to impress us with the fact that nursery-age children are social beings and that one good reason for placing a child in a nursery school is to encourage and guide a child's growing understanding of himself in relation to other people. I was, and still am, constantly astounded at what young children at play learn about what it means to live in a world with other people: how to be fully oneself, to develop one's own interests and strengths and at the same time to participate in life with others. While the children I was now observing had minor contacts with each other—sitting at the same table doing individual puzzles, or three or four sitting with a teacher learning about numbers—until it was time to "go out and play," there was no really healthy, robust collision of child with child in anger or affection or selfishness or compassion. This was not a laboratory in which one could learn about oneself in relation to others. There was no real traffic, no animated conversations—no yelling at each other! How do any of us know that we are truly alive until we begin to bump into other people? How can we really learn to be polite and caring when half our feelings are kept under wraps at all times? The atmosphere was reminiscent of pre-Freudian days, when children were repressed, when they were made to behave like miniature adults; these children were so careful, so polite, so un-free that they looked for all the world like their own grandmothers and grandfathers! There were no outward signs of restlessness or rebellion—except from the two thwarted garage-builders, who were saying "bathroom words" to each other when the teacher moved out of their range.

I became so restless and uncomfortable that I could hardly wait to leave. Where was the glorious world of nursery school that I learned about in college in the 1940's? Where was the experimenting with relationships, the rich profusion of imaginative play that helped a child understand his world? Where was the working out in play of ambivalent feelings? Where was the emotional working through of fears and confusions by the use of make-believe? Where was the lovely individuality of each child finding his own music, his own beat, his own world of dreams and hopes? The next day I raced eagerly up to

Westchester, back home to my own nursery school; and when a teacher came up to me and said, "Gee, I'm glad you're here today—I've *got* to talk to you about what to do about Peter—he urinated on Betsy again today!" I could have hugged her! Here was the reality of children being children, letting their feelings and problems show, so that we could help them learn to handle them.

So much for my indisputably subjective reaction; this personal experience was hardly grounds for any final conclusions. In order to make sound judgments, one must explore further.

The rebirth of interest in Dr. Montessori developed in the 1950's. A teacher, Nancy McCormick Rambusch, became interested in the Montessori schools that were reappearing in other countries. In 1953 *Jubilee*, a Catholic magazine, carried the first of a series of articles by her, and in 1958 she founded The Whitby School in Connecticut. She was also the founder in 1960 of the American Montessori Society. That something about the Montessori method was falling on fertile soil is attested to by the great interest evoked by the publication in 1962 of Mrs. Rambusch's book *Learning How to Learn: An American Approach to Montessori* (Helicon Press) and by the fact that in 1964 alone four or five books written before the First World War by and about Dr. Montessori were published without revision. In *The New York Times* on Sunday, October 4, 1964, appeared the following report:

When the liner *Cincinnati* steamed into New York Harbor on a crisp December morning in 1913, Dr. Maria Montessori, a young woman of regal bearing and assurance, stood at the railing. When she walked down the gangway she was surrounded six-deep by welcoming disciples who knew her work as an educator. Schools bearing her name had been established in many parts of Europe. . . . Now she had come to implant in America her idea that children from 3 to 5 years old were ready for classroom training. . . . Her educational system spread quickly across the nation . . . but a few years later both she and her system were virtually forgotten here. . . . [With the new wave of interest] educators wonder: Is a fad having a second flurry, or has the method been revived because it was too good for limbo? A Montessori classroom is not primarily a nursery or a playpen. It is primarily a place of learning. . . . The shelves are filled with the essential tools of learning. . . . A Montessori classroom is a place of almost mysterious silence and concentration. A visitor finds 20 or more tots each bending over some private occupation in deep absorption like so many doctoral candidates researching their theses.

In her book Mrs. Rambusch stated, "Montessori recognized that the early years, from 2 to 6, are critically important for the child's future education. . . . Some psychologists maintain that half of all the growth in intelligence takes place before the age of 4 and 8. Children need intellectual challenge in these years if they're to achieve maximum development." There is an obvious similarity between this statement and the pronouncements of the new flock of theoreticians so busily engaged in fostering accelerated mental development; if thousands of parents can be attracted by the prospect of teaching ten-month-old infants to read, then certainly they are more than likely to show enthusiastic interest in continuing this supposed "enrichment" into the nursery years. Mrs. Rambusch herself has said that the emphasis on "brass tacks education," especially scientific education, which she outlined in her book, may have stimulated the renewed interest in Montessori techniques.

Membership in the Montessori Society has increased by leaps and bounds, and Montessori schools have mushroomed all over the United States. The attraction of this approach is reflected in the brochure provided by the school that I visited. In describing Dr. Montessori's theories, it stated:

A basic tenet of her philosophy is that a child's growth is marked by "sensitive periods," . . . when he feels an inner drive to understand certain processes. . . . She also observed that children are happiest in a prepared environment where every object has its place and activities are performed in an orderly way. In this manner the confusions in a child's life are minimized and he is more free to learn. . . . Real progress in learning occurs only through his own actions. . . . In a large, peaceful and attractive classroom, where good manners and neatness are stressed, the children work at individual tables or on mats on the floor . . . working alone or quietly with others. . . . Group activities are never forced upon the child. . . . All materials are designed to develop the sense perceptions of the child so that he acquires the habit of observing the world about him accurately.

This was followed by a list of materials to be used in the practical application of these goals:

1. *Practical Life Exercises* (polishing shoes, silver, washing tables, sweeping, buttoning, pouring, flower arranging).
2. *Sensorial Materials* (matching colors, grading colors, measuring size, volume, width, length, weight).
3. *Academic Materials* (number rods, counting beads, cubes in units of tens, letters, geometric shapes, jigsaw puzzle maps).

What are some of the implications of this theory? It seems to me that this approach invites and encourages conformity and discourages initiative and creativity. "A prepared environment" can certainly make some children appear to be happy; any psychiatrist knows only too well how comforting compulsive orderliness can be. But the real world is full of *dis*-order, and while this may cause anxiety and confusion, it cannot be avoided. If we need to provide anything for our young learners, it seems to me there ought to be ways to tolerate the not-to-be-denied uncertainties with which we are required to live. In a larger social sense, Dr. Montessori could not have known that while her fellow countryman Mussolini would make the Italian trains run on time by a neat and orderly "prepared environment," there would be some terrifying side-effects! Life in a democratic society is not always comfortable, predictable or reassuringly orderly—but to many of us the alternatives seem far more undesirable. The miniature "cosmos" we create for our nursery-school children ought to reflect these conclusions.

There was no mention in this brochure of any goals for progress in feeling and relating. Do we not learn from others, as well as from what we do ourselves? Is motivation for learning not related to the human interplay of adult and child, to feelings of love, approval and acceptance? Aren't children encouraged to explore by the example of adults who are deeply committed to, and satisfied by, the adventure of learning? And as for "observing the world *accurately*," who has ever managed to do *that*? Isn't part of the wonderful potential of the human race the fact that each of us can perceive differently? Did Aristotle, Galileo and Columbus observe the world "accurately"? Only in the sense that they brought new observations to their own times—and each age has added or subtracted from their perceptions in terms of changing information and knowledge. Do we want to teach our children to make categorical assumptions about what is "accurate," or do we want them to understand change and to see life as fluid and always newly seen? This seems hardly the time in history to teach the worship of facts, when many of today's facts may be on tomorrow's scrap heap.

The "Practical Life Exercises" may have been a novelty to Dr. Montessori's slum children of fifty or more years ago. She was concerned with the fact that many of these children were being cared for by elderly grandmothers and were never permitted to do anything for themselves. Today's sophisticated youngsters are almost invariably provided with opportunities for such activities. Certainly any good nursery school takes it for granted that one of the goals is to encourage independent self-care and responsibility for housekeeping in the classroom; the real difference is that non-Montessori schools go far beyond these bounds. Reflecting information and understanding that Dr. Montessori would probably have found intriguing herself, they also provide materials for the development of creativity, socialization and emotional maturation.

There was a logical reason in Dr. Montessori's time to concentrate so completely on "the real world." The children she was dealing with were surrounded by superstition and fantasy; they had quite enough of the world of fairy tales in their homes—and Dr. Montessori felt a need to counterbalance this influence with a greater awareness of the practical and rational side of life. We now know that feelings of self-competence come just as much and just as importantly from learning to master one's feelings as from swinging a mop or a broom!

One of the problems in evaluating the Montessori approach is that any setting in which children are cared for with genuine concern for their welfare is more than likely to produce some fine results. Whatever the fundamental philosophy and goals, any child is likely to blossom if he is lucky enough to attend a school where there are enough teachers to provide a great deal of individual attention, and where those teachers are deeply motivated and committed to encouraging a child's instinctive appetite for learning. The question is whether Montessori schools accomplish more, and the exact nature of their accomplishment.

I came to understand this dilemma when I attended several lectures given by a perfectly charming, highly intelligent, warm and personable Montessori teacher. She obviously loved children, she had a most attractive manner and a good sense of humor and she made the whole orientation sound so absolutely reasonable that I began to think of myself as a stubborn idiot not to join the faith. She said, "One must constantly refreshen oneself, look at the child, what serves his appetites for growth." That's a very fine statement. She talked about helping children to be relaxed and at peace with themselves. She wanted to make the environment appealing to children and to give them the pleasure of discovery. The words sounded so sensible—and it was only hours later that I realized the omissions, the absence of real concern with relationships and feelings. As I reread my notes at home, I was able to see that, while many of the things she said were just fine, there was an underlying theme: the development of a mystique—a perfect set of answers to the problems of an imperfect world.

Much the same reaction was expressed in an article by Edward Wakin in *The Saturday Review* (November 21, 1964) entitled "The Return of Montessori." He wrote, "Even without the Montessori philosophy, a nursery school with such advantages (fervor and enthusiasm of teachers, small classes, well endowed children) would produce results." He discussed the tendency of its enthusiasts for overselling and for presenting this kind of education as a panacea. He concluded that this approach had lost its first round in America by unfair and one-sided criticism of John Dewey and progressive education, and might lose the second time around in the United States from overzealousness.

One probable aspect of many of today's Montessori schools tends to make the results look deceptively successful: a weeding-out process. Those children with high energy and vitality who become restless and bored very easily, and who are able to express their inner feelings of anxiety or hostility quite openly, frequently do not succeed. Their parents are forced to take them out of such schools and place them in more informal and permissive settings. The children who seem to be most happy and who succeed in a way that is most satisfying to the Montessori teacher are those who, being somewhat more passive and compulsive, find security and safety in dusting tables, arranging doilies and being left alone. While many of these children may be perfectly normal, healthy children who happen to be somewhat quiet and orderly loners, others may be youngsters who are retreating from serious emotional problems. In an overly standardized and organized nursery classroom, it is hard to differentiate between, or evaluate, these important differences. At any rate, to some of the parents who visit such a school, it may well look like heaven on earth to see children so quiet and well-behaved. What such a visitor must keep in mind is that the natural-born "hell-raisers" have probably been "drop-outs" or "transfers"!

One little boy who did not last was Paul, four years old, who came to our nursery school after five weeks in a Montessori school. He became very anxious because he had trouble learning to tie his shoelaces. However, after two weeks of struggling with this assignment, he came home, ecstatic with excitement, and told his mother, "I *learned*, I really *learned* to do it!" That night he fell asleep, completely exhausted from the strain he had been under. He woke up in the middle of the night shrieking, and when his mother rushed into his room, he cried out, "I dreamed I forgot how to do it!" This is not to say that anyone was putting constant or punitive pressure on Paul to tie his shoelaces; it is possible that he was simply the kind of child who puts unreasonable demands on himself. Such a child needs an environment that understands his special feelings about himself and provides him with a variety of experiences that will counterbalance his inner uncertainties. The rambunctious, lively, acting-out kind of child who cannot control his perfectly normal impulses to shout, jump, tease and punch would be a problem in most Montessori settings, and, slinking off miserably to a more informal nursery school, he and his parents are left wondering why he is such a failure.

The two following observations exemplify my own feelings about the new Montessori movement in America. Dr. Henry Haskell, Dean of Wheelock College, stated (in *Today's Child*, March 1966) that he felt that the Montessori system's emphasis on orderliness, quiet and obedience was more appropriate for training authoritarian societies than for life in a democracy, where there is a desperate need for creative individuals. He also felt that the stress on early reading and writing was the attraction for so many ambitious middle-class parents to this approach. He held that a fundamentally Puritan approach appeals to parents who want their children to be quiet, clean, neat and well disciplined. Dr. Haskell questioned the system's reliance on structured materials and situations, stating that he would rather see two children struggling over the possession of a bicycle, an unstructured situation providing the kind of human interaction and problem-solving experience needed in today's world.

In a review of the republished works of Dr. Montessori, Penelope Pinson wrote in *Parents' Magazine:*

> Some people, fearful that American children are not learning enough, think we should adopt all her teaching methods. . . . What . . . was in a Montessori classroom? . . . Furniture, some plants and lots of Montessori "toys." No easel with paints. No doll corner, no toy trucks, cars, boats, building blocks, puppets or dress-up clothes. Maria Montessori was strict about the use of her teaching devices and had little interest in children's imagination . . . each device was designed

to train muscles, educate the senses, or prepare for
writing and arithmetic. Each device must be used in
only one way. No child could take the tower of blocks
and build a ship. He could use all the exciting colors of
the rainbow—but only to put them in the exact order
of the spectrum. . . . Today we know that pre-
schoolers need more than a trained brain and body and
the "calmness" that Montessori admired. They need to
play with other children . . . discover the world
through trips, books, music, conversation. Above all
they need to communicate with other people . . .
with a teacher there to help them manage the raw materials of group living; fear, anger, love, excitement,
jealousy. . . . We also find that most children of six or
seven can write as neatly with two weeks' practice as a
Montessori child who has spent two years struggling
to train his immature muscles. . . . Many of Montessori's theories were excellent . . . but in practice she
fostered only neatness, order and self-control. We may
need a revolution in education today, but Montessori's
revolution happened sixty years ago. Her method is
tempting to experimenters because it is so easy to set
up. All the rules are spelled out, all the equipment prescribed. But today we must make new discoveries that
fit our crowded, fast-changing world. Her books make
fascinating history . . . but let's not mistake them for
blueprints.

However pure the motives of its advocates may be, the
new Montessori movement has developed for the wrong
reasons. It has caught on because it is simple, because it
promises academic achievement, because it is neat and be-

cause it manages to evade some of the most challenging and complex problems about child development. It invites young children to masquerade as adults—a classic example of the conspiracy to eliminate childhood.

FOUR

Getting into the
Nursery School of Your Choice

NURSERY education is "in" at long last. For those of us who have felt that going to nursery school could be a profoundly meaningful experience for most young children, this should be a time of great exultation and triumph. It is not. The current vogue to support pre-school education has very little to do with the values which motivated the pioneers in nursery-school education, who saw it as an opportunity to help young children explore their own three-to-five world; to encourage creativity and self-understanding; and to provide opportunities for learning to live well with other people.

None of these goals is related to the current wave of popularity; academic pressures on elementary, high-school and college students have simply seeped down to the nursery-school level to such a degree that being turned down by a nursery school can cause almost as much parental distress and misery as being turned down by Harvard or Yale. An

article in *The New York Times* (November 2, 1962) reflects the mounting hysteria.

The mother of a rather young man called upon the
headmaster of the Cisqua School in Mount Kisco,
N. Y., last year. "She started to talk about her aims for
her child and his need to get forth in the world," re-
called Henry O. Milliken, Jr., whose school embraces
nursery through primary grades. "Suddenly I discovered that her son was 20 months old. I had to calm her
down and explain how young her child really was and
that he wouldn't be ready for Harvard tomorrow but
when he was 18." This tale, with small variations, is
familiar to all those in the New York area who are
closely identified with early childhood education.
. . . So-called "prestige" schools are engulfed by applications, sometimes five for every available space.
Hunter Elementary School, which is tuition-free and
admits children solely on the basis of intelligence
scores, has 2000 applications for 70 vacancies. . . .
"We try to give mothers the feeling that their children
have not been rejected," said Eleanor Brussel, a founder
and former director of the New York School For
Nursery Years. [She said that] most of the candidates
were acceptable, but that the growing flood of applications had made admission largely a matter of chance.
[Dependent on what a school may need for a balanced
grouping] . . . There is the conviction, for some,
that the road to a prestige college and economic and
social success must be plotted early.

A mother called a nursery school and was told that she
had to apply a year in advance and have her child tested for
admission. The admission process in many nursery schools

is now more complex, or at least as complex, as getting into college. I.Q. tests are administered, parents and children are interviewed and observed, clinical reports evaluating the child's personality are sometimes required. Another mother who called a nursery school to inquire about enrollment for her three-year-old was told, "We only accept applications from children with college potential." A parent wrote to me recently, "I thought you might be interested in how far down the scale the pressures go. We just started our daughter at nursery school and after three months we got a formal report from the school in which she received letter grades in such subjects as 'sitting still,' 'attention span,' and 'singing in unison.' She is just 3 years old."

Such nursery schools reflect the expectations and demands of a growing number of parents who have been greatly influenced by the general climate of our times. It is again the syndrome of "Let's get on with it and get these kids grown up!" At the nursery school where I work, on the first day of school in the fall two parents brought in psychological test reports on their four-year-old children. The tests "proved" that according to their "mental age" the children should really be in second grade. These mothers hoped we would try to provide "an enriched program" so that their children might be permitted to at least skip kindergarten the following year. One of these children was still wetting her bed every night; the other spent the first three months at nursery school learning that biting was not a satisfactory method for getting your own way. Every year when they come to register their three-year-olds more parents ask if the nursery school has a reading-readiness program. One mother told us, "I just can't stand it when Jerry's not doing anything." She said she was concerned because her child had too little drive and ambition and would not do well in school because he spent too much time "making believe." Her son was four years old.

Another reflection of the current hysteria is the "boredom theory in education." This is expressed by the constantly increasing number of parents who ask if a child who has been in nursery school for one or two years won't be terribly bored in kindergarten. They are somewhat startled if I say, "Well, you were a housewife and mother last year, you are again this year, and you will be again next year, so I guess you are bored and can't learn anything new." Apparently the idea that doing any of the same things two years in a row means that it has to be boring only applies to children, not to adults. In adulthood we seem to be more likely to recognize the fact that time changes the way that you do something and what it means to you—that maturity and experience make similar events totally different and that we can go on learning. Repetition of an action or an experience seems perfectly appropriate and normal in adult life.

One senses the inner tensions, the compulsion of many parents to push for growth, not only in the nursery school, but in day camps for young children as well. At one day camp the director built a large wading pool for the three- and four-year-olds on the theory that many children of that age are afraid of the water and need a gradual introduction to this experience, rather than being confronted too abruptly with getting into the regular swimming pool used by the older children for more formal swimming instruction. She was nonplussed when she was bombarded by telephone calls and letters from outraged parents who did not want their children to be using "the baby pool." In a typical letter she received, the irate mother of a three-year-old wrote:

When I registered Jimmie at your day-camp, I was
clearly under the impression that he would receive
swimming instruction in the big pool. I cannot understand what you are waiting for—there are only *three
more weeks* left. I am very displeased with the swimming program and cannot see any constructive purpose in keeping Jimmie in knee-deep water when he is
perfectly capable of learning to do the "dog paddle,"
if he is taught. I feel very strongly about this and want
the situation rectified at once.

When any young child expresses a genuine interest and
readiness for a new experience, it would, of course, be ridiculous to hold him back, whether this be learning to write
his name, count to 100 or swim. The point is that, quite
aside from this issue, *where are we going in such a hurry?* A
child who develops such skills at three or four will not necessarily be any more skilled at eight than children who learn
such skills at seven. But whether or not he *does* perform at a
higher level, of what consequence is this in the life of a human being whom we have every reason to believe will still
be writing, counting and swimming at eighty?
    Unfortunately the original goals and purposes of nursery
education are being lost in an atmosphere that simply has no
patience with, or perspective about, growth as a life-long
process. The initial impetus for nursery education developed in relation to two major sources of insight and interest
in child development: the developing fields of psychology
and psychiatry, and the philosophy of progressive education. In the 1920's and 1930's we were discovering that a
child's play was his natural, instinctive way of learning
about himself and the world in which he lives; it was the

way in which the young child learned about his feelings, gained mastery over himself and came to understand and accept social controls. Educators became convinced that the young child's natural curiosity, his inventiveness, his wish to discover and experiment—his play, in other words —could be stimulated and reinforced in an environment that provided resources and guidance for his self-explorations. We looked on the nursery school as a place that could help each child develop his own special strengths, find outlets for his feelings, develop the skills that would give him self-confidence and begin the long tough job of becoming a civilized human being who could relate to others successfully, but not at the cost of sacrificing his uniqueness.

During those years, and into the early 1940's, there was a certain prestige in studying to be a nursery-school teacher; it indicated that one was aware of the new information becoming available to us in child psychology, which focused so much attention on the early years of life. Child-development researchers were telling us that the emotional climate in which a child lived during his first few years could have a significant effect on his mental health as an adult. In watching him play, we could learn about his needs; in guiding his play we could help him to find healthy avenues of self expression; in offering him opportunities for creative play in a social environment we could help him develop self-understanding and genuine concern for others. The nursery school was the place where parents and teachers, working together, could give each child a good start toward healthy maturation and self-fulfillment. A nursery-school teacher was not only an educator and a child psychologist, but a parent educator as well; parent education got its biggest boost from the early years of the nursery-school movement; here was the place to really study child development and learn new and better ways to help children grow well. Psychiatry was providing us with information about the early sources of adult emotional disturbance, and the nursery-school educator felt himself to be on the front lines in preventive mental health; here, in the early years of life, was the place to intervene, to "start things out right."

During the Depression, nursery education advanced with passage of the Lanham Act, through which the federal government paid unemployed teachers to work in nursery schools. This did not always enhance the original purposes which had to do with the needs of *children*, but it kept nursery schools going. During the Second World War there was another step forward because now mothers were needed to work in defense plants, and provisions had to be made for their young children. Again, the motivation was not to meet the needs of the children specifically, but they benefited from the needs of the community. By 1950 interest in nursery education seemed to be declining. This does not mean that there were not many nursery schools operating—middle-class parents especially wanted to provide this experience for their children, and did so, through private and cooperative schools. But there was little support for nursery education in local, state or federal governments to provide facilities for working mothers, and many college students planning a career in teaching looked with disdain on nursery education; the early impact of progressive education was waning, and since the emphasis in nursery schools had always been on "play" rather than on "learning" (as if the two could ever be mutually exclusive) teaching nursery-age children was viewed as "baby sitting"; the real rewards and satisfactions were in teaching "real school." There was a growing tendency in teachers' colleges to lump nursery education with elementary education, certifying teachers in both, without regard for the real and demonstrable differences.

By the early 1960's I began to see the marked change in attitude. When I started out as a nursery-school teacher in the 1940's, I felt it to be a fascinating and challenging profession, and one in which I could make a profound and significant contribution. In 1962, when I began working as a consultant in a Westchester nursery school, I found that new teachers, coming from colleges of all kinds, really felt that teaching nursery school was a way to fill up their time until they married or went to graduate school. Those who had certification to teach in public schools were waiting for kindergarten-to-third-grade assignments. Their attitude was that nothing of any real importance could possibly be going on in a nursery school.

Suddenly, in the last few years, this whole outlook has changed. With the increasing pressures for academic acceleration all along the line, the nursery school has achieved a new importance. Educators and psychologists who tell us that we are wasting the brain power of pre-school children, middle-class hysteria about getting children into college, the increasing concern about school failures among "disadvantaged" children, the general anxiety and confusion about "keeping up with the Russians" and the technological and scientific revolution that is causing such rapid and violent changes in the meaning and nature of work, have all brought about a new attitude toward the pre-school years. There is no question in my own mind that the sudden popularity of the nursery school is due to the promise, however covertly it may be made, that going to nursery school will prepare children for greater academic success earlier and for accelerated academic achievement.

The brains of three- and four-year-olds have become a "national asset"—to be exploited, to be pushed into more rapid growth, to solve all the problems of later school failures. We act as if we had found a relatively simple answer to one of the most complicated and terrifying problems facing education today. In an urban and industrial society faced with impossible problems of population explosion, inadequate teachers and schools, with educational programs that are unequal to the tasks involved in meeting the problems of rapid and complex social change, we have decided that the primary solution to our problems is to start formal education at an earlier age. Despite the fact that the increase in school failures is not only a problem of the "culturally deprived" child but is also occurring more frequently among his more privileged middle-class schoolmates, reflecting school systems in which classes are too large, in which educational services are drowning in a sea of administrative functions and in which, with the best will in the world, no teacher, however dedicated and gifted, can possibly meet the varied and complex needs of each child, we seem bent on making our three-to-five-year-olds solve the problem of the glaring inadequacies of our school systems.

Millions of dollars are being made available by the government for the education of pre-school children. Suddenly specialists in early childhood education are important and sought-after to administer Head Start and other anti-poverty programs affecting the lives of young children. It would be a lovely honeymoon—if one did not have to be so suspicious of the motives.

It seems to me a matter of great urgency to examine the new interest in helping the "disadvantaged" child in the larger context of what it is that we want and expect of all young children. It is true that children who are born into poverty, into social, economic and cultural deprivation, do fall behind in school achievement more frequently than do middle-class children. It is equally true that a sound, well-rounded nursery-school experience, which fosters general maturation, can be helpful to most children as an initial exposure to group living and learning, and that many of the teachers and consultants working in these programs feel this very deeply. It is also true that a democratic society must concern itself with providing equal opportunities for all children to develop their own unique and special gifts for competence in living and working and for inner self-fulfillment. But is this what we are now doing?

It seems to me that most of the programs now underway, including Head Start, have enjoyed their popular acceptance because they are conceived by the general public to be designed to accelerate academic achievement. Despite the fact that the top officials in the various programs may themselves be concerned with helping children grow toward a fuller and more meaningful life, this is not what most people find attractive or acceptable about the enormous financial investment they are making. We want to make children "smarter"; if we really wanted to help children become happier, more mature socially and emotionally, if we wanted to encourage an eagerness and an excitement about learning, we would be expressing far more concern than we are about the inadequacies of the new facilities we are creating. For example, in one Head Start program covering an area of twenty school systems, only two people had been specifically trained as specialists in early child development. This kind of procedure does not express a concern for the total needs of young children.

One of the reasons why all of us should examine and evaluate the new pre-school programs in relation to the general climate of attitudes toward young children is that in the long run we may be adding new defeats to old problems of school failure. Most of the children upon whom we are now focusing our interest happen to be Negro, Puerto Rican, Mexican and American Indian. A major concern is that these children, burdened by poverty and minority-status problems by the time they are three years old, have already developed a self-image that is very poor indeed. It does not take many years for a child to begin to see himself as he feels others see him—as a second-class citizen, as a human being who is somehow unworthy. If, when we provide "enrichment" programs, our aim is merely to put pressure on children for accelerated mental development, we may be adding to their feelings of unworthiness rather than relieving those they already have. The only way to help a child feel really good about himself, to enjoy being the person he is and to look forward optimistically to growing up, is to help him to develop *all* his strengths and to try to meet *all* his needs. If he feels that his worth is only to be measured in terms of how fast he can learn to read and write, and if he becomes frightened and anxious about these demands, then, in addition to having a low estimate of himself as a member of a minority group, he will simply join the increasing ranks of white middle-class children who see themselves as school failures by the time they are in second grade.

A Negro mother who had sent her four-year-old daughter to a Head Start nursery school told me that one day, when she went to call for her daughter at school, she was greeted by a sad and woebegone face. When she asked what was the matter, her daughter said, "I think I failed in orange juice today." Drinking fruit juices was a novelty for this child, and Fanny had apparently made it quite clear that she did not like the whole idea. But where did she get the idea that she was *failing?* How does a four-year-old arrive at such a conclusion? It seems to me that this is an example of the hazards involved in imposing middle-class standards on all children, whether it be in the area of academic achievement or in that of social custom. These children will feel that they are failing for all sorts of new reasons, unrelated to the color of their skin. Since this kind of experience will not help a child feel more confident about his strengths and potentialities, it will certainly not help him to become more open and eager for later school experiences. Instead of focusing our attention on developing readiness for academic achievement promulgating middle-class standards and behavior, we ought to be spending our time and our money on ways in which to help every child to feel that he is a *person*, that he is lovable and that he can contribute something of value to others.

The New York *Post* on May 31, 1966, carried a headline, " 'Must' Schooling at Age 4 Urged." The accompanying article stated:

WASHINGTON, MAY 31 (AP)—An education commission called today for mandatory schooling of four-and-five-year-olds and urged the federal government to provide general support for the revolutionary proposal. The Education Policies Commission said, "education in this two-year period can affect the character of the child and all his future life more deeply than his education at any later period." It added: "Early childhood education, properly conducted, promises significant benefits to American life. . . ." In a report titled "Universal Opportunity for Early Childhood Education," the commission described the current practice of starting children to school at the age of six as "obsolete" since most children that age "have already developed a considerable part of the intellectual ability they will possess as adults."

No one in the field of nursery education would dispute the notion that the years from three to five are an important period of growth—and the fact that the report starts out by mentioning character formation might lead one to believe that we see here a genuine awareness of the full scope of child development in the nursery years. But what is really meant by "significant benefits to American life"? The answer is expressed in the further explanation that children of this age have already developed "a considerable part of their intellectual ability." The emphasis is clearly on academic performance; if this were not true, the report might have stated that children need a good start in their emotional, physical and social growth in order to have better self-concepts, enthusiasm for learning, enjoyment of relationships with others, and the like. The whole tone of the announcement further accentuates the idea that everything important in the mental development of the child occurs at an early age, and if the intellect is not properly stimulated at that time, there is no hope. It is again a total denial of the true nature of life and of growth—a process which goes on all through life and that can be significant at twenty or forty or sixty or later. It may seem like quibbling to criticize the new interest in young children; but it seems to me that if anything is done for the wrong reasons, the results cannot be right.

That the renewed interest in nursery education is often only incidentally a reflection of genuine concern for the deprived child is borne out by the fact that the same new prestige is enjoyed by nursery schools which serve the middle- and upper-class child. We are not really thinking about *children* in either case, but of how we can make them grow up faster. Let me try to document this point of view; the following are just a few samples of the accumulating evidence.

1. *The New York Times,* October 7, 1962. An article bearing the headline "Intellect Found in Kindergarten" states:

> The days when nursery school and kindergarten children were satisfied with mere social development and fun are gone, according to a report published yesterday. Today's "space-age" children are not only ready for serious intellectual development but they even thrive on it. This was the conclusion of a study made by a research team headed by Dr. Kenneth D. Wann, professor of education at Teachers' College, Columbia University. The findings were announced yesterday in a book titled "Fostering Intellectual Development in Young Children" published by the college's Bureau of Publications. . . ." Today's children are bombarded by information," the report said. "The advancement of science, technology, the compactness of living, the ease of communication, the closeness of the entire

world, cry out to the children to look, test and learn.
. . . Too frequently we underestimate young children's readiness to investigate seriously and to understand their world. Perhaps it is because of undue
emphasis on children's ego-centricity and reliance on
fantasy." The research study, made in five private
schools in and around the city, showed that children
could be taught reasoning and logic, science, social science, language and vocabulary and the reading and
writing skills.

2. A statement made by a leading American educator,
Dr. George N. Shuster:

That learning to read at 3 can be for some children as
exciting as stringing beads or jumping was news to a
certain school of pedagogy until experiment began to
prove it was the truth. We have, in short, been wasting
a lot of the nation's time.

3. A statement by a leading psychologist, professor at
Rutgers University, Dr. Omar Khayyam Moore:

By the time an American child is 6 and in the first
grade, time is already running out for him. . . . Children must learn how to learn . . . if is not learned before the age of 6, it is questionable whether many children will ever learn it. . . . The child is in a constant
state of growth and metamorphosis, whereas the adult
has reached the norm of the species . . . the adult *is;*
the child is *free to become.*

4. An advertisement for Creative Playthings:

What kind of toy is a giant magnifier to give a three-year-old? Terrific! Research just published shows as much intelligence is developed in the *first four years* of life as in the next 13. If a child idles away these precious years in an ordinary, uninspired environment, the child will be an uninspired student. . . . [The magnifier] is one of hundreds of Creative Playthings that psychologists say can help add 20 points to your child's I.Q. rating before the first day of school. What a true Christmas blessing to give your child.

Even as I mention these statements, which I find so dangerous, I have the feeling that because these forces have been so influential, many parents who have just read the above quotations may find them quite sound and sensible. I feel compelled to pause long enough to say what I think is wrong with them:

1. There is no such thing as *"mere* social development" in pre-school children. This is the age at which children begin to learn some of the most fundamental lessons in what it means to live in a civilized fashion with other people. At a time when the greatest failures in society are social, not intellectual or scientific, we talk of "mere social development" as though it were some kind of disease rather than a central hope for the salvation of mankind.

2. The arbitrary relegation of "fun" to unimportant play activity is utter nonsense. Learning can be a lot of fun; play can be a serious business. In any event, the degree of seriousness of an act bears no relation whatever to whether or not it is a learning experience.

3. It is completely misleading to say that a new world of information is crying out to the child to be learned. Fifty

years ago adults already knew ten thousand things that their children did not. If they did not feel it was necessary to teach the law of relativity to three-year-olds, or to have them memorize all the physical elements we had thus far discovered, or learn Chinese or Arabic—it was because this knowledge seemed thoroughly irrelevant to a child who had only been able to look at the world for 36 months and who had a great many other things on his mind. It isn't an increase in knowledge that makes us think we have to teach more—we have *always* known more than our pre-school children—it is that our attitudes about what is important have changed. What is so fascinating about these reports of new findings concerning the learning capacities of children is that young children throughout the ages have tried to please adults—and in each culture and in each time in history they take on new coloration, like chameleons. Children are remarkable imitators and dissemblers; when you are under six, and completely dependent, you will go to almost any lengths to please the adults around you.

Jean Jacques Rousseau wrote:

The apparent ease with which children learn is their ruin. You fail to see that this very facility proves that they are not learning. Their shiny polished brain reflects, as in a mirror, the things you show them, but nothing sinks in. The child remembers the words and the ideas are reflected back; his hearers understand them, but to him they are meaningless. . . . Before the age of reason the child receives images, not ideas—images are merely the pictures of external objects, while ideas are notions about those objects determined by their relations.

4. There are still many educators and psychologists who do not feel that an emphasis on egocentricity and fantasy in the lives of young children is "undue" at all. It is entirely appropriate for a child who is just barely alive to be most interested in his mysterious, fascinating and growing self. There is also no lack of careful documentation and observation about the tremendous importance of fantasy in the young child's life and the long, hard struggle it is for him to deal more rationally and realistically with his feelings and his perceptions.

5. It is extremely disconcerting to be told that one is now a "norm of the species." This conception of the adult as a finished product and of a child as "free to become" is an unmitigated outrage, and arrant nonsense. If we are truly alive, if we want to go on growing and learning and "becoming," we can do so until the day we die. Those are my plans, anyway.

6. If you set much store by the I.Q. measurement, I suppose it sounds pretty impressive to add 20 points before a single day in school! If you understand that I.Q. tests are being given a status and prestige far beyond their original purpose or value, that they are in many ways unreliable and that all they really measure is a person's ability to take an I.Q. test, then the statement is less exciting. Dr. Lois Murphy, research psychologist at the Menninger Foundation, says, "Correlations between the results of I.Q. tests of the same individual at the ages of three and eighteen are distressingly low. This is now a matter of quite solid scientific confirmation."

Since there is such consistent and growing emphasis on early reading, it seems to me to be essential that parents and teachers of young children examine and evaluate the potential hazards. Some studies indicate, for example, that if children start to read before eye muscles are properly coordinated, they may become "one-eyed readers."

Today's Child, December 1966, reported on a speech by Dr. Helen Hefferman, chief of elementary education in the California State Department of Education, at a teachers' meeting in New Jersey, in which she said: "We have a mountain of evidence to prove that a perfectly 'normal' child cannot learn to read until he is about six-and-a-half years old. Any attempt to drive him may result in some evidence of reading, but at an excessive cost in physiological and psychological damage and at great risk of impairing his interest in reading."

In *Today's Child* (September 1964), Dr. Kenneth Zike, head of the department of pediatrics at Harbor General Hospital in Los Angeles, reported that only 25 per cent of all children in kindergarten are neurologically ready for reading instruction. He stated, "The eye may be ready to receive the visual image, but for more than 75% of the children, the neurological system has not reached the maturity needed to make connections between what they see and what they understand."

Also reported in *Today's Child* (September 1965) was a speech given in St. Paul, Minnesota, at the sixty-fifth annual meeting of the Minnesota Optometric Association by Professor Louis Jacques, formerly of the University of Southern California. From an optometrist's point of view, he said, early reading instruction is injurious to young children's eyes. He held that reading instruction should not be started before the age of seven. "The young child generally has to hold printed matter very close to his eyes and literally 'grits' his eyes. As a result, his eyeballs form in such a way that he loses his natural preparation to see far. This can permanently damage his eyes. . . . Experiments have shown that children who learn to read at eight get to college as soon or sometimes sooner than those who started at four."

In one further report in *Today's Child* (March 1966), Professor Nila Banton Smith, of Glassboro State College, New Jersey, speaking in Ann Arbor at a Michigan Education Conference, said that one out of every fifty children is ready to read in kindergarten or is already reading, which does not mean that the other forty-nine are ready. "When will we learn to respect individual differences? Any mass movement to teach anything to children at a certain age is contrary to modern educational philosophy, psychology and research." She further stated that when some children want to learn to read at an early age, there is no reason not to encourage this. In others "ripeness for reading" may not develop until seven or even older. "The bulk of the evidence that we have at present indicates that pressuring these children to read before the organism is ready is of no advantage in the long run and that it may have harmful effects." She reported on several studies that indicated that the academic advantages of early reading are not permanent. In one such study, in Grosse Point, Michigan, a group of children were selected by psychologists as sufficiently mature to enter kindergarten before the age of five. After fourteen years a study of the achievements of the children originally picked for early entrance showed that 25 per cent were below average or had repeated a grade.

To sum up this point of view, a classic and pointed comment on the whole subject was made by Mrs. Mary Haslam, Director of The Pengilly Country School in New Rochelle, New York, when, frustrated and weary after weeks of arguing with the parents of her nursery-school children about the age at which a child is ready to learn to read, she suddenly exploded, "Look—my daughter was *able* to have babies at 14—but I sure didn't think she was *ready!*"

In reporting on all the various pressures that have now become the constant, day-by-day facts of life in every nursery school, what we begin to see emerging is an important distinction: nursery schools may be "in," but *play* is "out"! Play is apparently to be postponed until retirement at sixty or sixty-five, when it becomes the full-time occupation of many unhappy men and women who have never had the opportunity to learn to play. Since play is "a waste of time," it is, however, appropriate that it should be lavished on adults, who cannot learn anything new anyway. As an inveterate troublemaker, I am not content to accept this point of view. There were and still are valid reasons for making every effort to re-establish play as a central and significant aspect of life during the pre-school years, to say nothing of its meaning in the lives of all human beings of all ages. It is *not* to be trifled with.

FIVE

Child's Play

WALK with me into a nursery-school classroom; let us see what a group of three-to-four-year-olds are up to. In the doll corner Robbie is curled up in the doll crib; he is sucking his thumb and talking baby talk. Patty is making believe she is his mother, and she says, "Now just stop making such a fuss—I'm fixing your bottle as fast as I can. If you start to cry, I am going to be very mad at you!" Dennis, who said he wanted to be the daddy, seems to have changed his mind. He is crawling around on all fours, and as he reaches the side of the crib, he says, "Don't worry, baby, I am a fierce and terrible lion, but I won't hurt you."

At a table nearby, three or four children are drawing pictures of guitars, drums, bugles, tambourines and bells. Their drawings are crude, and by the time their pictures have been colored in, cut out and pasted on a large board, they may look more like abstract than representational artwork; but they are making a poster which will announce to their classmates that tomorrow they are going to have a "concert." For several weeks they have been looking at, touching, playing with an assortment of instruments brought in by their teacher and shown to all the children. These are the children who were intrigued, who wanted to play with them, and they are very clear about which ones you bang and which ones you blow and which ones you "go pling-pling." While they are absorbed in their advertisement campaign, they are having a noisy conversation. Penny says, "At my house I have fifty hundred toys!" Jennifer replies, disapprovingly, "You do not—you're making that up." Peter says, "You stop yelling, or I'm gonna hit you both"—then, looking up surreptitiously to see if any teacher has heard him, he smiles sheepishly and says, "I'll let you come to *my* house. I got new skates. My Daddy doesn't live in my house anymore, but he says he's gonna take me skating in the park."

Two boys are lying on the floor, gazing at the ceiling. Nearby is a tower of blocks that they have just built. It is a "rocket," and they are pretending that they are space men, about to take off. Three or four little girls are washing doll clothes in the bathroom, laughing hysterically because "soapsuds look like pee-pee." Billy and David are racing two trucks across the floor; one is brand new, red and shiny, the other is much smaller, and one wheel is broken off.

Let us "cut the scene" right there. On the face of it, are these children "learning" anything? Before we decide that they are wasting their time in idle fancy and ought to be learning the alphabet, let us hear what the teacher can tell us about them. Robbie, the current crib occupant, is a shy, lonely little boy who for the first four weeks of nursery school stayed almost entirely on the sidelines. When invited to enter into an activity with the other children, he would smile but move quickly away. At almost four, he is the oldest of three children; his days for being the baby in the family must surely have been severely limited. Today, all of a sudden, Patty, a big, somewhat bossy youngster, said, "Robbie, I want you to play house and be the baby." Maybe Robbie had done enough watching to be ready to play; maybe the chance to play baby was just too tempting. At any rate, there he is, getting a chance through the marvel of make-believe to enjoy the gratification of being a baby and finding himself at long last a member of the group. Patty's mother has told the teacher that she often loses her temper; she is ashamed that she has so little patience with a young child, and she is afraid that Patty feels she pushes her too hard. Patty plays the same kind of mother; perhaps this is one of the ways in which she comes to understand and accept her mother's human fallibility. By playing a mother's role, she almost experiences a mother's feelings and can, perhaps, come closer to understanding herself and her mother. Dennis is a wild one! His parents are both European, and believe in being very strict; none of this soft-headed American nonsense for them! When Dennis is naughty, he gets the strap; if he talks back, he goes to bed without any supper. When Dennis arrived at nursery school, he was a very angry young man. During his first week of school, drunk with new freedom, he bit two children and kicked seven or eight others, and whenever the group went outdoors, he ran away from the teacher and tried to open the gate out into the street. Slowly his behavior has been changing; his teacher has talked to him calmly and affectionately about how all children feel angry sometimes, and it is all right in school to talk about it, but she cannot let him hurt other people, any more than she can let other people hurt him. Dennis has made clay figures of "big people" and socked and punched the clay into abject submission. He has tried, over and over again, to see what the teachers will do to him if he disobeys them, and each time that he has had to be separated from the group "until you feel steady again," he has seemed more friendly and cheerful about this. He seems now to believe it when the teacher says, "When you're little, you sometimes need a grown-up to help you be steady." Nothing has absorbed him more than playing with toy tigers and lions, and he has spent hours and hours building cages for them with blocks, "locking them up *tight*, so they can't get out." His teacher has agreed with him and said, "Yes, wild things mustn't be allowed to hurt people." A few times she has added, "Sometimes angry feelings are like wild animals," and Dennis has looked at her thoughtfully and then grinned. For the past day or two he has rushed into the classroom, given his teacher a bear hug and exclaimed, "You're my friend!" Now he is the lion-daddy, but he tells shy Robbie that, despite his wild feelings, he won't hurt him.

The music lovers have been drawing, cutting and pasting, practicing all the small-muscle controls that they are beginning to be able to master; they have worked in unison on a common interest; they have learned about wind, string and percussion instruments. They are even practicing the art of social conversation. Penny covers her uncertainties about herself by boasting; Jennifer knows this may be "real" to Penny, but she sternly makes it clear it isn't *"really* real"— as both children go on experimenting with fantasy and reality in order to eventually master the differences. And, for the first time since the event six months before, Peter has been able to say, out loud, to somebody else, "My Daddy is gone." Although his teachers have known of the divorce, Peter has been telling them at least once a day about how his Daddy is going to come home and play with him, tonight. His teacher has said, "Peter, I know how much you want that to happen," and now she exults as she hears that Peter has faced up to the holocaust in his young and vulnerable life.

Our two space men have never played together before. They are both big, blustery, restless children. At first they seemed overly aggressive and excitable; now it seems that perhaps they were bored until they found each other. They are bright, alert, curious, and now that they have discovered each other, the teachers know there will be hundreds of questions, books needed to look up information they want, all kinds of special adventures in learning that they can share and that they alone are ready for. They really love each other! How infinitely precious it is to each of them to have found such a friend.

The giggling laundresses were infants just a year ago; they could suck on their fingers, they could wet their pants —they may even, if we may assume they are normal, have had one heck of a good time smearing their feces on the side of the crib in some delightful undiscovered moment. It is still fun to feel things that are wet and squashy—and it is even more fun, when among friends, to talk about things that some grown-ups say are naughty. Their teacher has explained, "When you are alone, you may talk about bathroom things, but when you are with grown-ups, some of them may feel unfriendly if you talk that way." This kind of social distinction is just beginning to penetrate.

Billy and David, the truck drivers, had a big fight a few

minutes before they began playing together. Billy had the shiny red truck and David had to take second best. He didn't like that idea at all, so he had tried to take the red truck away from Billy, who howled in outrage at the first threat of a "punch in the stomach." A teacher had removed David, Billy and the trucks from the center of things, and after a serious council of peace, worthy of the United Nations General Assembly, they had agreed to take turns. Every few minutes the driver of the three-wheeled truck turns and asks the teacher if ten minutes are up—and each time it is, they switch. It is the first time that Billy, who always managed to get a coveted toy first, was ever willing to share his booty.

If these children are "wasting the nation's time," we are in more trouble than we know. Each in his own way, in *play*, is finding his own answers to some weighty and vital problems; in play that is fun and absorbing and challenging, each is learning. It is easy to recognize how a child may enhance his physical growth as he learns to jump, run, climb, balance, swing, push, pull or ride a bicycle. It ought to be equally clear to perceptive and sensitive adults that children come to a deeper understanding of themselves and others when they pretend to be storekeepers, policemen, wild animals, farmers, doctors or bridge builders. When a child moves into group play, when he shares or takes turns, when he recognizes another's pain or frustration, when he acts out his own conflicts, anxieties, fears and confusions, in a world of make-believe, he is doing the plain, hard, uncompromising *work* of growing up. He is challenged by his environment to create, imagine, explore, experiment, fail and succeed, and in the process he begins to learn who he is, what he can do, what it means to live and work in harmony

with others. This may well represent some of the hardest
work he will ever have to do—and if he can do it with joy,
with instinctive, playful pleasure, isn't that a blessing!

Speaking at the annual conference of the Child Study Association in March 1965, Dr. Eli Bower, a psychiatrist with
the National Institute of Mental Health, said, "Understanding the atom bomb is child's play compared to understanding child's play." How right he was! A young child's
play is so complex, so varied, in many ways so mysterious,
that educators, psychologists and psychiatrists have found
this a fascinating field of study for many years. For the
past thirty or forty years there has been great excitement
over the emerging discoveries about the meaning of play in
the lives of young children. In *Beyond the Pleasure Principle* Sigmund Freud wrote:

> We see that children repeat in their play everything
> that has made a great impression on them in actual life.
> . . . It is clear enough that all their play is influenced
> by the dominant wish of their time of life; *viz.*, to be
> grown up and to be able to do what grown-up people
> do. . . . In the play of children we seem to arrive at
> the conclusion that the child repeats even the unpleas-
> ant experiences because through his own activity he
> gains far more mastery of the strong impression than
> was possible by mere passive experience. Every fresh
> repetition seems to strengthen this mastery for which
> the child strives.*

At the time Freud made this observation, it seemed to be
a revolutionary idea; we felt that we were on the brink of

* As quoted in *Play: A Yardstick of Growth*, by Clara Lambert (The
Play Schools Association, 1948).

exciting new discoveries; the instinct for play served a very real and exciting purpose—it was a child's way of discovering the world and learning about himself. It was not merely haphazard, accidental activity, expressing youthful energy, but rather a vital and necessary life task. This view was confirmed beyond any reasonable doubt by research and experimentation in the field of psychiatry which led to the development of play therapy. Young children had emotional problems, we were learning, but the early experimental methods for treating adults were not applicable to children; it was not possible to say to a three-year-old, "Lie down on the couch and just say anything that comes into your head." Psychotherapy, whatever the particular school of thought, in the early days or today, depends primarily on verbal communication, and language is still too new and too limited in young children to serve this purpose. As Freud and his followers learned more and more about the unconscious feelings of adults, they were at the same time finding out a great deal about how these adults had felt as children; slowly we began to develop a body of knowledge about childhood feelings and needs that children could not tell us about themselves—but these early researchers began to realize that while children did not *talk* about their feelings and their problems, they did *play* them; play was the child's language for the expression of unconscious needs and feelings; and if we were perceptive enough to look and listen sensitively, play could also be the language by which a child communicated these things to adults. I remember very well my own excitement when, during the 1930's and 1940's, Susan Isaacs, Anna Freud and others began reporting on their observations of children's play. They were finding that all the remembered feelings elicited in the psychotherapeutic treatment of adults could be seen and verified in children's play.

The early researchers in psychiatry discovered, for example, that pre-school-age children are wrestling with problems of competition; as babies they feel themselves to be the center of the universe, but as they get older and wiser, they realize that they are going to have to share love and attention, and this knowledge can make them very angry, and then very guilty about their anger. With this knowledge available to us, we watch four-year-old Jan playing with a doll; first she kisses it and pats it and gives it a bottle—all pure mother love. Then, without a moment's pause, she picks the doll up by one leg and swings it around wildly, shouting, "Watch out, you bad girl, I'm going to chop your head off, and then I'm going to drown you in the bathtub!" That same evening her mother is giving her baby sister a bath. She asks Jan to watch Judy while she goes to get a towel. For "no reason" that the mother can figure out, Jan screams, "No, no, don't leave me with the baby!" She seems really to be panic-stricken. If we want to understand why Jan is suddenly so frightened, will it do us any good to ask her? No: a young child cannot be expected to understand the hidden meaning for her own behavior when even we big, smart, psychologically sophisticated grown-ups have plenty of trouble figuring it out! Is there any "language" through which Jan can tell us what she is feeling? Well, what did she "say" in her play about a baby? She showed very ambivalent feelings of both love and hate, protectiveness and violent hostility. Watching her play can help us understand what makes her refuse to be left alone with her baby sister; she is afraid the angry feelings may overpower the loving feelings.

Pre-school-age children, we learned from the early years of psychiatric research, get angry at grown-ups, too; but because adults seem so big and powerful, they may try very hard to conceal this anger. It has to go somewhere, so sometimes its "energy" or "force," or the tension it produces, may be expressed in unpleasant ways, such as in nightmares or bed wetting. Or we may see a child "working it out" in a more comfortable way, with a piece of clay; often he is not at all subtle about it! He says, "I think I'll make a Mommie and a Daddy"; and five minutes later he is gleefully dismembering these objects of his affection. Or he may say, "I am a big thundercloud and I am going to make terrible noises that will scare everybody!" In play, he is expressing some of his feelings about the omnipotence of adults and his fear and anger about being so small and powerless himself.

I remember one little boy with whom I worked in a child-guidance clinic many years ago, who had the most wonderful facility for getting right to the heart of the matter in his play. His father was a gentle, kind man, seen by his wife as ineffectual and a poor provider. Mama was definitely the boss—aggressive, outgoing, blustery, overbearing and over-controlling. One day, on his way to kindergarten, Kenneth saw a woman run over by a taxi. About a week later he began to have terrible nightmares and fears; he was terrified of the dark, he would not open a closet door, he could not bear to hear news reports about any kind of violence if his parents were listening to the radio. He became so anxious that finally his mother brought him to the clinic, saying that all his symptoms had developed shortly after the witnessing of the accident. Kenny was like his Daddy, quite shy and very polite in our first few sessions together—insisting that

I tell him what to do, becoming uneasy when I would not make some decision for him. After a few weeks Kenny began to be less polite; when we played a game, he wanted to beat me; when I said it was time to leave, he got angry. One day he decided to "wash the floor." When I realized that what he had in mind was turning the playroom into a swimming pool, I turned off the water. When he tried to hit me with the wet mop, I said, "Boy, do you get mad when a grown-up lady tells you what to do!"

That was the beginning of another kind of flood, which went on for many weeks—Kenny's unconscious anger at the overwhelming domination of his mother, who made him feel powerless and helpless. One day Kenny said that he was going to call me up on the play telephone. When he made the phone ring, I pretended to pick up an imaginary phone on my desk and asked, "Who is this?" Kenny at the other end of the room said. "I want you to guess what I look like." I asked a few questions—and finally, too impatient to play cat and mouse any longer, Kenny said, "It's really very sad, I'm half a boy and half a girl—hear my high squeaky voice?"

Kenny had for a long time been feeling both angry and helpless about his need to be an active, bouncy, aggressive little boy; when he saw the woman being hit by the taxi, for a split second it must have mobilized his own fantasies of what he might like to do to his mother—and since he also loved and needed her, this momentary flash had scared him half to death, terrified him of the "dark" part of himself, the angry part.

How did I know this? Because of our play together, over a four-month period, in which slowly but surely Kenny told me through his play about his feelings. I knew it best of all because of what he did the very last time I ever saw him. We both knew that Kenny was not coming back because his fears had left him; by becoming a part of his play, I had let him know he could be a boy even if he got angry sometimes; angry thoughts could not kill a person; anger was something that one could handle, without fear or guilt. Kenny's last message to me, to show me all was well, was one I will never forget. He took a doll-house figure of a mother and laid it on the floor. Then he took the biggest and heaviest truck we had in the playroom and, singing at the top of his lungs, ran the truck over the mother doll, over and over again. The song he was singing was, "I don't want her, you can have her, she's too fat for me!" Kenny, through humor, was expressing his more realistic acceptance of ambivalent feelings. And with this release and relief from guilt he would be able to accept himself and others with deeper pleasure.

No one who has ever done play therapy with young children can doubt the significance of play. But most parents are otherwise engaged, and somehow or other they must come to understand the deep significance of play if they are going to permit their children to have the kind of nursery-school experience they need. Hardly a day goes by at the nursery school where I work, without some visiting mothers looking around uncomfortably and finally saying, "But don't the children do anything but *play* all day?" These mothers have almost always visited the two local Montessori schools; a neighbor or the family druggist or the man who sells shrubs on Route 1 have already told them about such marvels and wonders as that each of their own three- or four-year-olds has learned to read a whole book, button his coat, and say five sentences in French—and be-

lieve me, these mothers are pretty impressed! At least half
their waking hours seem to be spent in worrying about how
Junior will ever make the grade in order to get into even a
second-rate college—"You know, even *state* colleges are
turning thousands away," they tell us as we stand looking at
a three- or four-year-old, sucking his thumb.

They walk from playroom to playroom with College
Boards on their minds, and they say, "But what are they
doing?" THEY ARE ENCOUNTERING LIFE—*that's* what they
are doing! In a free and open exchange, in a room that
offers all kinds of experiences and explorations, they are
searching for their own answers to their own vital questions. And what are the vital questions, in the lives of children from three to five? They are questions of such power
and significance that such skills as learning letters and numbers become dwarfed by comparison.

Pre-school children are learning to think in words. At first
language seems so powerful and magical that they must find
out if words can make things happen; like human beings
throughout history, children have a feeling that words not
only are thoughts, but can influence actions in the external
world. Plenty of grown-ups knock on wood when they
speak of some good fortune because they have never quite
gotten over the notion, gained when they were young and
just learning to use language, that words can bring about a
good or bad event. A friend tells me, "Yes, my mother is
feeling a little better—but I don't want to talk about it yet."
She means, "If I am too happy and relieved, if I *say* it, she'll
get sick again." This is exactly how a young child feels almost all the time. He is more influenced by his irrational
fantasies than by reason; and only through his play and in
his relationships with others, can he learn that thoughts do

not make things happen. A three-year-old gets angry when Mommie says that his toys have to be put away. He thinks, "I'm gonna make her dead, and she'll never be able to come back!" Anger-in-words is new to him—when he was a baby there were no words for such feelings. Now he worries: "But I love her and I need her; could my angry thoughts take her away from me?"

Pre-schoolers are discovering what it is to be a human being—to have mixed feelings, to hate and love, to cherish and to want to murder, to feel compassion and sympathy for someone who is hurt and to want to destroy someone who gets in the way of their own wishes. All human beings have all kinds of feelings. Some of those feelings may not be expressed in actions if we are to have any kind of civilized relations with others. What can be done about such feelings? If we just feel guilty and afraid of them, they make for all kinds of trouble. No child thinks all this out consciously, but it is the theme of his unconscious development and growth. Here is this little child, alive in the world for a few short years, wrestling with problems that have puzzled and disturbed—and even destroyed—millions of adults, for thousands of years. He is struggling to come to terms with the "angel" and "devil" within himself. If he is helped to accept all that he is, if he can be helped not to fear his less lovable impulses, if he is guided into acceptable ways of expressing his feelings, he will have at his disposal the energy and vitality he needs for subsequent concentrating on mastering the necessary skills of learning. If he represses his anxieties and fears and angers, he will be preoccupied by these feelings when he should be able to focus his full attention on other matters. If he can find no outlets for his feelings in his play, he may go on into his school years burdened by self-hatred, because he thinks of himself as a naughty boy instead of just a human being with normal feelings that need to be handled.

Pre-school children are learning about mortality; at some time between three and five they discover death; this fact has always terrified millions of adults, some of whom come to terms with it, while others may not. It is a kind of knowledge that overwhelms the strongest and the most mature of us. Once a child knows about this reality, he begins to try to cope with it. The most valuable resource at his disposal is his play; he has a funeral for the dead turtle—and then he keeps digging it up to see what is happening. He puts Band-Aids all over a doll, puts the doll in a shoe box, makes up all kinds of marvelous rituals and buries the box. He knows the game differs from his experience with the dead turtle, and he tries to figure out the difference. He shouts, "Bang, bang, you're dead," and he sees that making-believe dead is different again. When Grandpa, who was sick for a long time, really dies, he wonders with the normal irrationality of childhood, "Did I kill him because I didn't let him kiss me last time he came to visit?" He makes a clay ashtray and says that he intends it for his grandfather—but where shall he take it? Maybe he puts it next to Grandpa's picture, but he is still mixed up and scared, no matter what anyone tells him. He says to his best friend at nursery school, "Let's play being dead and getting buried"; and while this is also no final solution, it is a help along the way to mature understanding and acceptance.

The pre-school child discovers that there are real dangers in life; water is not always just fun to play in—if you sink in the pool, you can't breathe; cars can hurt people, fire can burn them, mean words can hurt your feelings, parents' going away on a vacation can make you scared they will never come back, that mean lady across the street says that saying bad words can "make you burn in hell." Sometimes there are visits to doctors, getting shots, feeling awfully sick. The world isn't so nice all the time—it has terrors in it. How do you endure the things that make you mixed up and afraid? Some sense of mastery comes with "make believe"—playing that one is scared or sick, or in danger.

The pre-school child is becoming more and more aware of the larger world outside his home; what do all the Daddies really do when they are away all day? Why do we need money? What and why are wars? What is the President, what is America? For that matter, what is Scarsdale or Harlem or Chicago? How do they make planes stay up? Why does the TV set make pictures when you turn a knob? How can you hear Grandma's voice on a telephone when she's in California, and that's a place that people tell you is far, far away? What makes people seem so different at different times? Why is it that one day Mommie can be smiling all day and then, suddenly, something makes her angry and sad, and you think she wishes you weren't even around? Why is the man in the supermarket always scowling at you, while the lady at the traffic light is always your friend? What makes some people like you and other people not like you? Why are some children your friends and others don't like you at all? What changes people's moods? How do people get born, and what makes them born boys and girls? This world is so complicated and confusing—will he ever understand anything about it? Rather than not having enough to learn, young children are overwhelmed with what they know must be learned and understood if they are to grow up. Again, play is the first road to mastery, to finding answers.

The pre-school child is becoming aware of himself; he wonders, What is it to be me, Jeffrey Frederick Smith, Jr.? Am I Grandma's perfect boy, or Sister's pesty little brother, or Mother's sweetheart, or Daddy's disappointing scaredy-cat because I need a night light? Am I smart or dumb, am I good or bad, am I the boy who paints beautiful pictures or the boy who is afraid to climb the jungle gym? Am I the mean selfish "brat" who won't let a visiting cousin play with my special Teddy Bear, or am I that wonderful generous boy that my teacher is so proud of because I gave David a turn with the wagon? This young creature, so new in the world, is wrestling with the universal, the profound and sometimes painful beginnings of self discovery—of seeing himself whole, as a person within and a person with other people—and all of this he also brings to his play.

Increasing consciousness and awareness of this world that one has fallen into makes the life tasks of three-to-five-year-olds overwhelming, in view of all these profound and complex questions they are beginning to face. And the best tool they have for beginning to find answers is play. If we sit them down at a table and say, "Be quiet and count these beads," we are robbing them of the opportunity to struggle with questions that need thinking about and studying, through the explorations of free, spontaneous, self-directed play experiences. Playing "going to the hospital" can relieve and release both real and fantasied fears about that recent tonsillectomy; pretending to be a mean tough cowboy with a gun can help a young child express aggressive feelings that must not be directed toward other people; making believe that one is a policeman can help a child internalize the controls he needs over his anti-social impulses; building a town with blocks can help him gain information and mastery of a small part of the world he observes.

Educators have known about these values in play for as long as the researchers in psychiatry and psychology, and the encouragement and enrichment of play have been of central concern to the large majority of educators throughout the past fifty years. I do not believe that most of the specialists who work in the field of nursery education have lost their commitment, their enthusiasm, for a child's right to his play anymore than I have; but they seem to have become less vocal about it in the past few years. I think that all of us have been too easily intimidated by a small but very vocal minority of educators and psychologists who offer today's parents the alternatives that so many parents want most— that seem to alleviate their anxiety about a child's academic achievement. Today's parents, caught in the general hysteria about the need for a college education and the lack of available resources to meet the growing number of prospective students, are open to any voice that promises a magic formula for making children learn quickly. The rest of us, too reasonable and too open-minded, I am afraid, have become passive spectators while our children are fed to the technician-lions.

One of the most sensible and wise and articulate voices raised in defense of play was that of Clara Lambert, who wrote a pamphlet published by The Play Schools Association in 1948 entitled, *Play: A Yardstick of Growth*. It remains a classic statement of what is still today a sound and rational view of the meaning of play in the lives of children. Mrs. Lambert discussed play as an outlet for a child's emotions, a socially acceptable means by which children can externalize their feelings, observations, confusions and uncertainties and learn to deal with them. She held that play is in essence a preparation for living, for comprehending daily life. She pointed out that dramatic or imaginative play is a bridge between the child's conscious thoughts and inner emotions.

> The expression of vague feelings through dramatization fulfills the same function for the child which conversation and thought do for the adult. As the child dramatizes he talks and probes and finally clarifies his own confused feelings.

He comes to grips with fears relating to birth, death, illness and separation. He "studies" family and other social relationships. He faces up to anger, resentment, jealousy and rage—and his natural fear of retribution for such feelings.

> Play, in its deepest and broadest sense, is the great bridge over which children must pass in order to grow up, to make a satisfactory journey from childhood to adulthood.

One of the remarkable features of this pamphlet was Mrs. Lambert's awareness, even in the 1940's, of the inroads that modern society was already making on children's play.

> Analyzing our present-day play problems in terms of our industrial culture . . . one conclusion is outstanding; despite the need for play, the enormous physiological and psychological drive toward it, children living in towns and cities have had this impulse warped.
> . . . Cities grew, industries expanded, living conditions became increasingly congested with each wave of immigration and industrial growth. As population grew, space for play almost disappeared. . . . Many forms of play, through which children learned the cur-

rent mores, occupations, arts and ideas . . . were lost.
What had been taken for granted as a "God-given
right" of all children, developed into a privilege for a
few, because space became costly—and space is a req-
uisite for play. . . . In the agricultural period of our
life in America, play was no problem. Space was cheap
and plentiful, and children found in everyday tasks
many of the satisfactions and learning opportunities
which are today only available in play. . . . Boys
learned occupations from their fathers . . . girls
learned household arts from their mothers. . . . They
did not have to *play* farmer, carpenter, shoemaker, tai-
lor, or nurse, for such work was close at hand, and
they participated in it. . . . There were frequently
animals to care for, wood to pile up in the shed, grass
to cut, gardens to weed, water to carry, fences to mend
or paint. . . . There were community gatherings,
husking bees, shucking parties . . . harvesting cele-
brations, and sociables at which work and fun were enjoyed by children and parents together as *play*. . . .
Children had a sense of continuity in human relationships and a feeling of "belonging." . . . The breaking
down of these large family groups has narrowed children's emotional experiences. . . . Much of the population has been removed from first-hand sources of living, and has become accustomed to seeing a movie
. . . listening to the radio [and we can add TV]. . . .
Our new civilization has surely and rapidly stripped
work and play of their rich content.

Mrs. Lambert, who died some years ago, did not know of
the new ways we would devise for making inroads into

child's play by our current preoccupation with academic skills. But her students and her co-workers—who know perfectly well that what she said and wrote is even more valid and important today—have too often seemed, in the face of today's climate of pressure on children, to have become silent and therefore acquiescent partners of those who seek to eliminate childhood.

I was one of those students—and I think it is time to yell a little! We simply must not stand by and see all such important insights about children discarded during an era of panic. It is my fervent and somewhat agonized plea that parents of young children will seek out those nursery schools for their youngsters that are still genuinely concerned with the *total* healthy growth of children. Such nursery schools still exist. Such schools recognize the significance of play as the most crucial and important tool available to the growing child in his struggle to gain mastery over his feelings, explore his environment and achieve a sense of personal identity.

If I were looking for a nursery school that would best meet the needs of my own child, these are the qualities I would look for:

1. I would want a child-oriented setting, which provides stimulation and opportunity for children to develop those skills that are appropriate to their age, needs and interests. There would be a great deal of equipment to encourage dramatic and imaginative play. There would be creative materials, such as paints and clay, to encourage expression of feelings. There would be equipment for releasing the energy and vitality of young children, helping them to develop the large-muscle coordination they want and are ready for. It would be a place with space, with room to run

and jump and move freely.

2. I would want a warm and accepting environment, peopled by teachers who know a great deal about the psychological needs of young children and can help them cope with their genuine struggle to become human—to be free and themselves but in a context of relating to others. I would want teachers who are ready to experiment, to explore, to let the child's curiosity and spirit of adventure lead to unplanned learning and discovery, where new questions are encouraged and answers found together.

3. I would want to know if the teachers are content to be with three- and four-year-olds and see enough excitement in this—free of a terrible sense of urgency to turn these children into six- and seven-year-olds.

4. I would want a school that is open to change and to new ideas but not easily swayed by the passing fashion of the moment. The teachers must feel free to experiment with new equipment, new methods, but only in the context of retaining critical judgment and preserving a basic philosophy that is well-balanced and clearly thought out.

5. I would want to see teachers who are not impressed by surface learning—who know that young children are wonderful mimics and can be taught to repeat information, but who know that this has nothing whatever to do with deeper understandings. I would want teachers who encourage a child to learn as much and as fast as he pleases, but who do not measure their own value or status by the learning they can see—teachers who are satisfied with their work only when they know that what is being learned is meaningful and is meeting all the needs of a young child, whether or not the satisfaction can be measured or seen.

6. I would choose a school where children are on the

move; where the program is flexible and relaxed enough so that children can begin to make their own decisions, where being quiet or active are choosable commodities most of the time. I do not want permission for chaos; there must be regulations and rules whenever groups of people try to live together. I want a room full of opportunities, where chatter and movement and changing interests and activities are not merely viewed as permissible but are deliberately encouraged. Reasonable rules about safety and respect for property and the rights of others should be enforced by grown-ups who do not expect young children to be capable of self control all at once.

7. I would seek an environment in which children ask whatever questions they want and where teachers help children find their own answers; an environment in which teachers are concerned about the child who *always* needs to be playing in a group as well as the child who *never* plays with others; about the child who never lets himself go and the child who is always at the mercy of his impulses and feelings.

8. I would want a school that is concerned with encouraging spontaneity and joy in self-expression as well as with helping children learn ways to live comfortably and creatively with others, respecting his own rights and the rights of others. Teachers in such a climate want to encourage each child to be different, to be himself, to find his own inner music, the things that will make his life significant to him; they want to help him solve whatever problems he may have that keep him from being unique and free.

9. I would look for a school in which teachers were not concerned with "raising I.Q.'s" but with raising a child's pleasure in the wonders of the world and the wonders

within himself; where their goal is helping children to live warmly and securely with others, both adults and children; helping children find pleasure in developing new skills; helping each child to feel good about himself—to feel that he is a worthwhile and growing person; helping each child to understand himself and others, to gain in self-discipline and, most of all, *to like the person he is becoming*. Such a world lets each child know that he has *time to grow*.

How I envy a parent in quest of a good nursery school! There are still many such schools, which have withstood the pressures of the times we live in. It is a great deal more difficult for those of us with older children to find grade schools, high schools and colleges that are still concerned with the whole child in his total growth and who have preserved as their central goal the making not of a *student* but of a *person*.

SIX

The Healthy Aspects
of Under-Achievement

WHEN I meet a parent who tells me that his child loves school and is doing beautifully, pleasing everyone with his work, I am reminded of the sign I saw on someone's desk which read, "Anybody who feels relaxed and confident doesn't understand the situation!" Rather than being surprised by the far more frequent tales of woe I hear, I find it quite remarkable that so many children seem to be able to take the current academic pressures so well. What seems more natural to me is the story of the little boy who, as part of an arithmetic lesson, was sent on an errand by his teacher to collect pebbles outside the school building; when he came home and told his mother about this special responsibility, he was excited and proud, but then became thoughtful and said, "Gee, you know I could have *escaped!*"

The expression "under-achiever" first came into use primarily in connection with the bright child who was unable to learn because of some psychological block. It was a useful concept insofar as it was used in a protective and compassionate way to help parents and teachers understand that there were times in the lives of some children when they simply could not function successfully in intellectual pursuits because they were too preoccupied with some emotional disturbance. It was certainly a more useful descriptive term than "lazy," "ornery" or "stupid."

Unfortunately, as our educational demands and expectations have increased, the term "under-achievement" has too often come to take on an entirely different meaning; it now describes any child who is not doing the level of work that adults arbitrarily assign to him. A typical example is David, age nine, who lives in an upper-middle-class suburb and attends an elementary school in a school system that prides itself on its accelerated academic program. The parents in this community are very ambitious for their children, not only sharing a conviction about the necessity of a college education but having also the expectation that despite the ever-increasing hordes that apply each year, *their* children will go to Ivy League colleges—or else. Like millions of nine-year-olds before him, David at this stage of his development is more of a doer than a thinker. Picturing himself as a grown-up is such a vague and unreal concept that he has little motivation or interest in getting into college or becoming a success in some business or profession. Once upon a time, in the dim past when we permitted children to "act their age," nobody would have been particularly disturbed because David was more interested in baseball than in geography, that he was a sloppy writer or that he balked at doing his homework. His restless energy, his enthusiasm for any adventure which took place outside of school, his insatiable but disorganized and erratic curiosity would have been viewed with indulgence and filed in the "boys will be boys" category. His parents would have worried a little and nagged, but everyone, including David, would have expected him to mature eventually; sure enough, by the time David was in high school, his own goals would have shifted, his interests would have changed, and he would have matured enough to take responsibility for the kind of work that was assigned to him.

That is not what is likely to happen to David today. He and his classmates are being tested at frequent intervals; he has undoubtedly already had an I.Q. test, and his teachers and parents, impressed by his score, feel that he is "too smart" not to be doing better work; he is therefore labeled an under-achiever. No one can wait; if David doesn't buckle down now, he will never be able to handle the work in high school. He is going to have to learn subjects in high school that his father didn't study until college; he is going to be expected to understand and memorize facts on subjects that even fifteen or twenty years before were taught in graduate school to students specializing in a particular field of study.

As a result many of today's "under-achievers" are yesterday's normal children; if they had been lucky enough to be born fifty or more years ago, they would have been considered quite competent in terms of some of the things they know that we now take for granted. Many of the children we now label as "not living up to their potential" have more information than their grandfathers had when they were adults.

In the mad rush for academic acceleration more and more nice, normal kids, are being labeled as under-achievers or failures without regard for the change in our expectations. We turn our schools into failure factories, insist that our children grow up according to an entirely new time schedule, demand a much higher level of achievement from nursery school to college—and then wonder why so many intelligent children cannot "live up to their potential"! Whose potential? What kind of potential? A potential for memorizing? A potential for sitting at a desk and doing homework for two hours in sixth grade? A potential for taking tests well?

In assessing the meaning of under-achievement, we have to view it from the vantage point of the times in which we live and in relation to our attitudes toward childhood and toward learning. Our children are living at a time when homework starts at the beginning of elementary school and increases until it amounts to as much as four hours a night in high school. They live in a time of tremendous competition. They are tested constantly. They are in classes in which they are grouped by ability as determined by aptitude and achievement tests. In many schools they experience "team teaching," which means that they are expected to relate to three or four different teachers each day in each subject that is being taught. They are likely to spend some part of their time in school "relating" to teaching machines. They live in a climate that seems to concern itself primarily with their ability to get into college from the day they start school. Tests and grades are the most important subjects they hear about in school. Memorizing facts has become a primary goal in most of their classrooms. How would such an environment affect us? It may help us gain a sense of perspective if we try to imagine how *we* might be labeled if we lived under the same conditions as our children, for it has occurred to me that I do not know any adult who doesn't spend some part of every day under-achieving and who could be said to be living up to some externally imposed, arbitrary notion of his potential! Whether you are a lawyer, a housewife, a secretary or a salesman, suppose you knew that every Friday you were going to be tested on everything you were supposed to have learned during the preceding week. You also knew that you would be graded on what you had accomplished—not in relation to your own growth or development over a number of years, but in relation to everybody else around you in your office, or your community—in other words you would be marked on a "normal curve" in relation to your peers. If you are a housewife living in an area where most of the women are college graduates, you can assume that your mark will be lower than if you live in a neighborhood where many of the women never finished high school; no matter how important some learning experience may have been to you personally, you will be marked on a curve in relation to those around you. If you are a salesman in a corporation that employs highly skilled and experienced men, your mark will be lower even if you know that your experiences in the past week have dramatically and excitingly increased your understanding of your work; if you are a salesman in a small and relatively new business, it is probable that even though you know you have really been goofing off all week and have accomplished almost nothing, you will probably get an excellent grade. Since, in this hypothesis, any clubs or organizations you belong to must be made up of people on your level of intellectual achievement, there will be a dramatic reshuffling of friends and acquaintances and many farewells.

In the course of daily living you have wondered about something; you want to ask some questions or get some advice or information. If the subject is not scheduled for the week, you can just forget about it. You will have been told by your boss what you are supposed to learn or accomplish this week and that any extraneous topics or activities will only interfere with your performance on the weekly test. Each night when you come home, you will bring at least two to three hours of work with you. This homework will consist of matters you have already worked on during the day, not new areas of interest. For example, the housewife will be required to memorize the price differences between the two supermarkets she visited, the lawyer will reread briefs he has already prepared and will memorize the most important facts, the secretary will practice her shorthand. There will be little or no time for reading a book that you thought might interest you or following a political campaign in the newspaper. And if you cheat and sit down after dinner to watch TV, you will know deep down in your heart that you are not living up to your potential and, feeling guilty, you may have a pretty sleepless night. Every time you stop doing something useful, something that will help you "get ahead," you will know that the defection is going to be recorded on your cumulative record and will interfere with future advancements or rewards. You will be assigned different instructors for every subject, and as you must contact these different specialists constantly, there will be no time to make any close friends. The housewife will have a list of people she may call who know a lot about a subject; this will mean that if Johnny has a cold and you want a recipe for Hungarian goulash and you would like to find a new laundromat, you do not call your mother or your best friend; you call a doctor, a chef and the Better Business Bureau. You might feel comforted by a friendly chat with Mama or the girl friend, but they are not experts in the subjects you are working on. If you are the secretary or the lawyer and you need some special information, you do not make a lunch date with a friend who might be able to advise you while you settle down together in a happy haze of dry martinis, nor do you spend an afternoon browsing through the public library; you find the right set of cards and sit down in front of a teaching machine, where you can test your ability to memorize the facts you need.

I do not think I need pursue this nightmare further. This should be sufficient to help us re-evaluate who the under-achiever is; he is more often than not a child who is telling us what is wrong with his world more than what is wrong with himself. He is rebelling against what is meaningless to him in his learning experiences; he is showing a sensitive awareness of impossible expectations and unrealistic standards.

In order to understand what is labeled as under-achievement in school performance, we need to examine how the world of school looks to our children. First of all, it is a world of absolutes, of success or failure. We are not asking our children to do their own best but to be *the* best. Education is in danger of becoming a religion based on fear; its doctrine is to compete. The majority of our children are being led to believe that they are doomed to failure in a world which has room only for those at the top. Dr. Gladys Gardner Jenkins, professor at the University of Iowa, in a speech at The Association for Family Living in Chicago, said:

"As I walk through the halls of our junior and senior high schools I see bulletin boards on careers—rarely do

I see posters encouraging boys to be plumbers, carpenters, masons, or sales clerks; rarely are there signs that housework is an honorable profession with good pay; where are the signs suggesting that work in one of our modern factories may be desirable? We do not really value all our children unless we can make it possible for all kinds of work to be honored and respected. We must make it possible for the boy and girl of average ability to walk with confidence and to choose his goal with pride even if college would not be a wise choice for him. . . . The re-emphasis of the concept that all honest work is honorable and worthy is long overdue . . . . Many of our school practices of grades, promotions, honors and curriculum expectations are still set up without sufficient acceptance of the real differences between children not only in their basic mental ability but also in background, drive, motivation and experiences. . . . We shall fail our children unless we can bring ourselves to accept a concept of success as relative. Rarely is success rated as giving of one's best by contributing and achieving what one can contribute and achieve. . . . Success is far too often equated with being best or better than someone else in a competitive situation, rather than in doing one's best. . . . With our present concept of success and the pressures which it is putting upon many of our children we must often pay a high cost. Children strive for what is rewarded. When the goals of success are arbitrary ones set by adults and unachievable by many children, youngsters who care may strive to reach these goals in any way they can. . . . We know, for instance, that cheating is becoming a very real problem in our

schools. If getting an approved grade is the means toward approval at home and at school there are children
who will take what means they can to obtain the grade
and avoid the hurt of disapproval or the humiliation of
having failed or having been left behind."

A recent study involving a number of elementary schools
in a large city showed that most children enjoy kindergarten
and look forward to first grade eagerly. By the end of first
grade and the beginning of second grade many of these
children begin to see themselves as failures, and by the end
of the third grade the number has doubled. Dr. George
Esty, working in the New Jersey State Health and Education Departments, recently reported that increasing numbers of school children of all ages are being given tranquilizers, "to help them avoid cracking under the pressure for
good grades."

Another major characteristic of the educational climate
in which our children live is a preoccupation with the learning of facts, with giving the "right answers" and with learning everything that is known about every subject. Dr. Eli
Bower, of The National Institute of Mental Health, calls
this the "Mug-jug theory of education." The teacher, the
mug, tips over and pours knowledge into the jugs, the
empty heads of pupils. In this approach the child is not
helped to relate facts, nor does he learn ways of looking for
information, processing, integrating, interpreting or differ-
entiating between facts when he acquires them. A horrifying
example of this approach was epitomized in a *New Yorker*
story: "Upon applying for reference material at a Philadelphia public library in order to do some special vacation
work, a prep-school student of our acquaintance was told

by the librarian, 'It had better be a school question, because we don't give it out just for curiosity's sake.' "

The superintendent of a school system in Westchester reported that he had asked a group of volunteer parents to visit 300 different classrooms, in all the schools, at the same time on a certain day, and to write down in one paragraph a "verbal picture" of what was going on in each classroom. The large majority of these reports stated that the teacher was talking *at* the children. The New Jersey State Education Department, in a similar study, found relatively few classrooms in which there were opportunities for children to ask questions or to discuss matters of interest to them. John Holt, in *The PTA Magazine*, wrote: "We make children so concerned with getting right answers, and so afraid of getting wrong ones, that we force them into all kinds of strategies for finding, or guessing, or prying out of the teacher the answer the teacher wants. Thus the chief business of class is not only pleasing the teacher but out-witting her, out-guessing her, reading her mind. And the more effectively you can do it, the more pleased she is."

Our preoccupation with facts and right answers is expressed also in the idea of team teaching at the elementary-school level. If there is one fact we thought we knew about school-age youngsters it was that they did their best learning in a classroom where they could identify strongly with a *teacher* who enjoyed *learning*. Still closely attached to their parents, grade-school children have seemed to thrive best in a close, intimate relationship with one teacher. Now, it is perfectly true that this arrangement has sometimes involved the children's living through a year with an inexperienced, unkind, neurotic, punitive or poorly trained teacher. But it seems to me that since we know such a mistake can happen, the logical next step would be to devise better teacher-training programs, better screening methods and better in-service supervision of teachers. Since that is not the road we seem to be taking, it is fair to assume that team teaching was devised because of a concern with *subject matter*, not as a way of exposing children to kinder, wiser, more gifted human beings. At a stage of growth in which the personal relationship with a teaching person has in the past seemed so important, we find children as young as seven and eight going from classroom to classroom, having less and less opportunity for developing a true friendship with any one teacher. The use of teaching machines at this age level simply goes one step further, removing the personal interaction altogether. If teaching machines had come into use at a time when we still felt that the teacher as a human being was more important than the subjects he or she taught, they might have served a good purpose as a device for helping some children move along at a more rapid pace, so that others could have more attention; in some classrooms machines are used sensibly and in a limited way. But in a climate in which subject matter has become so important, the dangers of excessive dependence on such devices seems to me to be very great.

An article in *The New York Times* of April 4, 1966, reported that a grade school in California was planning to introduce the three R's to 170 first graders by "an infinitely patient, infinitely tactful teacher who knows all the answers"—a computer. Every day these children, along with their regular teacher, would work with the machine for at least one hour. If a child "told" the machine that three plus three was seven, the computer would signal a "soothing pre-recorded voice" to tell the child he had given the wrong answer. "All right," the voice would say, "now let's go back and add up two and two." If the student decided to get "smart-alecky," the computer could be programmed to snap right back at him and even refuse to go on with the lesson. The article concluded, "Indeed, this is one thing about the machine that educators like best." Mentioned quite casually in the article was the fact that most of the children who would participate in this program were Negroes from "culturally deprived homes." There has been a good deal of evidence to suggest that a major factor in helping such children must be to provide them with an "ego ideal"—a warm and loving relationship with a person who can help them to value learning and give them a feeling of hope and faith in their own intellectual development. One can only hope that this machine, in addition to being programmed to handle chastisements, can also be programmed to take these first graders on its knee and tell them they are lovable!

There seems to be a new theory in education—one which I do not believe has appeared before—that everything we learn in every field of endeavor must be learned by everybody. We have made so much progress in scientific knowledge in such a short time—more in the last 100 years than in all human history—that it has simply overwhelmed us and seems to have robbed us of good sense and good judgment; in fact, the whole notion that we have to teach every child all that we know is sheer nonsense. I have grown up during an era in which the radio, TV, the airplane, penicillin, the theory of relativity and the splitting of the atom have been invented and developed. I understand nothing of consequence about any of them. I leave the navigating of a plane to the pilot, my doctor decides when I need penicillin and there is a radio and TV repairman at the corner. Most of us who are now adults have lived through a period of unbelievable change. Born into the time of Buck Rogers as a fictional character, we have lived long enough to know that his exploits were not fiction for long; scientific progress during our lifetime has already been enormous. How has it affected those of us who are now over forty? We have all remained specialists; we have learned what we needed to know for our own work; we have learned that part of the total knowledge available that interested us. We remain totally ignorant of some subjects and very knowledgeable about others, depending on our interests and talents. And though we do not know a great deal about almost everything, we do not feel stupid, incompetent or handicapped. When we need to know something, we look it up or ask somebody or get some books or take a course—but at no time do we feel that the tremendous force of all the new scientific knowledge must weigh on each of us personally. And it is important to remember that it *is* quite specifically scientific knowledge which has advanced so rapidly—not greater understanding of ourselves, not an ability to live more intelligently with others, not in finding new and better ways of solving human problems. An example of the sudden vogue to teach everything that is known is represented by a new high-school-level biology book which includes all the latest information about genetics. It is 460 pages long, replacing a book that was 210 pages long. Certainly textbooks should be revised and corrected and new information given, but not by heaping such detail on children; intensive treatment of *any* subject should remain for those who are going to specialize in that area. Actually, the more we learn, the more we must specialize, because we simply cannot ever, in one lifetime, know it all—and even if we could, why should we? Housewives manage to live rich full lives without understanding why the telephone works; there are pediatricians and musicians who do quite well without understanding how rockets are launched; there are excellent social workers and gifted ballet dancers who know nothing about the chemistry of protoplasm, English professors who drive their cars without knowing what the engine looks like, physicists who never read poetry, dentists who cannot speak French, on and on ad infinitum.

The compulsion to teach everything new is only half the picture; the general hysteria about getting everybody smartened up also means that we are teaching old knowledge faster, earlier and in more detail. I recently received a letter from a mother which illustrates this phenomenon:

> My 14-year-old daughter is in a special class for very bright children. This weekend she has been preparing a report on Greek philosophy and literature. My husband, a student of the classics, never heard of some of the obscure Greek poets she is studying. He glanced through the book she was assigned to read and discovered that it was written for college students at Cambridge University, England. This same brilliant child, who later got a 95% on her report, is scared to death of boys, spent one evening recently working with a friend on how to "hex" a mean boy by making a voodoo figure and sticking pins in it. She also is experimenting with fake nails and making phony phone calls. On the one hand she functions like an elderly intellectual and on the other she acts like a normal little girl who is just barely beginning to grow up in her feelings.

I am truly frightened by the widening split between what she is being taught and what she needs to live through emotionally.

While it is true that there has been a general acceleration and intensification of teaching in all subjects, the greatest emphasis has been in the area of science. A few years ago I went to visit the university that I had attended some twenty years before. I was amazed at the changes; there were veritable skyscrapers of chrome and glass all over the campus. I was told that these were all science buildings; the three largest and fanciest were for chemistry, physics and math. When I asked how so much money could be raised for such an extensive building program, I was told that government and corporation grants for research had made this possible, since both these groups in our society are greatly concerned with technological progress and are ready and able to support it. As we drove farther, I saw a little gray frame house that looked very familiar. Once a private home, it was tiny and ramshackle when I had been at school, and seemed only more so now. I remembered it immediately as the School of Music because my college roommate, having fallen madly in love, spent days on end in the record library, listening to Tchaikovsky's Romeo and Juliet Overture while looking soulfully into her boyfriend's eyes, and I had gone along to share this romance vicariously on several occasions. There it stood in all its beat-up glory—unchanged, only older— still the School of Music of a university that had tripled its student body and had spent millions of dollars on new buildings. I am not suggesting that the music school needed a new building; crotchety and old-fashioned as I am, I suspect that better music composition may emerge from old houses than from steel towers, but this experience brought into sharper focus the relative values we express.

The goal of acceleration goes on from nursery to graduate school. A first-grade teacher in a suburban school proudly told me that she had increased the pace for learning to read to the point where 90 per cent of her class were reading at the third- to fifth-grade level. She was giving homework assignments which involved writing themes of at least three pages. She told me that her principal was so impressed with her work that he was asking her to conduct an after-school seminar for the other first-grade teachers. I learned some months later that the training program had been given up because there were increasing reports from parents that their six-year-olds were becoming insomniacs or the victims of headaches, stomach aches and crying spells.

A friend of ours, who is in charge of a research laboratory at a well-known university hospital told us this story. "The other day our neighbor's son, Richard, came in to see me, to ask if he could borrow my hospital library card for a school project he was working on. He's only in the tenth grade, and I couldn't imagine why he wanted to use a hospital library. He explained that his science teacher had given him some obscure medical references from a German medical journal, and that neither his school library nor the public library could get this material for him. I started asking him some questions about what he was trying to find out, what he hoped to accomplish—and I realized he didn't have the slightest idea how research is carried on. All he kept saying was, 'The report's got to be thirty-five pages long.' I was so sorry for the poor kid that I gave him my card and thought that was the end of it. The next night two other boys showed up at our house—same teacher, same kinds of projects, same request. I was so exasperated with the teacher, that I said I wouldn't let them use my library card —and do you know, their mothers were so furious that they don't speak to us on the street anymore!"

As a natural consequence of increasing school pressures, homework has also increased in quantity and quality. One mother sent me a clipping from her local newspaper, reporting a PTA meeting of ninth- and tenth-grade parents, at which the principal had said, "Approximately four hours of homework should be handled each night." I have been collecting homework assignment sheets from both students and teachers, the way some people collect stamps or coins, and some of the contributions ought to be "collector's items." The following, contributed by a high-school sophomore, was typical of most of them.

Homework for Monday Night

Geometry—Read pages 231-233, 235, 236, know pg. 237, 238, read pg. 241, learn 243, do pg. 243-244 (1-14).

Latin—Vocabulary Test (study for), on Lessons 19-25. Homework—Page 104, study vocabulary, pg. 104-107 study grammar. Translate story on page 104. Study for test Friday (Vocab. Test is Wednes.).

English—Book report due in one week. Should have notes written on 3x5 card. Rapid quiz on first 200 pages Wed.

Social Science—Test Wednesday on all of the Economic Philosophies and also some current events questions. Due Friday—Answer what is meant by Great Britain, what are the 2 branches of Parlia-

ment, how many seats in the House of Commons, what are the 2 major Political Parties, who is Prime Minister, does the Queen of England have any real power.
Biology—Lab. Manuals due Wednesday, Investigations 15-25. Do Inves. 26 this week. Bio. Test on Chapters 13-14 on Wednes. Know all classifications (know all characteristics of the Spermatophytes, know Class 1. and its first 3 orders, know Class 2, its 2 orders, and their characteristics. Know pg. 143 (all tissues), cambium, phloem, xylem, pericycle, epidermis, endodermis, cortex, cork, parenchyma etc., and all their functions. Know woody and herbaceous plants. Know annuals, biennials, perennials, and their life cycles. Know fibrous and tap root systems. Know the root hair and how it is formed. Know longitudinal section of the root. Know the cross section of the root. Know all tropisms. Know adventitious roots and roots for propagation.

My favorite item in my collection to date is, "Read *The Third Reich* over the weekend."

Another major aspect of today's educational trends is a kind of disrespect for appropriate and normal individual differences in abilities, interests, rates of growth and ways of learning. We divide children up according to performance, for reasons of expediency, not because we really respect differences. Dean Willard C. Olson of the University of Michigan School of Education stated in a speech several years ago, "Seven-year-olds may vary from three to 12 years in growth ages. Ten-year-olds may vary from seven to 18. A high school graduate may be someone from the fourth grade to a college graduate in common learnings. These differences are not 'curable' in the usual sense." He added that "get tough" programs, advocacy of a narrow curriculum of so-called rigorous subjects and ability grouping have little relevance to individual achievement or successful learning programs. He pointed out that individual differences in growth timing, such as the "late starter" or the "slow maturer," have little relation to subsequent distinction. He concluded: "Wise programs work with differences instead of against them."

A friend whom I met recently told me how astonished she was at how well her son was doing in college. She said, "All his life he's been pursued by reports from school, saying that he 'never finished anything.' His teachers kept warning us that this was very bad for his college records, and we were so worried all the time that we never realized that the reason for this was that he was so *curious* about so many things, so interested in everything, that his attention kept wandering from one thing to another—like a kid in a candy store who wants to taste everything! Now that he's discovered the thing he wants most to do, he's ready to settle down and plug away."

Another example of the problems that arise when individual differences are seen as troublesome rather than thrilling is the story a father told me. He was in a state of turmoil about the fact that his sixteen-year-old son refused to take the mathematics courses that were required for high-school graduation. He wants to work eventually in the field of international law. He has written several papers on this subject—so good, as a matter of fact, that they have appeared in professional journals. He "eats, sleeps, breathes" international law, knows more than any teacher now available to him can possibly teach him. He corresponds with professors at many universities and with political scientists in this and in many other countries. His marks in history and related areas are always in the high nineties, frequently 100 per cent. He hates math and finds it torture to take math exams, which he invariably fails. The school has been unable to make him accept the seriousness of the situation. He wrote to outstanding figures in the field of international law asking if mathematics played any or much role in their work, and most of the answers he received (including one from Adlai Stevenson) tended to bolster his side, a characteristic answer being, "If you are wise you will marry a woman who likes to keep books; that's what I did." It is hard not to feel some justification for his point of view, but whether one does or not, one must admire his spirit and ingenuity. He will have to be helped to accept the realities and imperfections of life—but it may well be a waste of everyone's time and talents.

Even the most minimal variations in skills may jeopardize a young person's opportunities. Marion, a high-school senior, had to graduate with an 85 per cent average in order to be admitted to a city college. Her family could not afford to send her to a private college or the expenses of living away from home at a state college. Her final marks were 90 per cent in English, 88 per cent in History, 86 per cent in Chemistry, 80 per cent in French, 70 per cent in Math. How many English or history teachers would do as well in French or math? And yet, she did not have the needed 85 per cent average to gain entrance to a municipal college.

If our get-tough approach in education were to produce a generation of intellectual giants or creatively gifted human beings, one might concede at least an opportunistic justification, if not a moral one. But there is every reason to believe that the current approach is *not* a sound method for helping children develop the best they have to offer. A book entitled *Lessons from Childhood* by Cynthia and Ronald Illingsworth, published in England, reports that "the child who is backward today may be the genius of tomorrow." After an analysis of 500 famous persons, the authors came up with these facts: Picasso has never been able to remember the alphabet; Einstein was four before he could speak and didn't learn to read until he was seven; Beethoven's music tutor told his parents, "He never has learned anything and he never will learn anything. As a composer he is hopeless." Winston Churchill and Isaac Newton floundered at the bottom of their classes. The authors also pointed out the mysterious inconsistencies of growth by reporting that others of the world's greatest men had been very bright when they were children. Mozart composed a concerto at the age of six, and the philosopher David Hume began his university career when he was eleven.

The newsletter of The Association for Family Living published several years ago an article entitled "Reaching Your Potential" by Edgar Dale:

> What future would you predict for a man who as a little boy roamed the streets of San Francisco, sometimes going into saloons with his father? The father died and the family moved back East. The boy enrolled at Dartmouth . . . however he soon quit, . . . and took a job in a mill. Next he entered Harvard but quit in his second year. He married, taught English superbly well in a high school; next taught at a Normal

School. He then decided to chuck the whole business, sold his farm, and took his family to England. Here, at the age of thirty-eight, he published his first volume of poetry and Robert Frost's distinguished career was launched. What was the potential of another man who stated in his autobiography that "(I was) considered by all my masters and by my father as a very ordinary boy, rather below the common standard of intellect. To my deep mortification my father once said to me, 'You care for nothing but shooting, dogs, and ratcatching.' . . . During the three years I spent at Cambridge my time was wasted, as far as the academical studies were considered." This was hardly an auspicious beginning for one of the world's greatest scientists, Charles Darwin. . . . Albert Einstein's early scholastic career was also inauspicious. At sixteen he failed the entrance exam to the Zurich Polytechnic. He . . . eventually took a good degree, although not good enough to gain him a post in research. One of his professors really did describe him as a "lazy dog" and his Professor of Physics did recommend him to try biology or medicine instead. . . . Peter Ustinov's term report from Westminster, a prestigious British public school, read: "He shows great originality, which must be curbed at all cost!"

Lack of respect for differences in ways of learning penalize children who learn more slowly. In his book *The Culturally Deprived Child* Frank Riessman wrote: "It is time to put an end to the negative description of the term 'slow' in the learning process. Slowness can reflect many things. It can indicate caution, a desire to mull things over, an emphasis on the concrete and physical."

He goes on to say that slowness is not always intellectual inadequacy and that we must study the nature of slowness. Because a child takes a long time to arrive at an answer does not mean that his thinking is retarded. It may be that his thinking is more circuitous, that he is easily distracted, that he will not venture an answer until he is certain. While our culture emphasizes speed, there is really no reason to assume that everyone can or must learn rapidly or perform rapidly. Some people take a long time to learn basic concepts, but when they finally do so, they may use these ideas in a thoughtful, penetrating fashion.

One of our major difficulties is that we have tended to equate intelligence with creativity, as though they were interchangeable. Recent studies indicate that nothing could be further from the truth. Typical of many such reports is that of Dr. Emmy E. Werner, Assistant Professor of Child Development at the University of California. She stated that a number of studies revealed that only about one third of the children from nursery through high school could be regarded as highly creative and highly intelligent as measured by intelligence tests and academic performance. More frequently there was a difference of about 25 I.Q. points, creative children performing at the lower level on I.Q. tests. She reported that children who were judged in these studies as being highly creative were frequently regarded by their teachers as having wild or silly ideas and as being less ambitious, hard-working and studious than the high-I.Q. children. In an article in the *Nursery Education Journal*, Dr. Werner wrote: "When we contrast youngsters who are gifted in the traditional sense—those with a high I.Q.—with children who score high on tests of creative thinking, we find one group seems to be better at finding the one right, recognized answer (convergent thinking) and that the other excels in thinking that takes off in new directions (divergent thinking)."

Dr. Donald W. MacKinnon, Director of The Institute of Personality Assessment and Research, carried on a long-term research project studying creativity. He concluded that "a certain amount of intelligence is apparently necessary, but above that it doesn't make much difference." On the basis of a study of 530 creative persons, among them some of the nation's most outstanding writers, artists, architects, mathematicians, engineers and industrial research scientists, Dr. MacKinnon concluded, "It is certain that our most creative subjects haven't been grade-getters. The architects have ranged around B averages; research scientists from B to C. Many don't have the academic record that would get them admitted to most graduate schools today."

In a book titled *Guiding the Creative Talent* Dr. E. Paul Torrance discusses the qualities that seem involved in creative thinking. He sums them up as "adventurous thinking" —getting away from the main track, breaking out of the mold, being open to experience, permitting one thing to lead to another. It seems to involve curiosity, imagination, openness to discovery, innovation and invention. Dr. Torrance holds that we must differentiate between talented conformists trained as "brilliant enhancers, embroiderers and manipulators of ideas and others" and talented nonconformists "who may make imaginative breakthroughs to new knowledge."

Our present trends in education support the first group wholeheartedly and discourage the second group. The creative personality usually includes adventurousness, independence, disorganized habits, inability to make long-range plans, questioning of authority, playfulness—a kind of divergency that most teachers find exceedingly difficult to handle. In addition, these children are often bogged down in some phase of development, frequently experiencing difficulties in learning to read and write. Their strong need to question and to test facts and ideas can be threatening to teachers who are concerned with teaching skills and facts.

All these forces in education tend to foster an aristocracy of achievement, not of intellect or creativity. We encourage those who are clever and smart, rather than those who may become wise or profound. When I was discussing this problem with a psychologist recently, he told me that he felt we could see the issues more clearly if we were to study "*over*-achievers." He told me about a research project which had been undertaken to study the personality characteristics of under-achievers, but in order to do this, both very low and very high achievers were studied and compared. The researchers discovered that they were learning just as much about the high achievers, and one observation was that high achievers have a very low tolerance for failure. These were the youngsters who stayed up half the night studying, who showed enormous tension and anxiety about exams. Typical of this group was the fifteen-year-old girl who had a study period first thing in the morning but who could never leave any homework for that hour and always completed all her work the night before. When asked why, she said, "I always worry—suppose there was a fire drill or something, and I couldn't get it done during that hour?" The psychologist commented to me, "We have often wondered why such a large proportion of high achievers in high school and college don't produce on a higher level later in life—why they are not necessarily those who succeed at the highest level or become our leaders. It may be because of their lack of tolerance for failure—which is such a necessary ingredient for creative work in any field."

It is all very well to criticize "the system"—but I am well aware that such criticism doesn't change the facts or solve our problems; the decisive factor is what we do about it. All over the country parents and teachers are concerned; the voices of many leading figures in education, psychology and psychiatry who are deeply disturbed by our present direction are beginning to be heard and listened to; the worst of the "sputnik hysteria" is over; and if we are willing to express our opinions and work for changes, we can begin to bring them about.

We can certainly make a difference where our own children are concerned by keeping a sense of perspective and refusing to let them view themselves as "those most likely *not* to succeed." Until we return to some sense of balance, many parents will have the difficult (but not impossible) task of reassuring their children about their worth as individuals with different needs, abilities, styles and rates of learning. Because our young people are too caught up in the problem to have any perspective about it, it is up to us to provide the needed counterbalance; to insist that all is not wrong with the children who cannot take the pace. We need to feel this deeply ourselves and then to communicate the fact that it is not that our children are inadequate but that the environmental demands are too rigid. If ever there was a time for parents to enjoy and celebrate, encourage and reinforce the qualities and strengths that their children do possess, this is the time.

This does not mean that we condone or accept irresponsibility, excuses for poor work, laziness or indifference. We must of course help our children face reality even when we are not entirely in sympathy with that reality. We may do this by providing special tutoring or an opportunity to attend summer school; we may encourage a child to repeat a year of school—but we have to make it clear that such steps are necessary not because the child is just too stupid to learn, but because the demands are so much greater than ever before.

Not only do we need to reassure those children who are in difficulty; it is equally important not to become smugly contented about those children who are doing very well. Both groups of children must be helped to understand what we value most in life, that no matter what achievements may be at the top of the national popularity poll each year, *we* are concerned about such qualities as honesty, compassion, imagination and integrity.

We can help other people's children as well as our own by offering our services as volunteer teachers. In the past few years this program has grown very rapidly—a good example of how a positive gain can result from a bad situation. Faced with increasing numbers of non-learning children, school systems have turned in desperation to an idea that would be good under any circumstances: to enlist the services of people in the community willing to spend a few hours a week working with an individual child. It is one of the many ironies of life that these volunteer programs are so successful. What does the volunteer do? Although he receives some supervision and guidance, he has no uniform or standard methods that he must use; he is encouraged to invent and improvise, adapt and experiment as he gets to know the child. He has an opportunity to develop a warm affectionate relationship with the child. As we begin to see quite excellent results, we are forced to conclude that in the absence of advanced graduate courses in teaching techniques, it must be love that finds a way! In other words, the volunteer teacher is having the opportunity to do the creative teaching, while the classroom teacher must often devote much of her time and energy to struggling through her prepared syllabus.

There are many opportunities for letting those discouraged under-achievers know how good they really are. The guidance counselor in one high school asked some of her under-achievers to write an essay on what they thought was wrong with their education. They showed such eminently good sense and sound judgment that their essays were mimeographed anonymously and distributed to the faculty, the parents and the school administrators. So long as such examples of "under-achievement" as the following samples exist, we are in pretty good shape.

> 1. . . . The predominant part of my life is school. I wish instead, that it was the nucleus around which my other activities revolved. . . . I want every course I take to be interesting and stimulating enough to make me want to do the work. I do not feel for instance, that I should be taking a math course just because it is required, which is pure drivel for me. In it I learn by memorization and repetition. I would prefer to take a course which stretched my mind. . . . This year, I have not had time to read. . . . Last year I read 40 books for pleasure, yet after two months of this year, I have read only one. To me, this is a dismal situation.

. . . I would like time to be myself. I want to spend time with my friends, talking and ironing out mutual problems; going to the city to see an art gallery or a play, or just watching the people go by; or taking a bike ride or a walk in a park.

2. . . . The greatest service the community, my parents and the school can do is to GIVE ME TIME. . . . Perhaps the rush can be eased by setting a ceiling on the amount of homework to be given. I think that more than 4 hours is exorbitant. One of the worst times to have homework is on the weekend. It is on Saturday and Sunday that there is a bulk of time that could readily be used. I know that if the load on those two days was decreased, I would come back on Monday feeling very refreshed, and ready to start the grind all over again. . . . I believe that to mature correctly, a person at my age must, more or less, "soak up" life as he sees it.

3. . . . I think all people my age want to be of use to society, but I think they all believe also that to achieve this they must be a doctor, politician, lawyer, teacher, etc. This I think is the fault of parents and the community. Most parents have stressed that their child should go to college, even if he doesn't have the ability. This is wrong. Wouldn't it be better for the child to be a good plumber or electrician than a poor doctor or lawyer? I think the stress should be switched from college to be a success at whatever you do!

For myself, I think I would like to see the term "under-achievement" barred from the English language completely, even as applied to those children for whom it was originally used, who are unable to learn because of emotional distress. Such children must be given special help, of course—but all children would gain from a general viewpoint that everybody is what he is and does what he can, from moment to moment, changing and growing constantly, failing and succeeding, but moving ahead, so long as he can believe that he is good and that life is good.

I recently saw Dr. Louise Bates Ames of the Gesell Institute on a television interview program in which she said that she and her colleagues were suggesting that as many as 50 per cent of our elementary-school children be put back a grade. When I heard this, I did not know whether to laugh or cry. First we accelerate the academic program, scream about wasting time when we could be teaching reading and writing, shout gleefully when we figure out a scheme for teaching calculus in second grade—and then, a few years later, when we happen to notice the children, we discover that "50 per cent are too immature for their present grade level"! There *must* be a simpler solution; and for a starter, I suggest that we follow the advice of Dr. Ernest Melby of Michigan State University, who stated: "One of the most important things a teacher can do is to send a pupil home in the afternoon liking himself just a little better than when he came in the morning."

SEVEN

Any Dope Can Have a High I.Q.

A NURSERY teacher and I were having a conference recently with the mother of a perfectly charming normally endowed four-year-old girl. We had nothing but good things to say about Jessie; she was friendly, spirited, enthusiastic and happy in school. Her mother was pleased but not ecstatic, and finally she said, "In other words, you're really telling me I have an average child." She sounded so crestfallen that I found myself feeling somewhat ashamed, as though I had insulted her child. She went on to tell us that in her neighborhood all the mothers knew their children's I.Q.'s, and as it came closer to the time when Jessie would enter grade school and be tested, she was getting more and more nervous about having to know "the verdict" as to how smart the child was. "Suppose it turns out she isn't as brilliant as her father thinks she is?" she asked. I confess to having lost my professional objectivity when I snapped back, "Well, there's obviously only one thing you *can* do— throw her back and try for another!"

Nowhere does our collective madness about education show up more blatantly than in relation to tests and grades. Dr. Harold Taylor, at that time President of Sarah Lawrence College, once said that our demand for measured academic achievement is a "national defect . . . to identify growth with grades is to deny the meaning of life." A grade school principal told me that he realized he had made a terrible tactical error when he mentioned at a parent-teacher meeting that at some time during the course of the year, the children would be given group I.Q. tests; he discovered that many of the parents were having their children "cram" for the test. The fact that advertisers have discovered the secret hopes and dreams of parents was attested to by an advertisement for a children's encyclopedia bearing the headline "How to Increase Your Child's I.Q. in 30 Days." The specter of tests hangs over the heads of our children like a nightmare, haunting them from nursery school to graduate school. Phyllis McGinley described this atmosphere: "Tests sort them, classify them, winnow them out as if they were gradable peas from a commercial garden." I was shocked a few years ago to hear my daughter and a friend, both in the first year of high school at that time, discussing how they hated to face another week of school; the friend said, "I wish we could just have exams all the time and no classes—that would simplify everything." Neither of them seemed to find this view at all ironic or sad.

A child psychiatrist, consulted about the effects of tests on children, told me that every year she sees increasing numbers of children who are more and more frightened by school examinations. She said, "You know, testing is becoming such a big business that one of these days it will be taken over by the 'syndicate'! How could the racketeers keep their hands off such a juicy plum?" She was certainly correct that testing is big business; the publication of school exams alone is an industry involving well over $25 million a year. Over 100 million standardized grade-school and high-school tests are given each year, averaging about three tests per pupil from kindergarten to twelfth grade. An additional two million multiple-choice tests are given for college admissions and scholarship competitions.

In a paper presented at the Annual Convention of the American Psychological Association in New York in September 1966, Dr. Ohmer Milton, Director of the Learning Resources Center at the University of Tennessee, reported:

> "In round numbers, there are sixty million students in schools today. If each of these youngsters is required to take twenty classroom tests during the coming school year, then one billion, 200 million educational tests will be administered. . . . In round numbers, there will be six million undergraduates this fall. If each student carries twelve courses during the year and is required to take three tests in each one, there will be 216 million college . . . tests. . . . Classroom testing is "big business" on the basis of numbers alone; more importantly, it is "big business" because of the sorts of decisions about students that are based upon test scores. . . . The grade point average—the final result of numerous tests—determines to a large extent such matters as financial aid, honors . . . graduation, graduate school attendance, choice of jobs . . . and even entry into the armed forces.

An article in *Look* for March 22, 1966, "Testing vs. Your Child" by George B. Leonard, tells the story of a graduate student who was teaching in an experimental class in a large university. He reported, "There's a story in Greek mythology about the goddess Circe and how she turned strong, brave men into swine. I saw that happen in a classroom. I watched students—human beings—turned into swine." The class was designed to encourage learning for the sheer joy of learning, without testing or grading. A professor who was very uneasy about this approach and who was not sure that the class was reading exactly what he assigned each day, surprised the class by walking in one morning and announcing a quiz. He reeled off ten factual, petty, simple-minded questions, reminding the students of his precise attitude—he was the teacher, they were the students, limited, slightly less than human, expected only to regurgitate facts and opinions that he stuffed into them: swine. The author goes on to say:

> As the process called education keeps getting lengthier and more crucial to the life of your child, the science of testing is outrunning the art of teaching. Your child's teacher stands in danger of becoming not a connoisseur of learning, but a custodian of examinations. . . . The teacher who relies heavily on tests and exams does not have to concern himself with the learning process. He can simply assign lessons, then later test his students to see what they have learned on their own. *This is not teaching.* He can continue to use the lecture method, that outmoded, one-way form of non-communication that may be defined as the easiest way to get material from the teacher's notebook to the student's notebook without touching the student's mind. *This is not teaching* . . . the present situation, with

its heavy emphasis on tests and its insane pressure for grades, is less an invitation to learn than an invitation to cheat. . . . A Columbia University study of more than 5,000 students in 99 United States colleges found that at least 50% *admitted* cheating. William J. Bowers, the author of the study, estimated that an even greater percentage of students cheat in high school. . . . Our children are simply responding—generally quite appropriately—to the world we have made for them.

If we are to understand the uses and abuses of tests, we must have some perspective on their background. At the heart of the matter is the intelligence test, and just as with the description "under-achiever," so too the term "intelligence quotient" or "I.Q." started out to be a means of communicating about children with special problems. Binet and Simon, who devised the first intelligence test, never dreamed that they were creating such a Frankenstein; Simon said as much, a few years ago. Their original purpose was to design a test that could help the classroom teacher discover cases of mental retardation and check the general abilities of the students. They spoke of it as a "minor tool," as an adjunct and a check on the teacher's personal observations and judgments, its primary purpose being to "identify children with less than the usual school ability who might need special help."

The test was based on a relatively simple design; for example, a large number of children, all ten years old, are asked to answer a question. If 50 per cent can answer it, the question is considered reasonable for ten-year-olds. Numbers of such tests or questions involving information, reasoning, memory and various kinds of manual and perceptual skills are assigned to every age group on this basis, resulting in an examination in which at any given age level 50 per cent will get a score below 100 and 50 per cent will get above 100. In other words, there is set up an arbitrary division of the entire population in order to find an average. The Intelligence Quotient is obtained by dividing the "Mental Age" (a child's score on the test) by his chronological age and multiplying by 100. If the mental age is higher than the chronological age, the score will be above 100; if the mental age is lower than the chronological age, the score will be below 100. The main point to remember is that *50 per cent of the population must get 100 or below—* that is how the test is designed.

We Americans are crazy about games and gimmicks; we love to standardize things, to play "number games." The story of the intelligence test is the story of the gun no one knew was loaded or the "sleeper" that became a best-seller. Since its development it has grown to unimagined proportions, providing employment for thousands of psychologists. It was and is a useful tool when used as a supplement to human judgment, as a way to verify or substantiate opinions and impressions gained in direct relationships. It can offer clues and directions for further exploration, and it can serve as a flexible guide in evaluating behavior that is difficult to assess by direct observation. But it is not a permanent judgment of an entire future. The I.Q. is an arbitrary number, not a life sentence. Perhaps more importantly, if you happen to have gotten one of those coveted high numbers, it is no guarantee that you have received your ticket to heaven; high test scores do not discriminate between heroes and villains.

It is absolutely essential to remember that I.Q. scores are frequently very poor predictors. Even within the limits of their usefulness they are often incorrect. When I first started practicing to administer intelligence tests, most of my subjects got scores which seemed to indicate that they were feeble-minded. As I learned to use the tool better, it was amazing how much smarter became all the children of the students and professors at the college where I was taking a course in testing. An experienced, warm and generally approving examiner gets higher scores from his subjects than do inexperienced examiners or one who finds it difficult to relate easily to his subjects. If the examiner has been told that he is testing mentally retarded children, or exceptionally bright children, his expectations may play a subtle and unconscious role in the test results.

On one of my first jobs, working as a child-welfare worker in West Virginia, I was assigned supervision of a little girl placed in a foster home. She had lived in another state for several years, and when we were faced with some difficulties in her adjustment, I wrote to an agency that had had contact with her before she was returned to West Virginia. I received this report: "Betty Hayes [not her name] is a mentally retarded child and was given a psychometric examination showing her chronological age to be nine years and four months and her mental age six years and two months, giving her an intelligence quotient of 66. We trust that this information will be of some help to you in planning for this child." By exploring further, we also found out that Betty had been abandoned by her unmarried mother at the age of three and since that time had lived with her alcoholic father in what was euphemistically called "an unlicensed boarding house" in which whatever supervision she had received was given by the chief "Madam"—who happened, we learned much later from Betty herself, to have a strong propensity for attempting to stab with a large kitchen knife any customer who was a little slow in paying up. When Betty was nine, her situation was finally reported to the authorities, and it was at this time that she came under our supervision for foster care. After about a year of intensive psychotherapy and supervision in a foster home in which we were able to work very effectively with two warm and compassionate foster parents, Betty was retested. Her I.Q. was 115. In a sense this story is an example of a *good* use of testing; it was obvious to the foster parents, to Betty's teacher and to me, that if she was mentally retarded, we *all* were—and the test was a way of confirming what we felt and saw. But the point I want to make is that, as in the original test, very serious errors can occur if a test score is accepted without very careful evaluation of many other salient factors.

In his book *The Culturally Deprived* Frank Riessman writes: "Intelligence tests measure how quickly people can solve relatively unimportant problems making as few errors as possible, rather than measuring how people grapple with relatively important problems, making as many productive errors as necessary with time no factor." As one very wise guidance counselor explained it to a group of parents, "A child's I.Q. test score really measures a child's ability to take an intelligence test—nothing more." I was very happy to hear this since, when my husband used me as a guinea pig for practicing the art of testing, my score was 94; at the time I was in graduate school—and I graduated. I have always been a classic example of a terrible test taker; I get nervous as soon as I hear the word "test"; my mind wanders, I cannot concentrate, I think of answers that are very original but have nothing whatever to do with the subject at hand. At the age of six, when I was given my first intelligence test for entrance into a progressive school, I was later asked by my mother what I had thought of the test. I reported that it had been all right, except for one very puzzling question. I said that the teacher had asked me to draw a lion between a chair and a pail drawn on the test page; I didn't think I could draw a good lion, so I had drawn a daisy instead. When my mother said, "But, Eda, they probably wanted you to draw a *line*, between the chair and the pail," I replied, "Oh, but that would have been too *easy!*" It was a testament to the school's faith in human potential that I was admitted—especially since it later developed that on a simple arithmetic question, "When the fox ate two little rabbits, and then he ate two more little rabbits, the fox had eaten —— little rabbits," I gave as my answer, "The fox ate the *poor* little rabbits." When my mother suggested that I should have said "four rabbits," I replied, "Oh, but Mommie, the *poor* rabbits!" As you can see, I have always been a troublemaker when it comes to taking tests, which undoubtedly accounts in part for my jaundiced view of the whole procedure!

In the original conception intelligence tests were not viewed as suitable for group administration. Except in special cases, where an extensive individual evaluation is felt to be needed, group intelligence tests are now administered by many schools. Given individually, it was possible for the examiner to view the test results in relation to an individual child's level of anxiety; confusions and misinterpretations of questions could be noted. Even important variables, such as whether or not a child seemed to be tired or was getting a

cold or tended to be shy with a stranger, could be incorporated into the evaluation of the results. We are faced, therefore, with a double problem in group testing; there is no
opportunity for these observations, and as testing has
gained in importance, children taking them tend to become
more nervous and uneasy about them. The child with a
consistent tendency to become flustered by testing situations is often penalized unfairly.

There are, of course, many other kinds of tests, designed
to measure aptitude and scholastic achievement as well as
assessing personality. In a Public Affairs Pamphlet titled
What You Should Know About Educational Testing the
author, J. McV. Hunt, summed up some of the similarities
and differences:

> Tests of intelligence or aptitude are commonly distin-
> guished from tests of scholastic achievement: intelli-
> gence and aptitude tests are supposed to measure ca-
> pacity to learn, often conceived to be innate; achieve-
> ment tests, to measure what is learned. Actually these
> two kinds of tests differ less than commonly supposed.
> Intelligence and aptitude tests reflect the amount
> learned from incidental experiences before the student
> has had an opportunity to receive special training in a
> given skill or subject. The abilities tested are presumed
> to be common to children regardless of their schooling.
> Achievement tests, on the other hand, reflect the
> amount learned in school courses. In both intelligence
> and achievement tests, however, the abilities tested are
> products both of the individual's inherited potential
> for learning and of the opportunities for learning
> within his experience.

Personality tests, such as the Rorschach Ink Blot Test, are by nature more flexible and versatile and can often be better predictors of future interests and abilities—but here again, the value of the results depends very greatly on the skill, the point of view, the breadth of knowledge and the insight of the examiner. Such tests must also be used as adjuncts to other kinds of observations and information; and in cases where the test interpretation seems completely alien to everything known about a child, we ought to question the test, not the child.

One of the most serious problems in the use of so many standardized tests, which usually offer multiple choice answers, is that they tend to benefit "non-thinkers." The poet John Ciardi once said, "A fool is a person with short answers to long questions." Even examinations in which essays are required can fail to assess some of the most genuine talents. A newspaper story about Bel Kaufman, author of *Up the Down Staircase,* illustrates this point very well. In an exam for her teaching certificate she was asked to interpret a poem by Edna St. Vincent Millay. When the examiners failed her, she wrote to Miss Millay and described her interpretation. The poet replied that even she could not have interpreted her own poem as well. Miss Kaufman had Miss Millay's letter photostated and sent it to the examiners, but they did not reverse their decision. Instead, they decided in future to use only the works of dead poets.

With such masses of children to educate, with the inevitable necessity for some means of assessing readiness for each new level of schooling, we must rely on tests to some degree. Especially in such a mobile society, where families move from one place to another, it is necessary to find some relatively rapid way of placing children into new school systems. Used with discretion, tests can be a convenient and reasonably efficient way to handle some of the Herculean tasks of mass education. But we will defeat these sensible purposes if we worship test results, viewing them as final answers or as having a mystical validity handed down by God. In his book *They Shall Not Pass* (William Morrow), Hillel Black states: "Much of the alarm and concern over mass testing has been misplaced. It is not the tool itself that is dangerous but how we employ it. The real danger, which the use of tests reflects, is our attitude toward education."

Classroom grades and report cards can be as misleading as standardized tests. They are frequently based on the "normal distribution curve," which means that the individual child is being marked, not on the basis of his own performance, but in relation to the performance of the whole group. A report in *The New York Times* (November 17, 1966) pointed this up sharply:

> Margaret Mead surprised more than 600 Yale undergraduates in her introductory anthropology course today by giving out almost all A's and B's on the midterm examination. "Anyone who gets into a highly selective school like Yale, should be able to do A or B work unless he just didn't do the reading," Dr. Mead said. "To curve a grade automatically is absolute nonsense. . . . I'm not training people to be anthropologists. . . . I just wanted them to learn how to think like anthropologists. I was very pleased with the exams. Everyone deserved what he got."

In a survey of 300 institutions of learning made in 1958 by the University of Michigan, it was found that approximately 25 per cent of the freshman class in every college failed, whether the school was Harvard or some small college with very easy entrance requirements and a much less selective group of students. What this means is that most schools and most teachers are wedded to the idea that they must give a certain percentage of A's and F's, quite independent of both the background and the performance of the student. In *Evaluation in Higher Education* (Houghton Mifflin) Paul Dressel wrote:

> In one university, the decision was made to section engineering students in calculus on the basis of previous grades. One professor, not knowing this, was assigned a group of students . . . who had received A's in all preceding mathematics courses. Although recognizing that this was an unusually good group . . . on the first examination, he ended up with the usual distribution of grades from A to F. The reaction of the students forced him to reconsider . . . the grades at the end of the term showed 40% A's, 50% B's, and 10% C's. Knowing the caliber of the students, the professor still could not bring himself to report a distribution of grades in which almost every student would be given an A.

Every parent knows what such an attitude means in practical terms: "Keep your kid in the dumb group, and he'll do brilliantly!" In the previously cited speech by Dr. Milton before the American Psychological Association he quoted from an article written by a college junior which appeared in the University of Tennessee *Daily Beacon:*

> I am increasingly appalled by the near-cutthroat competition that is becoming even more inherent in our

whole approach to education. For example, grading in introductory psychology classes is geared to the ideal of a normal distribution. . . . Since any individual score is relative to the performance of the entire class, your neighbor's loss is your gain. The logical extreme of this situation will be when students no longer study together for exams for fear of helping each other. No one will lend his notes to a student who has missed a class or tell him an assignment. . . . Can there be no basis for evaluating a student's academic progress other than his relative performance as measured against that of his classmates? . . . The practical and ethical implications are disastrous.

Grades and report cards are notoriously poor at predicting future success; scratch almost any "famous" person, and you will find that somewhere, tucked away for safekeeping and brought out for an occasional self-satisfied chuckle on a rainy evening, is a well-preserved packet of neatly tied *terrible* report cards! On a somewhat more scientific basis, a research report which reviewed forty-six studies dating back to 1917 of the relationship between college grades and later success in a variety of careers, led the author, Donald P. Hoyt, to the conclusion: "Present evidence strongly suggests that college grades bear little or no relationship to any measures of adult accomplishment."

Despite such observations, parents tend to view report cards with a "this is IT" attitude; despite all that they may know about the children they live with twenty-four hours a day that may be contrary to the report card's evaluation, they accept it as THE VERDICT. Not only is such an approach unsound, but considering the difficulties the human race has always had in communicating with each other, written report cards tend to be misinterpreted unless there is a direct contact between the parent and the teacher. And once we have instituted this person-to-person relationship, the report card becomes unnecessary. A classic example of the potential for confusion is the story of the mother who was satisfied when under the heading "Classroom Social Behavior" the teacher had written about her eight-year-old son just the one word, "Trying." She assured the boy that all she wanted to know was that he was making an effort. Six months later a second report card arrived, and under the same heading there were now four words, which classified the situation but were far from reassuring; they were "More trying than ever."

A significant change in education is the fact that an increasing number of specialists apart from classroom teachers are becoming involved in the child's life in school. The addition of guidance personnel, such as social workers, psychiatrists, psychologists and guidance counselors (three out of four of whom at the present time are former teachers, with varying degrees of special training in educational counseling) has been increasing rapidly. Here again we have an example of a movement that started out with exemplary purposes and goals, to help children with special problems, but that has been corrupted to some extent by the general climate of pressures in education.

A mother recently told me this story. Her son, a third grader, seemed to be having a great deal of difficulty in school. He had always been somewhat shy and a worrier, but much to her surprise at a school conference with his teacher early in October the teacher said that Kenny was insolent, uncooperative and failing in his schoolwork. Very much distressed, Kenny's mother made an appointment with the school psychologist. "That was the beginning of three nightmarish months," she told me. "The psychologist said she would observe Kenny in his classroom, and then speak to me again. A week later she called me in and said she thought Kenny was a very upset little boy and she wanted to give him some tests. After another week she suggested that I come in to talk to her once or twice a week, to see if she could help me to understand some of Kenny's problems. She said he was over-identifying with me, and a lot of other things. I felt so guilty and upset—I couldn't understand how all of a sudden, I could be doing such terrible things to this child. But now I could see he really *was* a miserable person. He couldn't do his homework, he cried all the time, he worried so about school that he was making himself sick. It was terrible, because he was getting two to three hours of homework every single night, and his teacher was giving the children marks on tests almost every day. She was some perfectionist—once he did a report on something, and he really worked on it, so she marked him B/F, which meant it wasn't a bad report, but he failed because his writing was not neat." When Kenny's mother saw the shocked expression on my face, she said, "Don't you dare say one word about what a dope I was to think this was reasonable work for a third-grader! I can't explain it myself—I figured all the other children must be doing all right, and after all, a psychologist is supposed to understand these things. Then two things happened. At a club meeting I met five other mothers with children in that class, and their children were in trouble too. That psychologist was observing and testing and discussing with half the mothers in that class! For *the first time*—isn't that terrible?—I thought to myself, Maybe it's the teacher, not Kenny. Then came Christmas vacation, and next thing we hear—Kenny's teacher's been 'transferred.' The new teacher was just wonderful and that boy hasn't had one problem in that classroom since then."

Conceived of as the direct source of assistance to "underachievers" with emotional problems, or of help for children with problems that might express themselves in other ways as well, such as in delinquency or truanting, many guidance counselors find themselves providing emergency first aid for otherwise normal children who are cracking under the strain of accelerated learning schedules. Because of the additional numbers of youngsters aiming for college, and the limitations of such facilities, high-school counselors also find themselves spending as much as 75 per cent of their time counseling students on college selection and admission.

An item in *The New Yorker* commented succinctly on the emerging role of the school guidance department: "Overheard in a local classroom during Open School Week, a young, flushed teacher to a restless child: 'If you don't sit still and behave yourself this minute, I'm going to march you straight downstairs to the Guidance Counselor.' " Despite the best of intentions—a wish to offer unconditional acceptance, emotional support and encouragement to children with learning difficulties—guidance programs have under the current pressures almost inevitably tended to find themselves in the position of supporting school administrators who want to encourage uniformity in learning and achievement. When a youngster is in trouble, too many guidance counselors seem to feel that it is their job "to get this kid achieving again"—not to question the system, which may be contributing greatly to the problem. Some of the most dedicated and hard-working coun-

selors, who seriously question some of our current educational policies, have admitted to me that they are spending
much of their time trying to teach children how to study,
how to take exams, how to "get by," rather than being able
to concern themselves primarily with special and often
pressing psychological needs.

There are many wonderful guidance counselors, some
who are pretty good and some who are terrible; there are
guidance programs that are truly geared to encourage the
fullest personal growth of each child and others that sometimes seem more hindrance than help. Almost all guidance
counselors are overworked; there simply are not enough of
them to meet the constantly increasing demands for such
services. Therefore even the most skilled, creative, warmly
human counselors very rarely have the time or the resources to do the kind of job they would like to do. Because
the guidance department is part of the official school administration, and because we have tended to invest the "helping
professions" with a kind of mystique, there is a danger that
parents may be overwhelmed by the prestige and status of
guidance personnel. Instead of using the good judgment
with which they evaluate the effectiveness and good sense
of lawyers, dentists, pediatricians or any of the other specialists they rely on, they too frequently come into the
school scared, guilty, self-conscious and passively accepting
whatever they are told.

Parents must realize that while the services of a guidance
department can be of real help, they can also be inaccurate
and misleading. When a mother walks into a school building for a conference about her child, she is not going to
meet an oracle from Delphi! She is going to talk with a human being, who may or may not have good judgment, who

may or may not be able to be helpful. If one is lucky, the guidance counselor may be an artistic human being—a person with warmth, humor, good sense—possessing in addition special skills for eliciting information and guiding a child toward genuine personal fulfillment. He may also be an unimaginative, rigid, limited person, who uses the tools of his trade in the most inflexible and mechanical way. Few parents seem to realize that there are just as many variations in skill among psychologists, social workers and guidance counselors as there are among any other group of human beings. In every profession there are wise and stupid people —some who are mean or kind, happy or bitter, creative or cloddish.

In an article in *Woman's Day*, "The Guidance Counselor: A New Power in Education" (March 1965), Alan Hynd reports that there are now about 35,000 counselors, the majority of whom work in high schools. Even if there were 10,000 more, they would be unable to allot more than an average of six hours to each child during the year, and within the next few years we will be lucky if we can make the ratio of counselor-to-student one to every 300 or 400. Under such circumstances no parent can expect the guidance counselor, however kind, sensible and experienced, to chart a child's educational future.

Despite the realistic limitations of facilities and time, there are thousands of counselors who somehow manage, with imagination and dedication, to provide the kinds of services to children that are loving, protective and strengthening. I think that this group would agree with me that it is important for parents to know that in their relations with school guidance programs they must be prepared for making intelligent judgments about what is or is not good use of guidance services. In this connection Mr. Hynd says, "Watch out for the guidance program that separates children into groups based on ability—don't let a counselor pigeonhole your child!"

Too often these days, under the aegis of the guidance department, many school systems are accelerating their academic programs by using tests and interviews for placement of children into ability groups as quickly as possible. It is in this area that I think guidance programs can be most detrimental to children; the era of human engineering has produced assembly-line psychologists just about as efficiently as the technological age has made it possible to mass produce automobiles. Roaming some of our school halls and classes are dangerous "beasts of prey," who should have gone into computer operations but who decided, God help us all, to streamline and mechanize psychology! They appear to be human beings—they can be very charming and affable and put us at our ease; they are therefore doubly insidious, for we find ourselves hypnotically drawn into conclusions about our children that are horrifying. Let us use one school to describe the kind of result I mean: A few years ago a new principal (let us call him Mr. Birch) was assigned to The Bryant School (as we will call it). He was a young man with big ideas, thoroughly convinced that we are wasting too much time, teaching too little. He brought with him a psychologist-guidance counselor (we'll call her Mrs. Pierce) with whom he had previously worked, and who shared his views. The Bryant School is in an upper-middle-class neighborhood, the children are bright and intellectually stimulated and their parents are very ambitious for them. Mr. Birch and Mrs. Pierce knew that it would take a number of years to execute their new ideas and plans for the school, and they figured quite rightly that the place to start was with the incoming kindergarten class. At a parents' meeting Mrs. Pierce, an extremely attractive and charming woman, explained her point of view: that by finding and assessing problems early, learning difficulties could be greatly decreased; in addition, early assessment of extraordinary talents and abilities would make it possible to accelerate the curriculum for children who would be bored and restless unless given enough intellectual stimulation. The parents were, on the whole, delighted; they were flattered that their children were going to get such special professional attention, and worried as they were about competition for getting into college, they considered such a program an excellent one.

That spring every incoming kindergarten child was tested by Mrs. Pierce, and the mothers were interviewed either by her or by one of the kindergarten teachers. Test and interview involved about twenty minutes each. On the basis of these, decisions were made as to whether or not a child was to come to school for half a day or a whole day; the "bright" children were to come in the mornings only; "immature or slow" children were to come back in the afternoon for a special program. Since most of the boys and girls in this community attend nursery school, the three or four neighboring nursery schools very quickly began to feel repercussions of this project. Some of the more shy, or tentative, or easily upset children reacted very badly to the testing situation, and mothers reported back to their nursery schools that their children had "failed" the test and were in the all-day group!

At this point I heard about the school from a parent living in the community, and after contacting several nursery schools and gaining their cooperation, I began to collect stories from them about their relationship with the parents of their "graduating children" and the Bryant School. Feeling as I do about the dangers of early labeling, of arriving at a fixed position as to any child's future performance, I thought this seemed an excellent opportunity to see what happened in a situation which proposed to make judgments about children before they even entered their classrooms. The following are typical of the informal reports that were sent to me by nursery-school teachers in several neighboring nursery schools:

1. Yesterday Mrs. K. came to see us in a state of complete hysteria. She had a conference with us several months ago, and when she called and asked if she could come in again we were mystified. Dennis, we had told her, had had a good year at school, and we felt he was an imaginative, sensitive, volatile child. We had told his mother that life would probably never be easy for Denny—he was the kind of child who felt things very deeply, worried about things ahead of time, and would be somewhat unsure of himself in new situations; that was, from our point of view, a quality that he was born with, that made him the unique and special person he was, and we optimistically assured his mother that like millions of adults with similar tendencies, he could have a good life. Two days ago, Denny went to Bryant for his test. When he got to the school, and saw that he was to go into a strange room, with a strange woman, he became apprehensive. The more the psychologist insisted, the more he retreated, until, in tears, he tried to escape. Mrs. K. was told to wait in the hall, while Denny was

taken (forcibly) into the classroom. Fifteen minutes later, he emerged, subdued, wide-eyed, sucking his thumb. His mother was invited to come in, while Denny waited in the hall. Mrs. K. was then given the following report: Denny was very immature and would be a slow learner, he also was deeply insecure. He showed signs of being overwhelmed by a dominating mother-figure. Denny's mother told us all this and asked, "Why didn't you *tell* me that Denny was so disturbed?" We told her we didn't tell her this for the simple reason that such a thing never entered our heads. We knew darn well that Denny would be apprehensive about a new and strange experience—so are plenty of adults who are living exemplary lives. We knew he was sensitive, easily upset—so are a lot of other people including Presidents of the United States, and Nobel prize-winners!

2. Bobby's mother called us—she is beside herself. After his interview at Bryant she was told that he was immature, poorly coordinated and had a severe speech problem. Mrs. Pierce said he was inattentive, obstinate and insecure. Bobby's parents have been planning a vacation trip and when Mrs. S. mentioned this to Mrs. Pierce, she said she would recommend that they cancel it. She said Bobby was too anxious about this impending separation. She also said she felt Bobby wasn't getting enough intellectual stimulation, and that it was not good for him to play with his seven-year-old brother, who dominated him too much. Mrs. S. was furious at us because we had never told her any of these things, during the two years Bobby's been at nursery school.

In watching Bobby for two years, we had seen considerable growth; he wasn't Olympic star material on the jungle gym, but his coordination had improved dramatically. Yes, his speech was not perfect, but his mother has a foreign accent and it was often difficult to understand her speech; Bobby's speech seemed imitative, not exactly a major disaster at three or four years of age. We knew it would take watching, but did not see this as an immediate cause for great alarm. Bobby tended to be easily overstimulated, he often got excited and wild, but so do a lot of other energetic, active four year olds, and this also seemed no major disaster. He seemed to enjoy himself, he asked a million questions, was curious and adventurous, had a marvelous sense of humor, and many friends. He could be devilish and rebellious, but he could also be reasoned with. All in all, we thought he was a pretty normal specimen. This past year his mother has had a series of illnesses—at one point it was feared she had a brain tumor. Later the severe head pains were diagnosed as an allergic reaction to certain foods. One can imagine her relief and joy when this diagnosis was made, and the impending trip was by way of celebrating the good news—and as a restorative for the months of pain and terrible worry. Even if we had felt that such a separation would disturb Bobby, we would have done everything possible to encourage the parents to go. Children are resilient enough to endure such periods of deprivation—they have to be, because parents have a right to live too. Also, how could anyone suggest that it might be possible, in a family, to keep two brothers from playing together, even if there was a sound reason for doing so? A family is a family, and whatever problems there may be can't be solved by artificial separations.

3. We really had fun today with Valerie's mother. She has a wonderful sense of humor, and she was telling us about her interview at Bryant last week. She came in with Valerie, and gave her name to Mrs. Pierce, who looked in her files and took out a card with information about Valerie on it. Mrs. Pierce commented, "I see that it was an induced birth." Valerie's mother looked blank. "I don't know where you got that information, but it isn't true," she said. "It was a perfectly normal birth." "But I have it *right here* on this card," the psychologist replied, making it quite clear that anything that was in her files had to be so. Mrs. G. refused to accept this and kept insisting that she had been there, and knew whether or not it was an induced birth! (She gave Mrs. Pierce her obstetrician's name and telephone number. A day later the doctor called Mrs. G. and said he'd had a call from school, and when he also denied the induced birth, he was asked to check his records again!) Valerie's mother was asked what she expected from kindergarten. Among many other things she mentioned that she felt that by the end of the kindergarten year Valerie should be ready to begin reading, or on the brink of it. Mrs. Pierce said, "You know she couldn't even recognize this word." The word she pointed to was "plant." Mrs. G. said, "I didn't say she should be on the brink of reading *now*—but after kindergarten." Mrs. Pierce said she had asked Valerie what the individual letters were, and she knew them all except she wasn't sure about the p which she

thought might be a b. "You see, she has a long way to go," she said severely.

Of course in all the nursery schools there were also many triumphant reports by proud mothers whose children had behaved beautifully and passed every test with flying colors. But are we prepared to say that we can make *any* final judgments about a child at the age of four and a half, or that children who do not measure up to such a challenge are to be regarded as "abnormal"?

The Bryant School is no unique den of horrors. The school has a good reputation and has always been considered in the forefront of new approaches; the current program is hailed by most people as efficient and successful; most of the children who are predicted to be successes are; most of the expected failures occur. (It reminds me of the scientific experiment in which two groups of white mice were given to two groups of psychology students, who were told that one group of mice was "maze-trained" and the other group was not. Then each group of students were told to try to train their mice to go through a new maze. A marvelous thing happened; the maze-wise mice learned the new test much faster than the untrained mice. There was only one problem; the facts were not true—neither group had had any training beforehand! So much for the effects of the attitude of the experimenter!)

One of the most horrifying aspects of the episodes I have mentioned is the degree to which otherwise intelligent and reasonably well-balanced mothers accepted so readily the pronouncements of a total stranger who had spent twenty minutes with their child. Denny's mother did not say, "Why, Denny has been in nursery school for a whole year and loves it and is eager and curious about the world." She did not say, "I've lived with this child for more than four years and you don't know what you are talking about." Instead she asked the nursery teacher why she had not been told about her son's neuroses.

The episode of the file card is perhaps the most upsetting. It is a kind of mechanization and depersonalization that does not belong in a school. Depersonalization is anti-childhood. Children are warm flesh and blood, all themselves, uncatalogued, unpredictable, unorganized. As the manipulators take over, it is hard to know who suffers more, the child who is being automatized or the automaton who struggles to do it!

Finally I asked to see Mrs. Pierce myself. I said I was writing a book on education and would be interested in her views. She was most agreeable to making an appointment, and the following are my notes, written immediately after the interview:

It was a strange and kind of eerie experience—Mrs. Pierce seems on the surface to be a perfectly friendly and charming woman, devoted to children, talks about wanting them to have good "self concepts," not to feel they are failing, etc. And yet she seems oblivious to the ways in which she and her activities contribute to increasing the children's anxieties. She has now been at the school for four years and has two assistants in the guidance department. All classes are departmental in grades 4, 5 & 6, and the children are placed in ability groupings based on achievement levels in arithmetic, language skills and social studies. The children do not have any special grade-level teacher. Incoming kinder-

garten children are seen by three different people in
the spring—the school nurse, a kindergarten teacher
and by Mrs. Pierce or another psychologist. Each of
these people sees the child for about 10 minutes. The
psychologist's tests are designed to assess "visual and
motor coordination, spatial visual ability, concept-
formation, judgment, dexterity and general maturity."
The test results are then discussed briefly with the parent and suggestions are made for home activities and
parental handling of the child. . . . Behavior during
the testing session is recorded in detail. She showed me
one answer on a sentence completion test, "When I see
my mother . . . I get mad." "There it is, the whole
story," she said, looking at me significantly. She is very
proud of the special kindergarten group for "deficit
children." This class consists of from twelve to fifteen
children, with a highly skilled and "well motivated"
teacher. This group gets a great deal of attention from
other school personnel, each child is worked with "individually and lovingly," all kinds of special methods
are introduced for individual needs. She believes that it
is the early screening and the special skill training that
helps these children advance rapidly. It seemed to me
that if you created this kind of environment in every
single class, almost all children would thrive! You realize slowly that for all the kind and sensible-sounding
words, there is a basic assumption here that tests are
always accurate—that they are a magic way of knowing. One mustn't trust human judgment, no matter
how experienced—only the tests. I had the feeling that
as soon as the first contact was made with the school,
both children and parents were being measured and

judged constantly—and yet, at one point, with a straight face, Mrs. Pierce said, "I am very troubled by all the parental anxiety I see. I just don't understand why parents get so upset." Mrs. Pierce is a product of the technological age. She believes in tests, facts, statistics; she would not trust herself to make any judgments without them, but she feels confident in judgments based on twenty minutes of testing.

At a conference attended by several hundred New York State educators everyone was given a copy of the following case study:

Billy Jones is in fifth grade. Since 2nd grade the teacher has been telling Mrs. Jones (Mr. Jones never comes in for conferences or PTA meetings) that Billy doesn't seem to be motivated to do well in school. He comes to school without his homework and often does not bring teacher's notes home. He is a child of average ability and does below average work in all areas except art and science. Other children seem to like Billy, but he is likely to avoid participation in group activities. Billy has a brother in 11th grade who is preparing to go to college and who does well in school.

Then the conference participants were asked to respond candidly to the following questionnaire:

TYPICAL ANSWERS

1. On his way to school *Billy* thinks to himself ——   *"I wish I could run away."*

2. When Billy's *teacher* looks at Billy she thinks to herself ——   *"His parents will probably blame me."*

3. After a conference with Billy's teacher, Billy's *mother* thinks to herself ——

"That teacher just doesn't like Billy."

4. When Billy's *father* is asked to come to school he thinks to himself ——

"Don't they know their job?"

5. When the *guidance counselor* hears about the case of Billy he thinks to himself ——

"Something must be bothering Billy at home."

The results were fascinating; the majority of responses indicated that these educators felt that Billy hated school and would probably be thinking of some way to escape or to find some acceptable excuse for his poor work; the majority of responses indicated that these educators thought the teacher would feel quite threatened and on the defensive—something must be wrong with the way Billy's parents are treating him; the majority of responses indicated that these educators believed that Billy's parents would either feel very guilty and convinced they *were* doing something wrong, or they would be defensive and blame the teacher for not doing a good enough job. It was evident during a follow-up discussion of the responses that a child's failure is a threat to all the adults who are involved, that the adults in Billy's life were resentful and angry at him and saw his failure as a personal attack on them. One principal, summarizing the feelings expressed, said, "Let's face it—if he doesn't fit in, he's a pain in the neck!" Almost no one in the discussion raised the question of what might be wrong with the system, rather than what might be wrong with Billy. Even more interesting was the fact that after going around and around trying to figure out what ought to be done about Billy, the general conclusion was, "Let's send him to the guidance department!"

This seems to me to be the heart of the matter; whether or not school guidance personnel can submit to serving as the dumping ground for the academic failures that occur more and more frequently among children who would not have been failing if they had been in school twenty-five or more years ago—children who have a normal range of emotional problems and variations in speed of a growth and maturation but who are not seriously disturbed, who are reacting to increasing academic pressures. It seems to me that the role of a school guidance department is not only to offer therapeutic assistance to children in trouble, but also to serve as interpreter to the schools and the larger community concerning the growth needs of all children and the necessity for creating an environment in which a genuine love of learning can take place.

Dr. Sidney Jourard, a professor of psychology at the University of Florida, expressed to a group of psychologists, his feeling that, in the past, tests and guidance programs have sought to understand behavior in order to manipulate and control it. They have been used in the service of "the establishment" to spy on people and to change them. He described this effort as "an anti-human posture." He suggested that a new approach ought to be the development of a dialogue between the counselor and the counselee —"fellow explorers" trying to find avenues of creative fulfillment for the individual who is in difficulty, not trying to "adjust" him to some external, arbitrary and often useless or damaging demand. The counselor or therapist must not be "an invalidator of dissent," calling every quality of difference "maladjustment." In dealing with problems of failure, of human suffering, we ought to be committed to an enlargement of the scope of human possibilities, rather than seeking for or encouraging conformity to social demands and expectations. A guidance counselor, responding to this idea, remarked, "You know, it's really true. When a kid is referred to me because he's failing, or wants to leave school, or won't cut his hair, or is considered a rebel, I assume that the price he has to pay for being different is too high, so I do everything possible to encourage him to return to a more conformist position. Maybe the least we should do is find out if the price *is* too high for the *youngster*—maybe it isn't. Maybe he's willing to pay it and needs to, to be himself."

It is this kind of question we need to grapple with, in trying to nurture human potential.

EIGHT

Are They Dropping Out
or Are They Dropping In?

ONE day as I was reading a sign on a bus exhorting the city's youth to stay in school, it occurred to me that we have developed a new epithet synonymous with "bum" or "scoundrel" in the word "drop-out." Few words in the English language are more derogatory. When we visited the home of some friends recently, their twenty-two-year-old son greeted us at the door, saying, "You better not talk to me—I'm a law school drop-out. Do you think I'll ever be allowed to join the human race again?"

Like the term "under-achiever," "drop-out" must be viewed in the context of the times we live in. If we mean a person who does not finish high school, then 100 years ago practically everybody was a drop-out; if we mean someone who refuses to finish college, then fifty years ago almost everybody was a drop-out. All of a sudden, in the last twenty-five years, we have come to the conclusion that going to school for twelve to twenty years before ever holding a job is necessary and good for everyone.

In our current hysteria about education, with our excessive devotion to standardization, we seem to have decided that anyone who drops out of school is a failure, running *from* a situation rather than running *toward* another. Characteristic of this point of view is a Public Affairs Pamphlet entitled "School Failures and Drop Outs," which states, "In general it is the relatively stable youngsters who cope with the school's program and the relatively unstable, whose scholastic attainments tend to be poor, who leave." This refers to high-school drop-outs, and the statistics are very convincing; it is perfectly true that particularly at the high-school level drop-outs tend to be those who are failing. The question is, however, *why* they are failing and *why* they leave. It seems to me that one legitimate answer is that the schools have failed in meeting the needs of these young people. For example, the pamphlet reports that many drop-outs "have a consuming desire for ready money for dates and cars." What is really so hard to understand about that? Put into the perspective of history, 100 years ago *and in every other period of human history* most sixteen-year-olds *were* working and earning money; they were regarded by society as young adults who *should* be out on their own, making their way in the world. It would seem that judgments about an individual's goals depend more on the social context in which he lives, than on any intrinsically human qualities.

Expressing the basic anxieties about the need for education in today's world, Secretary of Labor Willard Wirtz wrote in his book *Labor and the Public Interest* (Harper):

[There is] a fallacious assumption that the dropout problem is one of increasing numbers of boys and girls

leaving school prematurely. To the contrary; each
year, for the last twenty-five or thirty-five years, the
number of dropouts has gone down. In 1960, the percentage of dropouts was only half what it had been in
1925. . . . The dropout problem is not that more are
dropping out. It is that there is significantly less demand for unskilled workers in the work force today
than there was before. . . . Today, boys and girls
simply have to be trained to fit into an economy which
no longer includes the unskilled work they could get
before. Anybody who drops out of school may very
well be committing economic suicide. Automation demands that the educational system assume the responsibility of seeing to it that nobody leaves school until he
or she is prepared to do the kind of work that is now
available.

On the face of it, that approach sounds reasonable
enough; it is perfectly true that job opportunities have
changed. But how many high schools are actually doing
anything about training young people for the jobs that are
available? Why is it necessary to set up the Job Corps
Training Program as a separate educational agency? Why
is it that the United States Army is able to take semi-illiter-
ates and train them for useful and necessary work, often in
less than a year's time? Why is it that there is no extensive
apprenticeship program in skills that are desperately
needed, such as plumbing, electrical work, carpentry and
expert homemaking? For one, the unions must bear a
heavy burden of responsibility for keeping our young people imprisoned in schools they hate, studying subjects that
seem entirely irrelevant to them, because they are afraid of
change in the labor-market balance. For another, we have

held rigid, inflexible ideas about training and education that bear no relationship to reality. In one city, as part of the anti-poverty program, semi-literate men and women, considered unemployables by the employment agencies, have become nursery-school teachers, teachers' assistants and recreation workers in less than one year's time because of the creative leadership in the community and the setting up of a work-training program that was imaginative and daring and that showed a genuine faith in human potential. Learning facts, passing tests and getting degrees are outmoded and thoroughly unintelligent as a single approach to job training. There are literally thousands of jobs for which people who are not academically inclined can be trained— and they can be *well* trained.

It is not dropping out of school that is the central problem, but rather our inability to allow young people who are not essentially book learners to start job training early enough or to grant them opportunities for on-the-job training. The most undernourished part of our entire school system is in the area of vocational training. If we want our young people to stay in school, all we have to do is make that schooling relevant and meaningful to their own individual capacities and goals, while also providing work opportunities through which they can gain direct experience and enjoy the right to earn some money as well. Automated we may be, but even the most automated equipment can be handled by someone who has had specialized training, whether or not he finishes high school or college.

What intellectual snobs we have become! Virtue is now in the number of degrees you have—not in the kind of person you are or what you can accomplish in real-life situations. To hear some parents talk, one would think that getting into the "right" college, or obtaining a graduate degree, were some kind of key to eternal paradise. In the mad rush for higher education for all, we have scared ourselves silly. With all the hysteria about getting children into college, a survey of 1,200 colleges made recently showed that there were over 30,000 vacancies in two- and four-year colleges across the country. Our real problem is first of all one of distribution, and secondly one of facing up to the fact that the few prestige schools in the country are receiving more applications in one year than they received in ten years some time back. Standards of acceptance have also shifted dramatically, so that failure to get into an Ivy League school is in no way a reflection on the young applicant, but simply a gigantic change in requirements. A Dean at Harvard commented several years ago that in all probability neither Franklin Roosevelt nor John Kennedy would have had the grades that would have gotten them accepted today. Dr. Owen B. Kiernan, Massachusetts Commissioner of Education, stated recently: "Educators have oversold the idea of college education for everyone to the point where parents now feel that a child who is not enrolled at college is destined for second-class citizenship . . . human dignity and worth are not monopolies of the collegiate world."

In our zeal to equate success with degrees, there are a great many questions that we have failed to ask ourselves about school drop-outs. As holds true for the under-achievers, there are some young people who are in serious trouble emotionally, for whom dropping out of school is merely a symptom of inner turmoil. There always have been such special problems, and I do not believe that their numbers have increased, except insofar as the increase in external pressures may be contributing to their psychological burdens. But if we take a candid look at the experiences and the values that make up a large part of the high-school and college scene, it seems to me we might well be inclined to call our drop-outs drop-*ins*; we have been too callous and too casual in our assumptions; dropouts may very well be leaving something that is at best useless and at worst harmful while sometimes eagerly, often desperately, seeking for something better.

For many young people staying in school endlessly, with the financial dependency this involves as well as the frustration of learning from books rather than from life, is simply unendurable. *The New Yorker* quotes one Barnard College co-ed as saying, "I'm sick and tired of being potential!" Why should it surprise us that young people of sixteen to twenty-five should become restless, eager to begin to live in the real world?

One young woman I know is terrified because her husband seems so willing to remain eternally a student. She told me, "Here I am, pregnant, and married to a boy who doesn't seem to care whether or not we ever stop living off our parents. Ken is almost finished with law school, but now he isn't sure he wants to be a lawyer—so the other night my father, who is a doctor, asked if he'd like to try medical school! I thought they were both kidding, but they weren't. Both of our families are very well off, and they enjoy our prolonged childhood—it's like letting us play house. All I want is for Ken to want to get out and work *someday*, but I think he likes being a perennial student— he'll never grow up unless he's forced to, and it scares me. Here he is, about to become a father—and the idea of going to school and being supported by our parents for another

ten years doesn't seem to bother him at all!" A little dropping *in* (to "real life") might be a good thing for this
young man!

Some of our young people are so deeply affected by the
incongruities, the hypocrisy, the shallowness of the life
around them that their general disillusionment is expressed
in a wish to rebel by escape. But we are making a mistake if
we interpret this attitude merely as immaturity or instability. The world in which we live is *really* so cock-eyed that
it doesn't seem to me at all surprising or alarming that so
many young people are in such distress. There is a group of
boys in Holland who call themselves "Provos"—a "beat"
group, who have been described as anarchists. When one of
their numbers, a young man of twenty, was asked what
kind of positive program he had to substitute for all the
things that he found wrong with the world, he replied,
"We have no blueprints for how to improve things—we
only know we cannot go on living as we do now." That
seems to me a perfectly reasonable statement. There is no
disgrace in wishing for significance in one's life and in crying out against what seems wrong in the world. And
whether we like it or not, our young people are going to
seek their own ways for bringing meaning into their lives.

Several years ago a high-school senior wanted to take
four days off from school to ride on a "Freedom Bus" in the
South. His parents and teachers told him that he was jeop-
ardizing his chances of getting into college. He went anyway—a temporary drop-out—and he also got into college.
A young man who was a junior at Stanford worked in
McComb, Mississippi, during that fateful summer of 1964.
He stayed for a year and a half, instead of going back to
school, and said, "I know I'm creating problems for myself

—but I just can't go back to that phony world." Another
young man, after completing two years of college and finding that he was still floundering and uncertain about what
he wanted to do, told his parents that he wanted to quit
college for a while and try to get into the Peace Corps or
VISTA, to have a chance to find out what it felt like to
work hard and to be really needed by others. His panic-
stricken father tried to talk him out of leaving school by
offering to buy his son a sports car—but realized he might
be missing the point when his son burst into tears.

Whether or not we may think some of their actions are
naive or misdirected, many college students who leave
school are trying to drop *in* to some idealistic vision of a
better world. They may very well be impractical dreamers,
lacking enough self-interest to do what will make them
most comfortable or successful, but in my opinion, many of
them represent the cream of the crop.

In its "Notes and Comment" section for October 29,
1966, *The New Yorker* offered its editorial congratulations
to two young men who had established their right, after
two weeks of penance on the detention bench, to wear their
hair long in high school:

> We have been set to wondering what there is about
> long male hair that is so menacing. Is it its tendency to
> pick up lint, soot, and bacilli? No, for the hair of long-
> haired boys we see looks, if anything, offensively
> washed, and anyway, the locks of ladies, however
> long, appear as far beyond sanitary considerations as
> the wavelets of the high, inviolable seas. Is it, then, the
> femaleness of long hair on males that offends us, turns
> us queasy? Yet what is so intrinsically masculine about

a close-cropped head? Do we think Charlemagne fey? Prince Valiant? Albert Einstein? John the Baptist? Ah, John the Baptist. Perhaps what we mind is being surrounded by . . . young persons uncomfortably reminiscent of Sunday-school oleographs. We have come a long way, nigh unto two thousand years, to get away from those people, and it is a shock to realize that the neighbor's son who used to mow our lawn has returned from Berkeley looking precisely like Jesus— that Jesus, in a sense, was in him all along, waiting to be let out. It may be that smooth chins, cheeks, and skulls represent to us something preciously modern— smoothness as an ideal, man as interchangeable, frictionless—and that all this bristling and flowing going on around us threatens to gum up the machine. Well, is the machine really that fragile? And was it designed to be eternal? We were furry primates before we were robots.

How grateful we should be to that portion of our youth who try to remind us of our humanity! A contrasting picture was provided by a friend of mine who was teaching at the Home Economics College of a large state university a few years ago. She wrote me: "The Marriage class drives me coo-coo as usual. It is loaded with sorority presidents, athletes, members of the marching band and other such other-directed characters. They simply ooze conformity and Rotarian togetherness. They are so well-adjusted to Babbitry that I yearn to flunk the lot of them. They are sunk in the apathy of the successful and accepted. I see before me the hideous result of good mental health. God save the nation if we ever get the whole population 'adjusted.' "

We have been and still are in great danger of labeling as "healthy" any behavior which is acceptable to us and makes us feel comfy-cozy and labeling as "neurotic" or "maladjusted" any behavior which makes us uneasy, which challenges us or suggests that perhaps we have fallen down on the job of providing meaningful experiences and values for our almost-adult children. As Dr. Abraham Maslow, Chairman of the Psychology Department at Brandeis University, observed recently, "My college students aren't suffering from the American Psychiatric Association's endorsed illnesses; their disease is frustrated idealism, a need for something to believe in, something to trust."

A guidance counselor at a large midwestern university told me that she was having a great deal of difficulty making judgments about students that were at all acceptable to parents or to the college administration. She said, "On my first day of work, I met the problem head on. A youngster was referred to me because he didn't want to go home for the Christmas vacation, and his parents were hysterical. They had gotten in touch with Jerry's advisor and together had agreed that maybe he was suffering from some emotional aberration. When I talked to Jerry, I found myself liking him immediately—he began to describe to me what would happen when he got home, how his parents would interfere with his plans, how they would try to arrange his life. He felt he was being infantilized by over-anxious, over-protective parents, who were robbing him of his own experiences, refusing to let him grow up and away. Jerry said, 'When I'm older, and more secure, I'll be able to fight more directly to be a person, to be myself, but right now I know that if I go home, I'll fall into all the old patterns of being the Fergusons' little boy.' The more I work with these college students, the more I come to realize that when and if they seem to us to be behaving in bizarre or hedonistic ways, they are frequently doing this because we aren't giving them enough room in which to grow on their own; taking LSD is one way of having an experience that isn't supervised by grown-ups! And failing or dropping out of school may be the one thing that they feel they can do on their own—it's something their parents and teachers can't take away from them!"

What are the "rebels" doing on college campuses? Some of them discover a book or a subject that fascinates them, and instead of doing the homework assigned to them, they spend weeks on their own, browsing, looking up other books by the same author, other work on the same subject. When they get a grade that reflects what they did *not* learn, rather than what they *did* learn, they stop caring about how they are doing. They seek out places where they can sit around and talk, share their ideas and feelings with others. They are, in a sense, philosophers looking for a forum where none exists, a forum for discussion of basic principles and values. As Dorothy Samuel described them in an article in *Contemporary Issues* (Spring 1965), "they would be Emersons and Thoreaus in a day when journals and podiums seem open only to statisticians and reporters."

Some young people enter college with impossible expectations; it was such agony waiting to be accepted, and such ecstasy to make it, that college has become over-idealized, an answer to all one's dreams rather than merely a next step in one's education. As one college professor put it, "They expect to meet Socrates in every class!" The sense of letdown and disappointment is overwhelming. In examining the problems of the college drop-out, we need to keep in

mind two important facts. The first is the current climate
of feeling about college attendance, and the second is that
one can make no accurate generalizations about *all* drop-
outs. There has been so much wailing and wringing of
hands that one would think that the rate of college drop-
outs had greatly increased in the last few years; this just is
not so. Dr. Lawrence A. Pervin, a clinical psychologist with
the Princeton University Health Services and Assistant
Professor in the Psychology Department, told me that approximately 50 per cent of the students who start college in
any given year do not graduate from the same institution
four years later. According to some studies, about 70 per
cent of those who leave their first college transfer to another school at once or complete their college education
later on. The percentage of return varies with the individual college, from about 59 per cent to 95 per cent in some
schools. Generally speaking, about 30 per cent of the drop-
outs never return to college. This statistic *has remained relatively constant during the past forty years,* according to
Dr. Pervin and other experts.

Why, then, have we seen an ever-increasing concern
about the college drop-out? Undoubtedly because we have
also seen an increasing concern about college admissions.
Parents and children live in a state of unrelieved panic during most of the high-school years, worrying about college
acceptance. Under such circumstances it is not surprising
that colleges are unable to live up to the impossible expectations of young people and that parents feel bewildered,
frightened and angry when their children want to give up
this sought-after prize.

Years ago, when a college education did not seem to be a
matter of life or death, young people were able to leave

college without such a total sense of failure. Many found jobs with bright futures, others were able to travel or work and return to college a year or two later without being made to feel like social pariahs.

As for the variety of motives and needs expressed by the drop-outs themselves, the following are samples of hundreds of such cases that I have been collecting for the past few years.

1. Alice was attending a state university, and in her junior year she met, fell in love with and married a young man who was a senior. They moved to another city when he graduated, and Alice transferred to another college for her final year, which she completed brilliantly; she is now a teacher. She is, statistically, someone who "dropped out" of her first college, but her subsequent plans and activities have been realistic, purposeful and satisfying.

2. Judy, an extremely bright, articulate and talented youngster, left college at the end of her freshman year to be married, and although her parents urged her to complete her education, she wanted to start having a family right away. At the present time she is 27 years old, divorced, having almost full financial responsibility for two sons, aged 6 and 8, unable for lack of a college degree to obtain the kind of job that would interest her or provide an adequate income. In her case leaving college was associated with escaping from reality, and the kind of lack of planning that was self-destructive.

3. Ellen barely graduated from high school, although she was an extremely bright youngster. Because of poor grades she could not get into the college she wanted and impulsively decided not to go at all. Her parents went into virtual mourning. After six months of working as a sales clerk, Ellen met and married a young man who was working during the day and studying at night. For a year or so, Ellen worked. A happy marriage, a feeling of real freedom and autonomy from her parents, led to a re-evaluation of what she really wanted for herself. Working part-time and attending college part-time, Ellen has now decided that she wants to become a social worker; her marks at school are excellent. She is a fine homemaker, and her employer sees her as one of the most sensible and responsible members of his staff. Life has a way of helping growth—if only we will have the faith and the patience to trust it a little.

4. Mark chose a college that turned out to be too small and not challenging enough; after his first year he realized that he would be much happier at a large university, with lots of hustle and bustle and competition. The college to which he wanted to transfer was unable to admit him until the second semester, so Mark went off in June to a student job in Europe, traveled for six months and returned to college thereafter. He is also listed as a drop-out. He adores the new college, is doing beautifully and says, "That six-month interlude was the most important part of my education so far. I needed to try my wings—I got something out of my system, and I found out what was important to me as a

person. What I brought back with me, inside myself, will make me a better student in every way."

5. Marion graduated from high school with no idea of what she wanted to do with her life—she had disliked most of her courses and passed them only by working twice as hard as most of her friends. She went to college for one year, hated it and refused to go on, much against her parents' wishes. She took a course as a dental technician, since that seemed to be as good a way as any to earn a living. A year later she had a good job and an apartment of her own. A friend invited her to join an evening adult discussion group, and Marion discovered that she was very intrigued with world affairs and politics; she subsequently joined a political club and wants to work toward becoming a delegate to her party's State Convention. She is now married, works part-time to help her husband finish his studies and says, "For the first time in my life I know exactly what I want—to be a homemaker and live in the country where we can have lots of children and animals!"

It is just as foolhardy to make generalizations about those young people who go to college and stay in college. Many of them are genuine scholars; others come with certain clear and fixed goals and are able to do the work necessary to achieve them. For many the college years are deeply fulfilling and extraordinarily happy. We need not worry about any of these. But if we want to understand those who do encounter problems, we must recognize that the mere act of staying in college is not necessarily an indication of a healthier or superior adjustment compared to those who drop out, temporarily or finally.

A psychiatrist who serves as consultant to a university mental-health clinic told me, "One way to get perspective on the question of drop-outs is to take a realistic look at the college *graduate.* Certainly the large majority do reasonably well, but many are anything but balls of fire, and some of the ones who do most brilliantly academically are crippled emotionally and do not manage very well at all when they leave the safety of the halls of academe. Many girls who go to college have no major goal beyond marrying a college man. Many boys who go to college are primarily interested in what the degree itself can guarantee in terms of higher salaries and greater financial security, not in increasing their knowledge. Many college graduates are not singularly ambitious or talented—they are, indeed, quite ordinary people!"

Some of those who stay in college are not so ordinary at all but may have serious emotional problems. Because we are so eager to keep our children in college, these young people are more likely to be neglected than those who drop out; they do not make us as uneasy or uncomfortable. Within a period of one month recently, three mothers told me the following stories: Dennis, a sophomore at an Ivy League school, called his parents one night in hysterics. His parents gathered from his somewhat incoherent tale that his roommate was behaving very strangely. They told Dennis to stay where he was in a friend's apartment, and they flew out to see him immediately. It turned out that his roommate —on the dean's list, the winner of several highly competitive scholarships—had purchased a rifle and was threatening to kill himself or Dennis. He had been having severe nightmares and had been behaving strangely for some time, but up until this point, Dennis had been able to "cool him down." Similarly, Linda had called her parents from a West Coast college, asking what she should do: her roommate was behaving very peculiarly, saying she was talking to God and was having visions. In this case the parents called the college's Dean of Women, who said the behavior had been reported to her and the school was watching the situation, but no action had been taken because the student *was doing very well in her classes!* In the third case, Jonathan, a senior in another excellent college, mentioned quite casually while home for Christmas vacation that his roommate was going to graduate Phi Beta Kappa, adding, "I don't know how that poor slob does it—he's off at marijuana or LSD parties every week end, and to my certain knowledge he has impregnated two co-eds during his four-year college career!"

The "stay-ins" are as vulnerable to pain and suffering as those who leave—and we ought to be just as concerned about the quality of life for those who are *in* college as we seem to be about those who are not. Dr. Marguerite Clark of the Cornell Medical College, citing a study of suicides among college students stated: "Surprisingly, the Cornell doctors have found that the student-patient who gets the highest mark is the one most likely to do away with himself . . . students with suicidal tendencies seeem, as a group, to be good students."

Among those who are not drop-outs, and who can help to give us a better sense of perspective on the total problem, are the following cases:

1. Betty was an A student all the way through college and graduated Phi Beta Kappa. She took a liberal arts major and was so busy studying that she managed

never to face the fact that she did not have the slightest idea what she wanted to do with her life. After receiving her Ph.D. in English literature she suddenly found herself face to face with a reality that she was totally unable to deal with—what to do now. She was stunted emotionally, having channeled all of her energies into intellectual pursuits because she was bright and because her accomplishments pleased her parents. At thirty she is an office clerk, earning just enough money to pay for the psychotherapy she is receiving at long last, to help her grow up emotionally.

2. Celia, a very able student, always assumed that she would become a teacher because her mother and grandmother were teachers and managed to convince her that teaching was the best work for a woman. She worked every summer from the time she was sixteen and went to a teacher training college. At twenty-one with her diploma clutched in her hot little hand, she suddenly became aware of the fact that she could not stand being around little children all day and was terrified of teaching! Now she works as a restaurant receptionist while attending classes in commercial art.

3. Fred graduated from college with high marks, just as he was expected to. Being a bright boy, he "got by" for four years with almost no studying, but he had a lot of laughs. His parents made him a partner in the family business the day he graduated; they gave him a house in Westchester when he married a year later, and he would be a most contented young man except for the fact that he has been wondering lately what he is

doing in Men's Underwear when the only field that ever really excited him was archeology! He is angry at himself, he is angry at his wife and children—he feels trapped in a life that bores him. He says, "All I can think of is that maybe I can get rich enough to retire at forty or fifty and go back to school."

4. Jeff is twenty years old and is finishing his sophomore year at an Ivy League men's college. He was a quiet, studious boy in high school who did very well academically, had a few very close and meaningful friendships but was never a "party boy." Neither he nor his parents were ever very worried about his getting into a good college; but with all the current pressures and dire warnings, there was great relief and joy when he was admitted to a first-class prestige school. During his freshman year he suddenly bloomed socially; he began to go out much more, served as a cheer leader with the football team, and the like. It came as something of a shock to him when his marks took a nose-dive, but by the beginning of his second year he had regained his balance. Studying was not difficult for him, and once he knew what the competition was like, he was able to handle the work. During his sophomore year he seemed to be a contented, mature and responsible young person, and it looked as if life would be smooth sailing for him.

However, during his spring vacation he seemed uneasy and tense, and when it was time to go back to college, his mother sensed that he was reluctant to go. Driving to the airport with his parents, he seemed morose, and when they got there, he did not seem to want to get out of the car. Suddenly the floodgates opened; Jeff poured forth a story of misery and of self-doubt, in the course of which he began to cry—for the first time in more years than his parents could remember. For many months he had been wondering why he was in college—the experience seemed to lack meaning. He was being pressured to choose a major for his junior year, and he had no idea what he wanted to do. He said, "I know I have a good brain—I can make it do whatever they tell me to do—but I can't figure out *why*—nothing means anything to me." He felt that he was not using his brain for anything worthwhile; he studied, turned in his papers, did well on exams but he was not really *thinking*, he said. Most of his friends seemed contented just doing what they were supposed to do—they memorized, sometimes they cheated if they got behind in their work. They did as little work as they could do in order to succeed and get high marks; they were "smart guys" who could take an assigned book, leaf through it briefly and write an A paper on it without ever really giving it any thought at all. "When someone assigns me a book to read," he said, "I like to assume there's a good reason. I want to read it and think about it—see what it really has to say. But there's no time—if I want to get a good mark, I've got to rush through it, not even caring, because there are five other books I've got to read right away, or an exam to study for, or a lab experiment to write up. There's no time for thinking—and I thought college was supposed to help you *think*—not just *produce*, like on a factory assembly line."

Jeff is one of the brilliant students—gifted in the sciences, groomed for an Ivy League college. At the age of twenty he finds himself in an identity crisis; his existence has become meaningless. He is shocked to discover that good brains are a dime a dozen at college, and suddenly he cannot stand the "smart boys" who do just as they are told, no questions asked, and get by, making everyone happy. He began to talk about leaving college for a while, of trying to find himself; maybe he ought to work for a year or two, see if he could find out what in life really mattered to him. His mother was terrified—if he left school, he might be drafted. His father told him that the only kind of job he could get would be boring and menial. Jeff accepted this advice; finally, the storm over, he took his suitcase, got out of the car and headed for the plane back to school.

There is nothing sick or maladjusted about Jeff. Quite the contrary; he has demonstrated a capacity for concern about values that many of his college friends will never have the wit or the courage to show. But as his parents drove away, they did not exult in this young man's maturity and sensitivity; and they died a thousand deaths until they were sure that this episode was over and that everything was running smoothly again. Jeff is one of those who did not fight the system; he stuck with it; in a sense he gave up. I would only hope that he has not given up for good.

With all the anxiety about getting our children into college, how many of us have really stopped to consider what college life is like today? Dr. Mervin Freedman, a professor at Stanford University, in an article published by the *Jour-*

nal of the American Association of University Women
(March 1964), wrote:

> It is my contention that the condition of students in
> the outstanding men's colleges is a dismal one indeed.
> . . . There is general agreement throughout . . . the
> United States that students should work harder and
> harder at earlier ages to absorb the knowledge of vari-
> ous disciplines and to prepare for college, where they
> will work harder still. . . . Since World War II the
> prominent men's colleges have participated increas-
> ingly in this ethos of college attendance, and the effects
> upon students have been devastating. With each pass-
> ing year students . . . seem more like Israelites groan-
> ing under the Egyptian's lash—humorless, leisureless,
> guilt-ridden drudges, harried on all sides by reading
> lists that are impossibly long, assignments that cannot
> be completed except by cutting corners . . . each
> successive freshman class faces tougher competition
> from fellow students and greater demands from fac-
> ulty. . . . Demands for earlier and earlier professional
> commitment have been intensified as well. . . . What
> is really disturbing about students is not their submis-
> sion to these demands—there is, after all, little else they
> can do, if they wish to go to a prominent men's college
> or remain in it after they are admitted. The disturbing
> fact is that they have absorbed this slave mentality and
> made it part of themselves.

With the exception of the traditionally small colleges, expansion has been the key word. In order to try to accom-
modate the ever-increasing numbers who want to go to college, the general tendency has been to further enlarge those
colleges and universities that were pretty big to begin with,

as against building many new, small colleges. Inevitably this process leads to a top-heavy administration, large lecture classes, fewer opportunities for genuine encounters between students and teachers. The poet John Ciardi put it succinctly (*Saturday Review*, May 21, 1966) in saying, "A university is what a college becomes when the faculty loses interest in the students." Because lecture courses of as many as 700 students have become commonplace, the situation has reached the point where many students are extremely uncomfortable if they are offered seminars; so geared to writing voluminous notes while listening to a lecture and committing those notes to memory, they are frightened and uneasy in an atmosphere of free inquiry—one of the most crucial roads to intellectual development.

Scientific and technological progress have resulted in large research grants from both government and private enterprise, encouraging colleges and universities to emphasize research rather than teaching. Many colleges give salary increments for publications. In attempting to improve general standards, most colleges now require that all or a very high percentage of the faculty have their doctorates. These credentials do not necessarily provide students with good *teachers*—that rare and remarkable breed of people who are primarily interested in, and talented for, awakening the intellectual curiosity of young people and encouraging them to experience the delights of intellectual exploration.

At a conference on the changing sex morals on the college campus, one professor commented, "If the students are seeking for more intimacy with each other, it may be because they have no opportunities for close personal relationships with faculty." One begins to see the inevitability of eruptions of discontent such as took place at Berkeley, when one considers that this university has more than 30,-

ooo students and may eventually have as many as 100,000. Typical of all big universities, at Berkeley departments which used to have eight members twenty years ago now have forty. One professor, who teaches a freshman course of 700 students, has a small army of twenty-three teaching assistants—graduate students who teach the section meetings that follow the lectures. This professor says that difficulties in scheduling mean that, at best, he can only meet with his assistants for one hour a week. Communication breaks down not only between the senior faculty and the students, but among the entire faculty as well. A senior in one such university said that in all his four years of school he had not had one single relationship with a professor that even approached being a genuine friendship. Dr. Wilson H. Elkins, President of the University of Maryland, although defending the large and growing state universities and denying that dehumanization is a necessary consequence of bigness, acknowledged receiving a Christmas card signed "Love, 035606."

One frightening outcome of the loss of Socratic dialogue between teacher and student was expressed in an incident. An instructor in a large university asked the entire freshman class toward the end of the year, "If you could have your degree now, would you take it?" Ninety per cent said yes. In other words, nothing had happened to them during their first year of college which made them feel that the learning process itself was something not to be missed; the degree was an entree to a job, and that was all.

Writing in *The New School Bulletin* (October 6, 1966) Dean Allen Austill stated:

The campus of ten or twenty thousand full-time students; machine-punched registration, grading and sorting; and the teaching television tube are extreme manifestations of the trend to treat the student as an object to be processed rather than an individual to be educated . . . the problems are compounded by the character and quality of the education offered. In the shorthand of students, they say: "It is irrelevant." By which they do not mean irrelevant to degrees, or graduate school, or jobs, but, rather, irrelevant to life—their life. . . . The student who seeks something other than a stepping-stone to graduate school or a "union card" for a job . . . frequently finds college a strangely disillusioning experience . . . his identity as a person and citizen is secondary to his identity as a prospective chemist, sociologist, or economist.

The emphasis on science and technology has been even greater in our schools of higher learning than in our elementary and secondary schools. What is in danger of being lost is pure scholarship; learning has become a commodity, not the pursuit of knowledge. Since the Second World War specialization has become so intense that the cross-fertilization of ideas between different disciplines, so necessary to human progress, has been all but lost in the shuffle. One professor of the humanities declared, "If I want to talk to someone with a broad, comprehensive view of life, I'd rather talk to an African aborigine than to a physicist." One gleaming sign of hope is the news that the board of directors of a newly formed medical school is insisting that all students take a required number of survey courses in the arts, history and philosophy in addition to scientific-medical studies.

A major danger related to college procedures is that every profession now requires graduate degrees. It no longer means very much to have been to college—that is just the beginning of the road. The danger lies in the fact that the acquisition of the degree itself is simply no adequate measure of ability. Any standardization of requirements means the loss of tremendous talent. As one college president told me, "It simply *kills* me that here, in this wonderful city, with all its resources of fascinating people doing wonderful things, I cannot invite some of the best of them to become part-time members of my faculty because they don't have graduate degrees—they've only been working in their fields of specialization for thirty or forty years!" In the same vein, a director of a mental-health clinic said, "I'm completely hamstrung by the most ridiculous regulations; my board and the state supervisors are perfectly happy to have me hire some callow youth straight out of social-work school, who isn't dry behind the ears yet and knows nothing at all about life, but when I suggest that there is a warm, charming, insightful middle-aged woman in our community who has raised four kids of her own and has worked as a volunteer for twenty-five or thirty years as a recreation leader in a community center and would be marvelous as an assistant leader in one of our group therapy projects for ten-year-olds, everybody howls because all she's got is a bachelor's degree!"

However, because of the shortage of people with the "right" credentials, more and more social agencies are finding that they *can* use people in the community with less than the required number of degrees, and can use them extremely effectively. One mental-health clinic deliberately went out into the community searching for women whose children were grown and who were interested in going back to work but who did not have any specialized training.

After a one-year intensive training program, it was found that these women were capable of serving as remarkably effective counselors. A university medical school has what is jokingly referred to as "a retread program" in which individuals with at least two years of college, retired or with grown children, are being trained to work with those who are mentally ill—and the plan is working out beautifully. Another example of the sheer stupidity of setting rigid and inflexible standards of what represents competence is something I see all the time in the nursery-school field. For certification in many states nursery schools must employ a high percentage of certified teachers. Frequently this results in the hiring of young women fresh out of college, who may not have had a single course in early childhood education but who have had enough education courses to give them certification as teachers, rather than the employment of mature, warm and loving women who may be available, who have raised their own families and who, the director knows, would respond with intelligence and dedication to on-the-job training. One director said, "I am fed up to here with these smart young kids who are just hanging around, waiting to get married, and spend half the day smoking and gossiping and who come in late and try to leave early—but no matter how many mature, sensible, responsible applicants there may be, I can't hire them."

Both on campus and off, by making degrees the only standard of competence, we are denying all the values of experience, of learning through living, of the wisdom that comes with genuine maturation. Another example of this defect is what has happened to some of our Peace Corps volunteers when they have returned to the United States after a two- or four-year assignment in other parts of the world. They may have overcome Herculean problems in bringing quality education to children in a South American village, they may have proved themselves to be courageous, resourceful, imaginative and dedicated—but when they return and try to get teaching positions in areas in which their experience would be most helpful—with some of our *own* deprived children—they are blocked because they lack some of the proper educational credentials.

In the light of this phenomenon, it seems to me that if we are really concerned about high-school and college dropouts, we are going to have to do some pretty honest and creative thinking about what we are teaching in the schools and what is really needed for satisfactory personal fulfillment and successful functioning in the world of work.

Not everyone should be expected to attend either the traditional high school or college; we must invent and find new and original approaches to education. A *New York Times Magazine* article by Dorothy Barclay titled "College—Who Should Go?" quoted Elizabeth M. Douvan, study director at the University of Michigan's research center, in connection with her feeling that there were many girls going to college for the wrong reasons: "Because we fail to provide adequate channels for gratifying their real aspirations, many girls are forced to assume a pretense of intellectual interest, to enter colleges and universities where they do not want to be and where they, indeed, do not belong in a time of short supply." In the same article Dr. Ruth E. Salley, of the New York City Board of Higher Education, is quoted as saying, "We have put so much stress on the traditional ideal of higher education—the four-year college course—that we have not been exploring other possibilities for continued learning."

This point of view does not at all imply that continued learning opportunities are unnecessary or are wasted on some individuals; every human being has the right to go on developing and growing and learning throughout his life. The problem is to break down the inflexible preconceptions about how and where and when and under what kinds of programs such opportunities can be provided. There is no doubt in my mind that many men and women who did not attend or did not complete a four-year college program have become far more "educated" people than many who followed this prescribed plan. I know many people who have read more widely, taken more courses in specialized areas and delved more deeply into such areas as art or music or history or poetry than many college graduates.

The *New York Times* Education Editor, Fred M. Hechinger, reporting on a meeting of the Association for Higher Education (March 20, 1966), quoted Frank H. Bowles, Director of the Ford Foundation's education program, as saying, "Democratization of education is not just the provision of more of the same." Mr. Hechinger reported on a growing demand for some form of universal national service—by no means exclusively or even predominantly military—after high school or at some point between college and graduate school. Such services, many educators believe, would utilize youth's demand for active involvement. Those who oppose compulsory higher education point out that sending too many young people to college under pressure—for reasons of social status or promise of better jobs—is already giving us trouble with frustrated students who want out. There was, however, widespread agreement that education beyond high school will be a necessity for the majority of young people. The question then is: can this be termed higher education in the conventional sense and, if given the college label, will it put the instruction into a conventional straitjacket? Many of the educators at the conference felt that much post-high-school vocational and technical training should be provided through various forms of apprenticeship, on-the-job experiences and internships. They also felt that there was a danger in making the two-year college an extension of the high school. Such a process might lead to a mere stretching of the conventional curriculum, without effectively introducing new and higher standards of either academic or vocational work.

An increasing number of young people seem, on their own, to be turning away from the traditional mass measurement of their abilities. Examples that I have heard of recently include a young man who left college after two years and obtained a job as an assistant film cutter. After several years of apprenticeship, he was able to earn more at this craft than he might have in many jobs which require several degrees. A girl of eighteen found herself a job as a salesgirl in a Greenwich Village jewelry shop, where the proprietors made all the jewelry they sold. Within a year or so she was designing and making jewelry herself, and she did this so successfully that her employers promised her an eventual partnership in a thriving business. Another young man who left college after three years, causing considerable anguish to his parents, went to work as an apprentice in an art gallery and became a master picture framer at an excellent salary. Handicrafts of all kinds seem to be having a renaissance; but of course there are hundreds of other kinds of work in the business world where experience and training (and basic talent) still count at least as much as college degrees. As someone pointed out in a recent newspaper item, parents should not be too distressed if their child does not go to college—he might still grow up to be President. (There have been nine of them.)

There is no reason to assume that the age of eighteen is the best time to go to college; in fact, there is considerable evidence that it is *not* the most desirable time. The GI's who went to college after the Second World War, with their wives and babies, tended to be the best students the colleges had ever seen; they were seasoned, mature people, with strong motivation, a sense of purpose, more discipline and a clearer notion of what they wanted to do with their lives. It may well be that we ought to think quite seriously of offering alternative experiences to many of our young people of about eighteen, and then make it easier for them to continue their academic education while they are working at a later period of time. I have rarely known more animated, excited, dedicated students than those who go back to school when their own children are all in school. The Peace Corps and VISTA might very well become a more extensive program—perhaps even becoming part of some required national service program, along with the draft—offering alternatives for two years of service to the United States. Over half of those in VISTA, for example, are from twenty to twenty-three years old, and many of these have had one or two years of college. One of the reasons they give for leaving school and wanting to work as volunteers is that they need time "to find themselves," to discover what really interests them most. With individual life so long, and with the likelihood that retirement will become increasingly a burden rather than a boon (sixty-five-year-olds today are just too vigorous and healthy to be put out to pasture), it seems to be not at all illogical to offer young people work opportunities and experiences at that point in their lives when they are most eager for direct experience and want most desperately to have some autonomy, some financial independence—and then seeing to it that institutions of higher learning are so set up that it will not only be possible but easy and convenient to continue one's studies while one is marrying, parenting and working for a living. If one is likely to want to go on working at something until the age of seventy or eighty, there seems little reason to be in such a rush to finish one's education by twenty or twenty-five.

An outstanding example of the kind of learning (and contribution to society) that can take place *outside* traditional learning institutions is this story by Jay Levin, which appeared in the New York *Post* (April 12, 1966):

Andrea is one of 12 poor youths, all members of a Neighborhood Youth Corps in East Harlem, who have brought their special vision and awful knowledge of poverty to bear in the making of a film on the city's anti-poverty programs. . . . "A Change is Gonna Come," they named it. It is a story, told with a clarity and reverence for life, of what it means to be poor in this town. The 12 amateurs, paid $37.50 a week to learn a trade in the Youth Corps Photo Unit, were granted $2,100 last fall by the city's Economic Opportunity Committee to make a short documentary on the "War on Poverty." What they came through with is a film that juxtaposes vivid scenes full of the sadness and despair of the poor with scenes flushed with the hope held out by the anti-poverty programs. Negro boys improvising games in a rubble-filled lot, framed by rotting slums, are contrasted with young men building a play-ground for Haryou-Act. . . . Then, the adults. A package changes hands, money is passed, and men lean back to drag dreamily at marijuana. Addicts and drunks stagger in the streets, the unemployed walk aimlessly, staring blankly. . . . It ends as it began, with the children. A little girl, her face dirty and her clothes ragged, sits mournfully on a tenement stoop. A new scene, and children play joyously in a Project Head Start classroom. "A change is gonna come," the narrator says. The film already is a success. The Office of Economic Opportunity in Washington saw it, pronounced it "the best film made on poverty," and has ordered prints for showing throughout the country. . . . The young film-makers (Puerto-Rican and Negro youngsters of 19 and 20) hope it is just the beginning."

Of course it is equally important to do all we can to help those young people who are in school and ought to stay there. One of the major problems is the way in which a college choice is made, and by and large this choosing has been pretty much a matter of hit and miss. A conference of educators at Princeton reported that they were concerned with selection as a key to decreasing the number of dropouts and transfers. They felt that the freshman year at college was being used as a screening for further college choice because of shortcomings in selection at the high-school level.

Dr. Margaret Devine, Dean of Mills College of Education, told me that "the large majority of young people who graduate from high school with reasonable success and are accepted into a college probably have the potential for graduating, *if* they are properly placed in a college most suited to their specific needs." She believes that as methods of selection improve at individual colleges and as the colleges cooperate more effectively in helping to facilitate necessary and constructive transfers, there will be fewer academic failures.

There are ways and ways of encouraging young people to "stick it out." This view was expressed succinctly by one young man, who said, "So long as my parents kept yelling about needing a degree to get a good job and earn a lot of money, I was sure I was going to leave. But then I talked to my advisor; I told him I wanted to leave school, so I could work in the slums and help people in trouble. He asked me what I had to offer them—what could I bring to them—and then he asked me if I wanted to bring myself as a mature, competent, trained person, or did I want to bring them *my* poverty—my problems and my weaknesses. I stayed in school." Some young people are leaving school because we have given them the wrong reasons for staying.

For some time now very able students who are doing remarkably well in high school have been able to get into college after completing their junior year; in other words, they skip the senior year of high school and go right on to college. It seems to me that a similar plan might be very effective with youngsters who are *failing* high school but who are clearly talented in some special area or obviously have the potential for doing better academically. Until we can improve the high-school curriculum, we might find that part of the problem of these youngsters has been boredom and impatience with a great many unimportant and meaningless tasks; possibly a small college, where each student's program can be given individual attention and where it is possible to begin to study some interesting subjects, might turn high-school failures into college successes.

Along this line, in an earlier chapter I mentioned that grade-school failures did very well working with volunteer tutors who could give them a great deal of individual attention and who were not hampered in their teaching by a lot of rules and regulations or by having to follow a prescribed syllabus. What it all seemed to mean is that creative teaching works—and it is a great pity that so much of it has to be added on as extras instead of being part of the educational system. Much the same kind of thing is happening at the high-school and college level. For example, in New York the experimental College Discovery Program is designed to detect and develop college potential; the experiment initially involved 581 high-school sophomores from culturally deprived backgrounds—under-achievers selected for special attention. They are taught in small classes and are provided with individual tutoring; their classroom teachers are not bound by curriculum guides or a syllabus—they are encouraged to be flexible in their teaching methods. The student's reward for successful completion of the three-year course is admission to a two- or four-year college in the city. First reports indicated almost no drop-outs or failures, "and the attendance record matches that of any college preparatory students." Whether at the elementary school or high-school level, one thing seems to remain constant and clear; provide a really *good* program, and the failures and drop-outs seem to disappear.

After watching a TV documentary on the work being done by the Job Training Corps, one high-school student commented wryly, "My whole problem is that we're not

poor enough for me to go to that kind of a great school!"
There is no question, of course, that whatever special
efforts we can make to undo the deprivation of some of our
nation's children are necessary—and still far from being
enough. But all children of all ages ought to have teachers
who are also friends and counselors, small classes, opportunities for special tutoring and a total educational climate
that is warm, affectionate and supportive.

Another aspect of keeping young people in school is giving them credit for some of what they do outside of school.
There are children who are failing in school but who are
not failing in life; who earn money, who give service, who
sing and play musical instruments, who dance, who paint
and write poetry, who take care of younger children responsibly, who can cook and sew or build ham radio sets,
who serve as volunteers in all kinds of capacities, who ought
to be getting credit for all the things they are, and can do,
beyond the walls of the school building. A failing student in
one town organized a group of her friends into a junior aux-
iliary to her mother's Braille group, and she and her friends
began working on books for blind children. A boy who
was barely passing in school persuaded a group of his
friends to take on the responsibility of earning enough
money with their rock-and-roll group to support several
Korean war orphans. I could go on endlessly citing such
examples, but the point I am making is that these kids ought
to have at least been awarded an A for citizenship, and that
this information should have been included in their cumulative school records.

One of the difficulties at the college level is that young
people become impatient for "meat and potatoes." They
have already been in school for twelve years—and here

they are in college, faced with taking more elementary required courses for at least another two years. And the elementary courses, in almost any field, are often enough to
discourage anyone from going on in that field. Introductory
psychology at college sure made *me* think that ditch-
digging might be a far more interesting and promising field
than psychology! If we would stop worrying about credentials and would have the good sense to bring into the
colleges mature, exciting, exeprienced specialists—people
who are actively working in fields that they love—for
freshman and sophomore survey courses, we might spark a
good deal more intellectual excitement and create a climate
in which students would begin to see why it might be
worthwhile to stick around and get educated. Teachers
who are *doing* something, and who love what they are doing, offer an additional dimension of excitement. At one
time my husband taught psychology to undergraduates in a
midwestern college; he was amazed, five or ten years later,
to see how many of his freshman and sophomore students
had gone on to become psychologists—he kept meeting
them at professional conferences, in numbers that seemed
unusually high. At one such meeting he told a former student how puzzled he was that so many of his students had
become psychologists, and this student replied, "I'm surprised you couldn't figure it out, it's really very simple—we
just never had another teacher who was so madly in love
with his work! You made it seem like the most exciting adventure anybody could ever have."

The way to encourage young people to stay in school is
really quite simple: to make the alternative unthinkable and
unbearable. It means offering learning opportunities that
are as full of life and significance as one can find anywhere.

It means offering students a direct encounter with teachers who love to teach, who have something to say, who have a zest for learning and for all intellectual exploration.

In an article in *Harper's Magazine* entitled "For a Reactionary Experiment in Education" (November 1962), Paul Goodman suggested that one step in the right direction might be to break up our big universities into small colleges all over again. Bigness at the university level has meant that there is on every campus a small army of administrators who do not teach and who, generally speaking, interfere with the opportunities for intellectual dialogue between teachers and students. Dr. Goodman wrote:

> I was asked to lunch with six senior professors, including the chairmen of departments, at a big Western university. The subject of grading came up and all were unanimous in the opinion that grading is injurious to both teaching and learning. . . . Grading, they agreed, destroys the use of testing, which is a good method of teaching if one corrects the test but does not grade it. When tested, but not graded, students are eager to learn the right answers, and they ask how to solve the problem. But if graded they become puffed-up, or crestfallen, while the subject itself sours. They agreed that the teacher should use tests essentially to find out what he is failing to get across. At this point I intervened and said: "Here you are, six members of the faculty. This university is theoretically self-governing, and each of you has a vote in its faculty council. Why is there still grading?" . . . The grading, they explained, was needed to determine progress, scholarships, admissions to graduate school, advice to employers, etc. The ad-

ministration of the school, it was clear, demanded a standardized scale of marking . . . the faculty would have to know the students personally, discuss them, even argue about them—and this was beyond them. . . . Thus the effect of strong administration is to weaken the college by keeping the students out of contact with the teachers; the teachers out of contact with each other . . . and both away from troublesome or embarrassing controversy with the world. . . . Whereas good teaching depends on close personal relations between scholars and students, modern administration isolates the individuals and groups on the campus one from the other; but, by using "scientific administration" to coordinate them, it reconstructs the campus as a social machine.

He goes on to remind us that historically the university was a small community of scholars in which teaching and learning involved intense personal relationships:

Then as now the student on leaving his family desperately needed older adults to whom he could transfer his affection—men whom he could identify with and imitate; who could show him ways to order his confusion by principled thought, and help him prepare for a meaningful career in the adult world. This is what teachers did. It cannot be done if they are cut off from students.

He suggests that we provide a faculty of full-time tenured teachers—people who have a special calling for teaching—and that to this group we add "practicing veterans"—writers, politicians, diplomats, journalists, engineers, bankers and the like, who are actively involved in professional life in the community:

> I am proposing simply that the students and teachers create a small university where they can associate in the traditional way, but entirely dispensing with the external control, administration, bureaucratic machinery and other excrescencies that have swamped our communities of scholars. . . . I propose that a core faculty of about five professors secede from a school, taking some of their students with them; that they attach themselves to an equal number of like-minded professionals in the region; collect a few more students; and set up a small unchartered university that would be nothing but an association. Ten teachers would constitute a sufficient faculty for such a community of scholars. (Jefferson's University of Virginia had eight teachers.) With individual classes of about fifteen, there would be 150 students.

Whether or not one may be ready to consider such an extreme proposal (many of Goodman's ideas have been incorporated in the recently emerging Free Universities), this does symbolize the kind of creativity and imagination that are essential in re-evaluating the educational opportunities we offer our young people, for they will, if they have any courage or sensitivity, continue to drop into life and out of our schools if we fail to respond to their challenge—that what they are offered inside our schools must have relevance to their lives and significance for their personal growth.

NINE

Life Is a Banquet:
The Real Meaning of
Human Excellence

SINCE I have been complaining so bitterly and long-windedly about pressures on children, and since I am not fundamentally anti-intellectual, I want to distinguish between pressures and enrichment of the mind and spirit—two entirely different matters. I am against the accumulation and memorization of masses of facts and information—but I am for thinking and progress toward maturation, knowledge and insight. I am against any notion of setting an arbitrary time schedule for learning—but I am for a long and full life of adventure in a world of intellectual and creative abundance.

In *Mame*, the musical version of Patrick Dennis' book *Auntie Mame*, that wonderful lady exclaims, "Life is a banquet—and too many sons of bitches are starving to death!"

The sad and awful thing about our current pressures on children is that in spite of all the facts we feed them, so many of them are starving to death intellectually. Worry has taken the adventure out of exploration; rigid, inflexible and unimaginative study programs have robbed learning of excitement; fear of failure has blocked a healthy, vigorous questioning, an honest search for new answers; cleverness has been substituted for profundity. Those who scream the loudest about "excellence in education"—and who mean by that "faster and harder"—are themselves standing in the way of genuine excellence; the truest and deepest life of the intellect takes slow nurturing, it comes with loving patience, with a deep and abiding acceptance of time as an essential element.

Excellence in life seems to me to be the way in which each human being makes the most of the adventure of living and becomes most truly and deeply himself, fulfilling his own nature in the context of a good life with other people. His mind is alert, his feelings can be profound; he is curious and unafraid, eager for discovery, capable of living an inner life that is full and rich. He is as eager to try to understand himself and others as he is to understand abstract ideas or objective information. What he knows and what he feels have equal importance in his life, and his intellectual development involves the understanding of current social issues as well as academic subjects.

Auntie Mame is horrified when she hears that her grand-nephew has never ridden on an elephant. "This boy has been *deprived!*" she says. Such is the banquet of life—not a narrow range of experiences that have to do with the absorption of facts, but a great adventure with rich possibilities, beyond measuring or anticipating. To eat well at the banquet of life is to have the zest of a true gourmet, who has a sense of renewal and excitement in anticipation of each new experience.

One part of the banquet is certainly the life of the intellect—the challenge to think and to learn. It can be, and is for many people, the most important part of the banquet, and I can understand very well when intellectuals insist that there is a certain vigor, a necessary discipline involved in the pursuit of ideas and of information in the arts and sciences, in exploration of history and philosophy. There is no doubt that about ten or fifteen years ago there was a tendency toward sloppy and lazy thinking about learning and education. That was "the age of conformity," when many parents simply wanted their children to be popular and were less concerned with how they did in their schoolwork; I remember very well mothers who told me that they were glad when their bright and talented children attempted to "hide their light" so as not to be labeled "a brain" and thereby lose out in the popularity polls. How quickly we turned from "group adjustment" to "mental wizardry" in just a few short years! Of course it is sensible and proper to hope for a high level of intellectual achievement and academic excellence from those who want it and are capable of achieving it; it is reasonable to expect that by mid-adolescence our children should be learning the kind of self-discipline necessary for study and can begin to set for themselves some challenging goals toward which they can work responsibly. It was right and proper, that we challenge the concept that being well-liked was enough. The problem now is to respect the tough work of learning without setting up such rigid and inflexible definitions that we negate or lose much of the very talent we want to celebrate and

enhance. Does respect for intellect mean everyone's doing
the same tasks at the same time? Does it mean identifying
intellect with studies in the arts or sciences only? Surely
not; human excellence can take many forms. In the classical
Greek period people did not believe that *doers* were as valuable as *thinkers;* artisans and craftsmen were considered
greatly inferior to philosophers; as a result, scientific progress was very limited in a time of great artistic advancement.
Today it is hard for many people to remember that poets
and philosophers are as valuable as scientists and technicians
and that each kind of discipline benefits from the others'
contributions. If life is a banquet, it is also a smorgasbord!
One of the most important aspects of a "banquet view of
life" is that we do not have to choose between different interests and talents; we need them all: the artist and the engi-
neer, the mechanic and the craftsman, the spaceman who
travels millions of miles in a few days and the Youth Board
social worker who serves a ten-block radius for five years.
Excellence in human beings requires a respect for all kinds
of people, all ways of living and working, all ways of viewing life. One of our greatest problems today, if we are really concerned with intellectual excellence, is in facing up
to the dangers of overemphasizing the sciences at the expense of the arts. Several years ago an Alumni Bulletin from
the University of Chicago stated:

> Counsel is heard—and it will increase—that our uni-
> versities must now intensify scientific training at the ex-
> pense of other branches of learning. This Chicago will
> not do. Your University would be proud to produce a
> man or a concept instrumental in giving the Western
> world superiority in space research . . . but the Uni-

versity would win the blessings of all the world were it to find a man or a means that could channel the great discoveries of our age away from the realm of terror into the service of mankind.

An incisive and moving plea for the return to an understanding and appreciation of the artist's view of life was expressed in an article by Arthur Miller in *Saturday Review* (June 4, 1966) entitled "The Writer as Independent Spirit."

> The writer today is closer to demoralization than in any period I know. He is being demoralized by the same forces that demoralize everybody else, but in addition he is face to face with a devilish and false ideology, running rabid in the world; the ideology of scientism, which would have us believe that the instinct of the writer to create a synthesis of meanings for life is false and trivial, and that the only truth is the truth that can be documented in statistics or an empirical experiment. . . . Some months ago I was interviewed by a psychologist who represented the National Science Foundation of the United States. . . . referring to a particular scene in one of my plays [he] asked, with some amazement, "How did you ever figure out the subjective connections between the two characters in that scene?" "What do you mean—figure it out?" I asked. "I imagined it." He went on, "But what was your theory?" "What do you mean, what was my theory?" "Well," he said, "do you feel that you're closer to Jung or Freud or the Behaviorists, or what?" It was quite clear that in his opinion human behavior and the analysis of it had begun somewhere around 1912. . . .

I pointed out that Oedipus (before he became a disease) was a character in a play, and that he had been invented by poets. That religion had been invented by poets. . . . Everything prior to the twentieth century is one long amateur hour; . . . I made a speech about three years ago before a congress of American psychologists in which I said, in passing, that without human values, one doesn't even come up with good science. (The Nazi doctors' experiments may have increased knowledge, but weren't science.) Afterwards about twenty-five people, all professional psychologists, gathered round me. "Why isn't it science?" they asked. This was not in Berlin or Munich; it was in New York City. . . . [The challenge to writers is] the preservation of the imagination itself and its legitimacy as a political and social force.

Let us look at the question of intellectual excellence from the point of view of what it is that we really want for our children—and whether they are getting it. At the same time that three-year-olds are busily typing away in research laboratories, teen-agers and adults are watching "The Beverly Hillbillies" and "Batman," which may be entertaining (I have never discovered why, myself) but can hardly be considered to be sources of intellectual stimulation. It seems to me that the phenomenon of millions of people willing and eager to use what precious time they have on earth to explore the world with "Gidget" and "The Man from U.N.C.L.E." and "The Munsters" raises the legitimate question of why we bother to teach French in first grade and geometry in third, since the majority of the population is obviously trying to deactivate their brain cells by such activities as listening to a car that talks.

The most learned among us need time to relax; and I am not for a moment suggesting that we should give up whatever forms of relaxation we find most satisfying; even Betty Friedan's girl intellects read movie magazines at the hairdressers, and detective stories and science fiction sales are highest near scientific research centers. I know one highly respected college professor who, for all his erudition, between lectures practices playing the flute; the fact that in the course of the first three years he was only able to memorize his favorite Christmas song, "Good King Wenceslas," never bothered him a bit! What I am really saying is that academic pressure on children and a general hysteria about the necessity for everybody to go to high school and college exist side by side with a period of frightening antiintellectualism. Timothy Leary tells his fellow LSD users that the purpose of his new "religion" is to help people "go out of their minds and come to their senses." What is he really offering? An escape from mind without feeling, a return to sensation without thought. Who are the people responding to this invitation? They are some of our most intelligent and talented people, college students primarily—those very young people to whom we have been directing our attention, those whom we have accelerated to such a point that they only want to go "out of their minds," having had more than enough of the computerized brain. Why such interest in psychedelic lighting effects such as at the Cheetah? Why the compelling attraction of our young people to "pot" and "horse" and "trips"? Why the more and more ritualistic, primitively sexual dances? Why the delight in the superficiality and cynicism of what is "pop" or "camp"? It seems to me that all these manifestations reflect at least in part a rebellion against the kinds of pressures I have described earlier; they are convincing testament to the fact that the pseudo-intellectualism of scientism has caused, not an increase in intellectual excellence, but a violent reaction against anything relating to mind and thought.

I do not think there is any writer of fiction in America today who has better stated the problem of pseudo-intellectualism's leading to anti-intellectualism than John Hersey. In *The Child Buyer*, written in 1960 (published by Knopf) he tells about a boy genius named Barry Rudd, who says, "To me things take on heightened reality after I have seen them on the printed page." A company, "United Lymphomilloid," which purchases gifted children for a special project, wishes to buy Barry. The "purchased specimens," who are eventually used as computers, must first undergo procedures which will eliminate all conflict, all human feeling, "to insure the utilization of their equipment at maximum efficiency." The first part of the treatment involves making the specimen forget the world; during the second phase of training the specimen "will never again look out at the complexity of nature, which would only confuse him." There is no contaminating contact with other human beings, all teaching is done mechanically, by whispering voices, tape recordings, and sleep teaching, and progress is very rapid because of the "emptiness of the receptive mind which has been freed from all irrelevancies." In the third stage the specimen is fed enormous amounts of data needed for problem-solving. A fourth stage involves major surgery, "tying off all five senses," because despite all the conditioning and the use of drugs which has accompanied the first three stages, there remains some danger that the specimen might still develop dangerous emotions, such as doubt.

These procedures, we are told, produced I.Q.'s between 974 and 1005!

When *The Child Buyer* was presented as a play off-Broadway several years ago, one of the reviewers commented that it's all very well to write science fiction, but that this idea of turning children into computers was really a bit too much—too wild an idea to have validity as a drama; all I could think of as I read this review was, Now *there's* a man who hasn't set foot in a school lately! While Hersey is using satirical exaggeration to make his point, the idiocy of the people in Barry Rudd's life, and their goals for him, seem entirely in keeping with some of our current attitudes.

In 1966 a new John Hersey book appeared, entitled *Too Far to Walk*. Here the novelist is telling us about John Fist, "a talented over-achiever" in his first year at college. This is a young man who eventually sells his soul to the Devil for "experience," for feeling. Most of the fictional characters who have sold their soul to the Devil have had as their reason their great thirst for knowledge. Why would we now have a story in which a young man who has vast quantities of knowledge wants to sell his soul for sensation and feeling? The story of Barry Rudd provides us with the answer; in order to make him the best possible "thinking machine," he was deliberately deprived of human contact, memory, senses and emotions. It becomes logical in the context of such a fictional theme to come to a "second installment," in which we are asked to face the fact that knowledge alone can be as damaging to the human spirit as ignorance.

John Fist becomes the logical aftermath of the goal of "instant brilliance" as exemplified by Barry Rudd. He is "smart," he can do any level of academic work that he wishes to do, he can produce anything that is asked of him academically. But he lives without meaning and without feeling; he has lost a sense of connectedness to life and to himself—and because this is unbearable, he tries LSD and a great many other bizarre, dangerous and impulsive experiences, under the direction of the Devil, in a destructive and disappointing attempt to regain what he has lost. The Devil promises him life; an end to being among the "walking dead." Hersey writes:

> He wanted to *feel*, to push his personal feelings out to the limits . . . to build up a store of experiences, of events of the senses of every kind and sort . . . soak them in, drink them all in, so that one could really get in touch with the solid hardpan reality that must lie underneath all the crap . . . all the walls would come tumbling down that most of the time shut John away from other human beings, from trees, from sea water, from light, from air to breathe.

As John begins to realize that "instant experience" is no more valid than "instant-knowledge, he comes into a classroom where the professor has taken as his theme for the day "classical passion." He quotes from Catullus, the Latin poet:

> I hate and love. You ask how that can be?
> I know not, but I feel the agony.

We are left with the unanswered question: is it going to be " too far to walk" for our young people, so full of information, so untouched by human feeling, to come full circle once again, and live with knowledge *and* sensation, as necessary balancing forces in human experience?

William K. Zinsser describes a different aspect of the problem in his book *Pop Goes America* (Harper and Row, 1966). He writes: "Pop is a point of view, an attitude of the 1960's. Pop means instant values. Pop is an enjoyment of the superficial. Pop says that form is more important than substance." In a chapter on the Barbie doll, Zinsser holds that she is everything that America's little girls want to become—long-legged, busty, button-nosed, rather dumb and smug-looking. He tells us that one can now buy a "Barbie College Campus" which consists of a dormitory room, a soda shop (with phone booth) a football stadium and a drive-in movie—*but no classroom!* "Anyone looking for deeper values in the world of Barbie is looking in the wrong place. With its emphasis on possessions and its worship of appearances, it is modern America in miniature, a tiny parody of our pursuit of the beautiful, the material and the trivial."

It seems to me that some of our new "Cultural Centers" also reflect anti-intellectualism in their preoccupation with appearances. Does New York City's Lincoln Center, for example, really reflect the honoring of excellence in the performing arts? The fantastic opulence, the preoccupation with technical brilliance, seem to me to deny the most essential ingredients of genuine creativity. The new opera house opened its 1966 season with new productions in which the costumes were so elaborate and cumbersome that it was a remarkable feat of human ingenuity that the singers were still able to sing; the scenery was frequently so complex and ornate that most of what we will remember of the early weeks of premières is how often the electronic turntables got stuck. Some of the productions were so elaborate in externals that the essence of the operatic experience—the aesthetic qualities of voice, music, color, drama—became dwarfed by the technicians behind the scenes, trying desperately to make the machinery work. The preoccupation with the new mechanical toys, the triumph of technology, seemed too often to outweigh the artistic aspects of the endeavor.

Another typical example was the production of the movie *The Bible,* which involved all kinds of brilliant technical tricks; every reviewer commented on the cinematic effects used to depict the creation of the world and the building of Noah's Ark; everything was ten times life-size; only one little detail was missing: what the Bible was all about—the fundamental simplicity of the moral significance of this drama of life. Clever tricks were there in abundance—all gimmicky and thoroughly superficial, and lacking in any genuine reverence for life, devoid of beauty and of inspiration.

Our so-called cultural explosion seems to me to be nine-tenths explosion—gaudy, impressive-looking, shallow and empty. There is little evidence to cause us to assume that the new masses of concrete, steel and glass are going to provide experiences that will inspire us or influence our values, that will help us to come to terms with the gigantic problems of our times. All they needed in ancient Greece was an outdoor amphitheater, with stone seats and daylight. In this setting Aeschylus, Sophocles and Euripides were able to shake up their world and to become a deathless part of our cultural heritage. *This* was cultural excellence—the creative force, not the furniture. Culture today is too often a kind of self-conscious and often snobbish ritual, it is not really alive or dynamic, it is not a force which helps us to understand or change our world.

A number of years ago, when my husband and I were touring one of "the stately homes of England," we marveled to the guide about the unbelievable beauty of the English lawns; we had never seen such thick, beautiful green grass, and we asked the guide for the secret. He smiled and said, "Well, first you have to start with a seven-hundred-year-old lawn." Time and cultivation—whether it be of grass or art—seems to be better understood in older parts of the world; in America we seem to have little patience with the past, and our confusion about speed as a measure of academic achievement is seconded only by our naiveté about creativity in the arts. Creativity is not susceptible to a machine-oriented way of life—it does not grow in that kind of garden. If anybody had asked me about how to begin building cultural centers in the United States, I think I would have said, "Find your artists and set up building your artistic enterprise in old lofts and storefronts; I'll even accept an old run-down theater, if need be; but don't build any new buildings for at least the first ten years—and even when you do, keep them simple." The intensity of the experience between performer and audience has little to do with the giant computers which work the sets and the lights.

Aaron Copland commented recently that putting music in irrelevant places makes music itself irrelevant. He was speaking of such absurdities as canned music on elevators playing Beethoven's Fifth Symphony. We are so proud of ourselves because technology has produced so many pleasant conveniences, such as canned vegetables, that we think any aspect of life can be improved by mass production and mass exposure to whatever riches may be available to us.

For those who say that intellectual excellence is in danger in America unless we get those three-year-olds on the ball with reading and writing, I say that "pop" and LSD and instant culture and the worship of technology endanger intellectual excellence far more devastatingly than almost any gap that our children may be feeling in their educational experiences.

I want intellectual nourishment for our children—nourishment that involves direct experience, direct *self*-testing, direct use of a child's own curiosity and eagerness to know more about the world around him. I do not believe that our children can be nourished by teachers who must follow a rigidly formulated syllabus or constantly administer tests. Many of our children, despite all their days in school and all their hours with homework assignments, are literally starving to death intellectually because what they are being fed bears little relation to what they want to learn or need to know. If we really wanted to nourish our children intellectually, we would set up programs of teacher-training which would outweigh in drama and cost our programs for getting a man on the moon; there would be a national search for potentially talented teachers which would call for the kind of enthusiasm shown by the millions who watch TV with baited breath each year to see who will be the new Miss America. If we are really concerned with the life of the intellect, we would somehow manage to get along with our old six-lane highways and divert taxes into seeing to it that no child was ever in a class of more than twenty children. With less concern for putting up more and more elaborate school buildings, we might be able to afford to train teachers to ask questions, listen, and help children find their own answers. Socrates managed very well in the market place without fluorescent lights, intercoms, electric type-writers, push-button windows and air conditioning. Children and teachers should be safe and warm and reasonably comfortable—but a lot of learning can take place sitting on the rocks in Central Park or putting on a Shakespeare play in an empty store.

On the night in November 1966, when there was supposed to be a shower of meteors, New York City's marvelously imaginative and creative former Commissioner of Parks, Thomas Hoving, invited everyone to come to Central Park for this astronomical happening. It sounded like a great idea, and off we went at midnight, with blankets, flashlight, a flask of something to conquer the late night chill, and several layers of clothes. My husband and I looked so unkempt, with all this equipment, that we were not sure we'd make it to the park without being arrested for vagrancy, but as we walked toward the Sheep Meadow we were joined by gay throngs in similar high spirits and equally strange appearance. There were so many young people, of high school and college age, and there was such genuine excitement. I cannot recall a time when adults and young people seemed more pleased to be in each other's company, more delighted with a shared adventure. There were thousands of people on the meadow; all were polite, courteous and thoughtful of each other. Where there might well have been pandemonium, there was none—even with the eventual disappointment that the clouds obscured the sight we had come to see. As I watched the children pouring into the park, I had the feeling that with this one gesture Mr. Hoving had done more for the intellectual development of New York City's children than had sometimes been achieved in years of school attendance. He had made nature exciting;

he had turned a learning experience into a shared adventure. Children who are bored to tears by lectures on astronomy might have become really excited about the subject if they had been able to experience this kind of direct confrontation with the miracles of our universe.

The educator Dr. Alice Keliher once said that the trouble with all schools is that the busses go in the wrong direction! How much more exciting learning would be if every day all the children were picked up at school and driven out into the world, to learn from direct observation and experience. How many more questions they would ask—how quickly they would see how much they want to learn! Who asks the questions in our schools? Children start out asking them, but this procedure is soon discouraged. Children seem to have the darndest tendency to ask questions about subjects for which we don't have the answers—and their curiosity is rarely in line with a grade syllabus. A "Candid Camera" crew asked a group of first-grade children what they had learned in the first few months of going to school. One child said, "I learned to hold up my hand"; another said, "To control yourself"; another, "How to be quiet"; and another, "My teacher yells even louder than my mother."

A research scientist once told me, "Education is a system for telling people what they *can't* do. This is the reason that so many of the really important new ideas, theories and discoveries are made by amateurs or beginners in a field, not by the established experts. The amateur doesn't know enough to worry about whether or not his own train of thought 'fits in,' and his naive questions sometimes lead to fantastic breakthroughs in knowledge!" Another scientist told me that most of the "facts" now being taught in our schools will not be regarded as true or valid in twenty years. "There is simply no point at all in cramming facts into kids' heads," he told me. "What they will need most is an understanding of *processes*—how do you go about thinking about a question, how do you explore relationships between things or ideas? Facts are what we have libraries and encyclopedias for—what we ought to be teaching children is how do you go about looking up the facts you need in order to understand." The life of the mind depends for its vitality on freedom, on lack of restraint, pressures, preconceived ideas of what is true or false. The world is changing so fast that rather than teaching all the new facts we now know, we must train children to examine, reject and accept facts, not to learn them by heart.

A news item in *The New York Times* (March 3, 1966) suggests an increasing awareness of this fact. Reporter M. A. Farber tells of the Inquiry Development Program initiated by Dr. J. Richard Suchman of the University of Illinois. This project, dealing with the physical sciences at the junior-high-school level, has the following goals as outlined by Dr. Suchman:

> What we want are free-swinging inquirers who will theorize and test their own ideas for themselves. . . . How a child sees himself as a learner is more important than what he, or his teacher, sees under a particular microscope. . . . Education is knocking something very good out of kids. The something is a child's fundamental and essential need to ask questions, to examine, and to make his world more meaningful through his own efforts. . . . Children are playing it safe and waiting for the teacher to take the lead.

Where, in our reward system, the premium is placed on being right, there is less willingness to run the risk of arriving at wrong, disapproved conclusions through the independent process of inquiry. We're not turning our backs on accumulated knowledge about motion, force, pressure, temperature or anything. But to tell a child he's right is to tell him he's reached the end of the road—which he hasn't. Science is always being rewritten.

These are hardly new ideas. Montaigne, in his essay "On Education," wrote in 1540, "Most commonly the authoritie of them that teach, hinders them that learne." Or, as I have suggested before, we need to listen once again, and harder this time, to John Dewey, who wrote: "The teacher's problem is to protect the spirit of inquiry, to keep it from becoming blasé from over-excitement, wooden from routine, fossilized through dogmatic instruction, or dissipated by random exercise upon trivial things."
Intellectual excellence starts, I think, with a kind of creative mental gymnastics. Undeniably, it must eventually be reinforced by self-discipline and hard work—but that is primarily for adolescents and grown-ups, not for young children. First, in order to encourage the kind of stamina and motivation necessary for hard work, one must set the stage for it. How do we encourage this first period of creative exercise? Certainly not by stuffing the mind with facts. No great discovery ever came about through merely adding up facts; the truly great scientist is not the one who knows more facts than the technicians he supervises; he is the one who can take the general knowledge in his field and see it from a new viewpoint, a new perspective. What he

does is to use his own special and unique creative perception, his imagination, to make new combinations of ideas. I once asked a scientist who had made an important discovery, how he had done it. His answer was, "I have a rich fantasy life." The true thinker, the intellectual explorer, knows there is no one road; he tries many; he free-associates until "something clicks." A mother told me that after her son had been in kindergarten for six weeks, she received a report that he was a dreamer; he was always looking out the window. The mother said, "There's nothing wrong with his work—he does very well. But what am I supposed to do about his dreaming? It's obviously driving the teacher crazy." All I could offer by way of counsel was, "If you're *very* lucky, he'll keep on 'driving people crazy' with his dreaming!"

Excellence of achievement in almost any field tends more frequently than not to appear as a somewhat narrow and limited talent. There are some exceptions—the "Renaissance Man," who finds many outlets for his creativity, and seems to be equally gifted in many different areas—but more frequently when we begin to study those people who seem to have some of the most outstanding talents, we find that they have centered their lives on one major interest and have often quite consciously and sometimes painfully, felt the need to deliberately cut themselves off from other activities. When a world-famous opera star was asked by an interviewer what she felt had contributed the most to the full development of her talent, she replied, "Well, of course first there had to be the voice, and then the hard work—but most of all, it was sacrificing everything else to this one thing in life—to sing." At the Nobel Peace Prize ceremonies one year, the wife of an award scientist was asked by a reporter how she accounted for her husband's professional eminence, and she replied with candor, "I think there are many men with great talent, but they must feel free of the usual responsibilities of life in order to attain great achievements. My part in this great moment is that I gave my husband isolation, protection from the ordinary pressures of the world."

Very few men of excellence have been "jacks-of-many-trades." The pursuit of excellence often seems to involve a narrow channeling of energies, a focusing on one special gift; it is a kind of funneling of creativity, so that it becomes distilled and refined. If this is so in general, and if we really want to encourage excellence in achievement in our children, then it seems to me that we must let our children become "specialists" to a greater degree. Certainly it is important in the early years to provide an abundance of opportunities and possibilities, but when a youngster begins to show very strong inclinations in a particular direction, we ought to at least permit him to focus his time and attention to the extent that he can begin to have the rewards of success and be less burdened by subjects that contribute little more than frustration and a sense of failure.

Charles, at sixteen, had failed two subjects in school, math and French. He had known that if he failed, he would have to go to summer school. He had wanted to go to a work camp in Appalachia, where he would have worked as a volunteer recreation leader in the anti-poverty program. His mother, in telling about the fact that he had killed his own chances by not doing enough work to pass, said, "It really serves him right—maybe this will teach him a lesson." His parents thought of him as lazy, indifferent, always making excuses for not getting his work done, unrealistic and irresponsible. What was Charles really like? It is true that he had great difficulty driving himself to do things that did not interest him. In addition, however, he had a marvelous wry wit, a delicious sense of humor, and a truly creative and imaginative mind for those things that intrigued him. He had many close friends; he could be counted on to help them in any rough situation. Three years before, he had taught himself to play the guitar, and at fifteen he was so good that he had been asked to be the guitar instructor at a sophisticated music camp with very high standards. He had worked at another camp the summer before—a drama camp, in which he took part in a different play every week. No job was too menial or dirty, and he had somehow managed to take additional courses offered in art. This experience had started him off on a new interest, and he wanted very much to take an intensive course in art history at a nearby college while still attending high school, but this plan had been forbidden because of his failing work in math and French.

To be realistic, Charles has to get through certain kinds of basic requirements; no matter how enlightened his parents or teachers might be, they will not be able to change "the system" in his lifetime. But it seems to me that if Charles must continue to struggle with subjects he despises, he ought also to be permitted to take that history of art course; such intellectual stimulation, such an opportunity for commitment and success, are likely to be contagious; rather than lessening his chances of passing math and French, doing the thing that he loves may give him the refreshment, the revitalizing that will make those hurdles easier to jump.

There is also no reason to indicate to Charles that taking

math in the junior year in high school is really going to test
his moral fiber or make a man of him; such a point of view
is sheer, unmitigated nonsense—a wasteful carry-over from
Puritan morality that has nothing whatever to do with reality. He might have a much better chance of getting this
chore over with if the adults around him would admit that
it is something he could very well survive without. Instead
of feeling wonderful and hopeful about himself and his future because of his very real promise, Charles is made to see
himself as lazy, stupid and irresponsible. To what possible
purpose? In all probability, once Charles has managed to
live through all the rituals of the establishment and manages
to escape from formalized education, he will keep narrowing his area of specialization until it is honed down to a fine
edge. Since by the time he is thirty, and an artist, there will
be nothing going on in his life that involves mathematics beyond long division, he could have been spending valuable
time learning to mix paints, perhaps, instead of taking algebra. French he has undoubtedly learned very well on his
own, with a summer at the Sorbonne and a French girl
friend!

I think it is reasonable and sound to want all our children
to be exposed to many different possibilities and to have some
groundwork in different ways of thinking and looking at
the world. But we need to be less rigid about the ways in
which we present this broad spectrum; sometimes a tasty
little tidbit can have more significance than a seven-course
meal. And certainly by high school, when a youngster begins to show some very special leanings, we ought to be
flexible enough to fashion a program tailored to the course
in which he is moving. His need and his right to move in his
own special direction seem to me to be just as great as is the

right of other kinds of young people *not* to make up their minds about where *they* are going until they get good and ready. At the other end of the line, there are children with many general interests who really need a great deal of time to mature, to experiment, to have a variety of experiences before choosing an area of specialization. The current trend to force college students to select a major at the end of their first year seems just as arbitrary and unrealistic as the refusal to accept a genuine talent when it appears early in life.

One of the most common complaints is that today's young people do not know the meaning of work. I would turn the sentence around and say *they know the work that is meaningless.* It may be true that very few children are eager to carry out the garbage or wash the dishes, but the large majority are certainly enslaved by many hours of homework; and because so much of that homework is dull, is unnecessary and interferes with genuine thought, our children *are* developing some detrimental attitudes toward work—primarily in rebellion, I think, against having so much of the wrong kind.

A friend of mine teaches ballet at a large university, and she commented recently that when she was a young ballet student, she expected to have to work and suffer in order to become a good dancer. "We worked at that bar," she told me, "until every muscle in our bodies was screaming in pain; there was a kind of dedication that I just don't see as often in my students. They aren't willing to work as hard for the results they want—they expect us to make it quick and easy for them." I asked her how she had felt about other kinds of work when she was in high school—had she been as willing to work equally hard at, let's say, her history assignment or in studying for a biology exam? "Oh, those were different times," she assured me. "We never had to work as hard in school as kids do today. No, I did what I had to, but it wasn't much, and I saved all my real energy for my dance lessons." I am convinced that some of the "make-it-easy-for-me" mood that we see among young people is not because they have not been made to work, but because we have forced them to work at meaningless tasks; work, as they have come to understand it, is a dirty word.

There is more than enough evidence to make it quite clear that, given a *meaningful* task, young people respond with a wonderful enthusiasm and are capable not only of sticking to a job, but also of doing so in the face of discomfort, boredom and even physical danger. There was one particularly dramatic example several years ago, during a flood in Illinois, when thousands of teen-agers entirely on their own poured into the stricken town, piled sandbags for two days and two nights without sleep and were largely responsible for saving the town. It also seems to me indecent to say that our young people are irresponsible or lazy in the face of the heroes and heroines of Mississippi during that summer of 1964. The Peace Corps and VISTA are further testament to the ability of our young adults to meet some real tests and challenges. A VISTA supervisor told me about a trip that she made to an Indian reservation in Arizona, where several VISTA volunteers were working. She was appalled when she got there—the temperature inside the hut in which they were living was over 100 degrees, there were flies, there were no facilities for taking a decent bath. "I thought I was in for it!" she told me. "I thought they'd all say they wanted to leave. In three days of talking with them, I didn't hear one word of complaint about the physical discomforts of their assignment. The only thing they were mad about was not having the resources they needed to help the Indian children. As I was leaving, I asked one of the boys how he managed to keep in such good spirits despite the heat, and the frustrations of the job, and the fact that he, a city boy, was stuck out in the middle of nowhere. All he said was, 'This is the first time in my life I really know some people need me. It's the greatest thing that ever happened to me.' "

A staff member of the New York State Education Department told me this story: In an upstate city there was a Negro boy of fifteen who had been truanting from school and failing in his work from first grade on. He had also been in trouble with the police and was on probation. To all intents and purposes there was no father in the home; he had eight brothers and sisters and an immature, emotionally disturbed mother. When the Head Start program began in his community, one of the nurseries happened to be housed in a building on his street. One morning he walked in, asked to see "The Head Lady," and told her he wanted to help. She knew who he was and was aware of his problems; she felt that with supervision he might be helped himself, and so she said that was fine. The following day Nick arrived in white shirt and tie and neatly pressed slacks. He came every day, all summer, and like a sponge soaked up all the love and affection of the teachers and the children. He played with the boys and girls, he cleaned and swept, he built toy shelves, he mixed paints—he did anything any teacher asked him to do. He understood the children, he spoke their language; they were his neighbors, so that he was often able to comfort or discipline a child more easily than could the other teachers. At the end of the summer, when the "Head Lady" commented on what a wonderful job he had done and how well groomed he was, he confessed that he was wearing the only shirt he owned and that he washed and ironed it each night after school. If you are looking for a happy ending, you have missed the point. In the fall he started truanting again, and he continued to fail his schoolwork. Why should that be surprising? Some things are important to a person, and some things just aren't!

Teachers are not really so different from children. The principal of a school told me that he can gauge how hard his teachers are willing to work by the changing directives that come to him from the Board of Education. "Whenever we get some special service, or whenever I manage to wangle a little more autonomy for my teachers to do things in their own way, I find teachers staying late and coming early. The minute we find out that all our children must be prepared for a series of grade-level tests, or if we hear that one of our special service teachers is going to be given three additional schools to service, I hear complaints—I am reminded indignantly about union hours and overtime!"

There is no question that we face serious and challenging problems in interpreting the meaning of work to our children; we are confused enough ourselves, on the subject. We are living through a time in which the meaning of work is changing so radically that most of us find ourselves uneasy and conflicted about what work means in our lives. Automation has produced what one social scientist called "the new poor." People with little or no schooling used to be able to lead dignified and useful lives; there were jobs to which they could be apprenticed and in which they could achieve a high level of skill. One example was a Negro man who came to Chicago from the deep South at the age of fifteen and became a sheep-shearer's helper in the stockyards. By the age of thirty, he was earning $150 a week, despite the fact that he could hardly read or write. When machines took over his job, this man, who had lived responsibly and supported his family, became an "unemployable." The indignity of being on welfare, the sudden loss of status, have meant the veritable destruction of his life, his work and his world. Millions of people with talents for craftsmanship, with mechanical skills, but with little motivation for book learning, have become the displaced persons of the 1960's.

Educator and writer Paul Goodman has said that in 1900 only 6 per cent of our population graduated from high school; now the number is 76 per cent. He believes that about 85 per cent of our population do not learn best by doing lessons—they learn by participating in real-life experiences. We are therefore penalizing large numbers of children because of our current stress on higher education. We need to realize that middle-class status seeking may frequently account for the pressure on young people to go to college, rather than any genuine conviction that this experience is essential to their well-being or to the needs of society. Dr. Goodman points out that in 1900 one-fourth of one per cent of our population went to college, and if one were to look through a *Who's Who* of that period, one would find that the lack of a college education did not mean we were deprived of great men in high places.

Some people throughout human history have been doers, not thinkers; always before they have been needed; now they have no place in the scheme of things. Fifty years ago a boy who ran away from home at the age of twelve and got a job could, if he had drive and intelligence, achieve success in life; now we are forced to tell all our children,

"No matter what kind of person you may be, whether or not you learn better from books or from direct experience, you must stay in school because there is simply no alternative for you." Since this is so, we had better adapt more schools to meeting the needs of different kinds of human beings.

Work used to provide one's main sense of identity, the central force in one's life; it consumed almost all of the time when one was not eating or sleeping. How can we tell our children that earning a living will be the focal point of their lives when the fathers of many of these children are members of unions that are fighting for a three- or four-day week? With leisure time increasing at a lightning speed, how can we go on insisting that a man's worth can be measured by the number of hours he works at earning a living? Rather than piling on homework, what we ought to be doing is helping our children make the necessary transition to a new understanding of work—to find a value in work that is unrelated to simple wage earning. Work is essential in human experience—it is and probably always will be a way in which we satisfy a need for significance in our lives. Well, what shall we work at if we have so much spare time, if we face increasingly earlier retirement? There is one kind of work that never ends: service to the needs of people. There is not a single community, be it a small town or a large city, that is not faced with unmet human and social needs of its members; there is no place in the world where there are not children who need help in learning, adequate play facilities and well-trained recreation leaders, better resources for health care, more facilities for helping people with their social and psychological problems. It would seem to me that the best way to promote excellence in work would be to give children a new kind of homework, opportunities to work in the community—to let our young people know we need them, that there are real and urgent needs to be met and that their services are of genuine importance to us all. It would seem to me that one of the greatest contributions that might be made by a high-school guidance department would be to serve as the "field placement office" for after-school volunteer jobs for teen-agers, setting up a program in which every student spent several afternoons a week in service to the community.

There are faint beginnings; many schools have discovered that one of the best ways to help a third grade non-reader is to provide him with a tenth-grade teacher who is not doing too well himself! Some of the best volunteer tutors are young people who know exactly how it feels to be confused and frustrated about writing a paragraph, spelling or learning the multiplication table. The February 1966 issue of *Redbook* carried an article by Bernard Asbell entitled "Let the Children Teach." He reported:

> In Oakland, California, first graders who seemed unable to learn their A B C's and 1-2-3's in regular classes are learning them eagerly in daily 45-minute sessions with sixth-grade "teachers." Especially bright sixth graders? Not always. Some of the tutors are not only backward learners themselves, but also rebellious "problem children." But they are teaching effectively. Perhaps even more important, these "teachers" are themselves becoming better learners, showing remarkable improvement in their behavior, their dress and their attitude toward learning. Having responsibility for others seems to make them more responsible about

themselves. . . . In New York an antipoverty project, Mobilization for Youth, employs high-school students for afterschool homework help to grade schoolers; both appear to benefit.

Mr. Asbell spoke to some of these young tutors about their work. These were some of their comments:

"Teachers," suggested Debbie, "most always call on the smart kids who know the right answers. When a teacher finally does call on a kid who doesn't know the answer, she just embarrasses him and makes fun of him in front of the whole class. She's always so busy with the smart ones, she has no time for the ones who need help." "I've learned," added Janathur, "that it's best to teach somebody what he's interested in first. He really wants to learn the rest, but he may be afraid. I wanted to teach Robert the alphabet first. I kept thinking that's supposed to be learned first. But I'd ask him questions and he wouldn't answer. When I gave in to him and let him learn numbers, he answered. After that, I saw he wanted to learn the alphabet. He was just scared." I asked the girls how tutoring had affected their own work. "Now, after we're finished tutoring," said Debbie, "I go back to my class and think about the little kids who want to learn. If I'm ever going to teach them, I have to learn everything so I can help them learn it. That's why schoolwork is more interesting now." "It makes my work easier," said Janathur. "Like when we get new work in arithmetic, it looks so hard. Then I tell myself I might have to explain it to somebody else. When you have to explain it, it makes you see it more clearly." "When my

teacher does something that I think is bad teaching,"
said Debbie, "I ask myself now how I would do it.
Then I make myself my own teacher and I teach it to
myself the better way."

Some schools are beginning to offer opportunities to students to work under supervision in neighborhood centers,
social agencies, hospitals, nurseries, centers for the aged and
mental-health clinics. Not only would children get an opportunity to see new possibilities and values in work, but
coming in close contact with professionals in many fields,
they might find new and valid reasons for wanting very
much to get further education. We will never convince our
children that working hard and responsibly are important
unless we provide the kind of work that proves this point
honestly.

There is an added "legitimacy" to service jobs in that in
some measure they can be used as opportunities for those
who learn by doing, more than by studying. In a large city
in New York state there is a seventy-five-year-old man
with one arm who is called "Grandpa" by thirty nursery-
school children, three teachers—and most of the staff members of the local Board of Education and the anti-poverty
program. Every day he comes to a nursery school which is
set up as part of a brilliantly imaginative project supported
by the United States government's Office of Economic Opportunity. He sits in a rocking chair in a small playroom,
and whenever any child feels homesick or angry, cranky
or rambunctious, he goes and sits on Grandpa's lap until he
feels better. In his spare time Grandpa builds nursery furniture and toys, including a beautiful three-story doll house.
When a child gets sick at school and must be isolated from

the others, Grandpa is his personal nurse and companion until his family comes to take him home.

It is very difficult for the Welfare Department to realize that Grandpa is no longer on their relief roles. When the OEO project director sent out a call for "old reliable unemployables," no one really thought for one minute that Grandpa would make it—except the OEO Project Director, who happens to be an unregenerate, soft-headed idealist, who believes—*really* believes—that every human being has worth and can be rehabilitated. You see, Grandpa had been the most celebrated drunken bum on his street for about thirty-five years! He was in a car accident at about that time, had lost his arm, and could not continue in the unskilled job he had previously held. He was illiterate and was simply unable to overcome the deprivations of his early life in facing the challenge of readjustment to his physical handicap. A good part of his life had been spent "sleeping it off" in the city jail because he often became belligerent when drunk and was charged with disorderly conduct. He is earning a wage now, he has not missed a day's work in over a year, and every once in a while he calls the Project Director's office if he thinks of some way to improve the program. It occurs to me that one part of the answer to our current dilemma about automation, education and jobs may be to employ truanting teen-agers, unemployed sheep shearers, and other casualties of our times, as "grandfathers" and "uncles"; there have been worse ideas.

Meaningful work experiences are just as important inside the school as outside the classroom. Learning in school must relate itself to the real issues of life in today's world. As this begins to happen, we see a new vitality and excitement, an intensified motivation to achieve. Dr. John R. Seeley,

Chairman of the Sociology Department of York University
in Toronto, Canada, calls this "Leveling with Kids." In an
article published by the American Humanist Association he
writes: "How is it that the school does everything well—
except tell its pupils the most elementary, basic truths about
the world in which they live? When I have been asked
what the schools should do that they are not doing, I have
constantly returned one simple answer: Level with the
kids."

What is the nature of the society in which we live? What
are the changing attitudes and values in relation to sex, marriage and divorce? What do we know about power, about
wealth and poverty? What about ethical values in living?
What about business and finances, "human nature," social
class, the function of myth in society, social conflict, cultural anthropology, sociology, politics and government?
These are some of the many issues involved in the social
realities of our times—and these are the things that interest
our young people—but too often they are discussed in
coffee houses rather than in classrooms. If we are going to
consider ways to enrich the curriculum, it seems to me we
ought to start with such issues as self-understanding and
how to become a responsible and intelligent citizen in a democracy. Selfishly, I would feel far better about seeing
some "excellence" in voting than in the memorization of
chemical formulas.

At the heart of the matter of excellence in education is
the teacher. We have lots of good ones, and we need to free
them to do a significant job; we have some poor ones, and
we need to help them. Despite the size of our cities, the
population explosion, the vast hordes of children we must
educate, we have to find ways in which to personalize the

experience of teaching, so that a genuine encounter can take place between teacher and child. In a recent study several thousand adults were asked what kinds of teachers they remembered best, which ones had influenced their lives the most. The most characteristic kind of answer was, "The teacher who made me feel I wanted to grow up to be like him." In another study of 100 great teachers (as selected by parents, fellow teachers and administrators) it was found that they were between thirty-five and fifty years of age, had had five years of preparation for teaching, knew at least one subject very well, had worked at some time in their lives at something besides teaching, did a good deal of traveling, and owned at least 250 non-professional books. But the most interesting point was that they knew how to reason; confronted with entirely new subject matter which they knew nothing about in advance, they were skillful at finding ways to solve problems and getting information they needed. General expertise in a great many subject-matter areas was regarded as less important than understanding how to go about learning something new.

At the present time, in the large majority of graduate teacher-training schools, great emphasis is placed on subject-matter information. One recent graduate of a large university told me, "I know a lot about history, geography and English composition, but if I wanted to learn anything about *children*—how they grow, what they feel—I had to do that on my own time through my own reading." It would seem entirely appropriate to me to spend most of the time in teacher-training schools helping teachers find out ways to relate well to children, answer questions and help children to solve problems, irrespective of subject matter. If we can ever hope for smaller classes, we will also need teachers who understand something about the ways in which growth and learning occur through a *relationship* rather than through subject matter. We need to devise ways for encouraging initiative and imagination and we must prepare for and eventually allow teachers the freedom to develop the year's curriculum with the children. Within certain flexible guidelines it is possible, and has been proven successful over and over again in experimental progressive schools, to cover generally similar basic skills in many different and individualized ways. One educator told me, "My idea of a great elementary school is to walk into four different third-grade rooms and find them all doing entirely different things." This idea does not mean abandoning *all* grade-level expectations—all it means is diversifying the paths to this goal.

Effective teaching simply cannot go on in a school where each teacher spends as much as half his time filling out papers and reports, grading tests, making inventories, taking attendance and reading administrative memorandums. Good teachers need the help of small classes, assistants, volunteers, older children and specialists. They need time to develop an intense and warmly affectionate relationship with each child. Under these circumstances it would be possible to have heterogeneous classes instead of feeding our children into tracks, departmentalizing their classes and placing them in homogeneous groupings, which are basically undemocratic, unrealistic and, in the long run, not even helpful. What a strange world it would be if in our daily lives as adults we had contacts only with people who performed exactly as we did, in every sphere of life! How dull and uninteresting it would be! The value of one human being for another seems to me to be entirely unrelated to levels of academic achievement. A brilliant and overprotected youngster who does not know how to play can learn a lot from a child who has ten brothers and sisters and has played on teeming neighborhood streets since he was three years old; the child who has had little or no opportunity to be exposed to intellectual or creative pursuits needs the healthy stimulation of children who have had a rich cultural experience. If all of us must learn to get along in the world, we need opportunities as children to discover other children —dumb ones, smart ones, shy ones, bold ones, bullies and scaredy-cats, rich ones, poor ones, leaders and followers. When we set up an aristocracy of intellect in our schools, we deprive *all* children of the abundance of human experience, for all human beings have something to contribute to each other, and we are all diminished by separation and selection.

We need more experimentation in teaching, more daring experimental programs. What would happen if we assigned no formal homework but simply offered interesting individual projects to a group of children all the way up to sixth grade? What would happen if we were to change our requirements, so that children who were neither interested in or talented for science had to study math only until the eighth grade? Would the world come to an end? Suppose we were to stop teaching spelling as a separate subject for drill and memorization and spent that time in increased opportunities for creative writing and journalism? If we are going to have tracks in high school, why not try to do it on the basis not of performance, but of interests? A high-school student who seemed to have very strong interests and abilities could select a track in science or in the humanities or the social sciences. The curriculum in each track would have survey courses in all the other subjects, but each track would offer an intensified program in its own area. For example, a student selecting the science track would be obliged to take courses in history and literature, but these would be especially designed to attract his interest by dealing with the important implications of science to these fields, and they would be broad survey courses; an art student in the humanities track would have to have some understanding of scientific method, but his course in science would be geared to his special interests; he might take a course in elementary psychology, or take a biology course which focuses on the ways in which progress in medical science and research has affected literature.

The Jobs Corps is, I think, one of the most hopeful signs in the development of imaginative and courageous experimentation in education. The small classes, the use of teacher-counselors to help young people develop self-esteem, the emphasis on the creation of a total environment to give young people who have failed new hope, all suggest new directions for education in general.

I would also like to see some brave school system abolish all marks through the eighth grade, substituting two parent-teacher conferences a year, of at least fifteen minutes each. I would also like to see a general agreement throughout all education that marking on the normal curve is insidious and inhuman. I would like to see what would happen if no I.Q. tests were given to any children except in cases where special problems are apparent. And while we are at it, we might try full-time teaching and learning by cutting down on all forms of testing by about 80 per cent.

During the era of the flowering of progressive schools, they grew out of a felt need for change, they offered new possibilities, new ways of looking at learning and child development. Aside from such technological advances as teaching machines, and the various research projects related to accelerated learning, there has been very little going on in education that is as dynamic or as fresh as what was going on in the 1920's and 1930's. It seems to me that it is time for a new wave of experimental schools, and a good place to start might be small schools designed especially for those nice, normal children who are having "learning problems" in the traditional schools. We have become so overinstitutionalized that even when such projects appear, we discourage their development.

A column by James A. Wechsler in the New York *Post* on November 23, 1966, described one such situation:

A small "dream-school" sponsored by the Lower East Side Action Project (LEAP) is in imminent danger of strangulation by our local educational officialdom. . . . It all began last summer when Larry Cole, the missionary-psychologist who runs LEAP, managed to raise private funds to stage a summer expedition in learning and leisure for under-privileged kids at an upstate refuge. There were about 20 of them, mostly Puerto Rican, ranging in age from 12 to 15, and a staff of six excitedly watched these youths grow in an atmosphere of responsiveness they had never known. But the summer sunlight ended and they came back to the shadowed sidewalks of New York and to the ghetto schools in their neighborhoods. Cole swiftly saw the process of backsliding—the kids again sniffing glue and lapsing into truancy. So, in early October, he and some of his friends agreed that LEAP should launch the modest equivalent of its own junior high school, perhaps setting an example for other communities where the alienated and restless find no home in conventional schools. With the support of the J. M. Kaplan Fund and the Aaron Norman Foundation among others, the school came to life. About a dozen youths for whom LEAP has offered an island of affirmative companionship enrolled. In an effort to avert legal wrangles, all of them were required to secure letters from their parents authorizing their transfer for "private instruction" in the new, unofficial and unsanctified institution. Martin Greenhut—a former public school teacher—became director, Irving Oyle the medical director and Robert Ellenbogen psychological consultant. And Martin Shepard, who had formerly served with the Board of Education, evaluated psychological tests to give the small, earnest faculty a clearer glimpse of the nature of the kids. Certain unorthodoxies quickly characterized the school. There was no compulsory attendance; it was soon discovered that "truancy" was minimal. Youths who were notorious runaways from public school appeared with remarkable regularity. There were animation and dialogue in the classrooms. But it was seemingly all too good to be endurable in the bureaucratized life of New York's school structure. Suddenly truant officers who had ignored the perennial absenteeism of these kids were haunting their homes and harassing their parents. The Bureau of Child Guidance began demanding full copies of Shepard's psychological profiles of the pupils. . . . In essence LEAP's leaders were told that they could justify the school's existence only by establishing that the pupils were so psychologically disturbed that they required a therapeutic setting; LEAP, one might say, was to be branded a leper colony. This was exactly what it did not propose to be. It did not want its students stigmatized or its student body restricted to those labeled unfit or unmanageable by the public schools. . . . The matter of accreditation by the State Board of Regents complicated the problem. This is a long, cumbersome operation, often taking as long as two years. "We didn't want these kids to lose all of the summer's progress while we waited around 24 months or so for accreditation," Cole said the other day. And so yesterday afternoon came the ultimatum from a dignitary in the Bureau of Attendance. Unless Dr. Shepard transmitted his full psychiatric findings about the pupils at once, the bureau would begin truancy proceedings against them. . . . Certainly there are elements of defiant non-conformism in the LEAP adventure. It is based on the premise that at least a fraction of New York's children of the streets can't be handled by the public schools to which they are assigned, but can be salvaged by more private and, if the word be forgiven, more progressive methods. . . . But the educational establishment is a nervous body, hostile to daring dreams and beset by bureaucratic nightmares.

Paul Goodman reports that in Denmark twenty parents and a licensed teacher can set up a school—and the state will pay for it. In fact, 20 per cent of all Danish schools fall into this category. This seems to me to be the kind of courage and flexibility that might well be emulated by state boards of education in the United States. There might be a few pretty awful schools, and after accreditation studies, some might have to be closed, but the way things are right now, could this kind of endeavor really make things any worse than they are for thousands of our children? The road to excellence is paved with daring, venturesome ideas.

Human excellence is what makes the struggle to improve our schools worthwhile. The thought of what we could be doing is what makes me so impatient. If we can keep before us the image of "the excellent person," we will feel impelled to keep up the good struggle. For me, this is a self-actualizing person, who has had the opportunity and the encouragement to search for the treasures within himself, with no sense of time limits for personal growth, but rather with a certainty that he will go on becoming his "best self" all the days of his life. Such a person feels that life is worth living —he brings a zest and a vitality to each new experience. He has a reverence for life and a tenderness and compassion for the suffering of others. Respected himself, he is able to respect personality differences in others and to have faith in the potential worth of every human being. He is able to understand the meaning of personal freedom and accepts the responsibility that goes with it. He welcomes differences in people and variety in ideas and experiences, seeing here the seed of creativity. He is able to participate in a democratic group life—in "the just relations of unequals." He can accept frustration and the irrationalities of daily life with humility and humor. He can work, he can enjoy leisure and he can meditate. And most of all, with all the richness of his inner being and his exultancy in being alive, he can find the fullest expression of his human excellence in loving and being loved.

TEN

Everybody's Children:
The Stench of Social Neglect

A FEW years ago the psychiatrist Dr. Fritz Redl was speaking to a group of parents and educators about the fact that we seemed to be returning to a "get-tough" policy in relation to the handling of juvenile delinquency. Faced with the ever-increasing complexities and subtleties of community living, in a world of such challenge and change, it seemed easier to advocate a simple-minded "back to the woodshed" approach, and Dr. Redl concluded, "This is what we really want to do—we want to be punitive in order to forget the stench of our own real neglect."

Neglect of children? On the face of it, it seems an incredible accusation to level at American parents, but Dr. Redl was talking about *society*, in its role as parent to *all* of its children. It is one of the strange ironies of modern life that during an era in which we find ourselves so concerned about the psychological needs of our own children we seem to be failing in our collective responsibility for meeting the human needs of all of our children.

The bigness of things—the anonymity of city life, the population explosion, the loss of small-town connectedness in community living—have given a low visibility to the unmet needs of all of our children. We are vaguely concerned when we hear that thousands of schools have classes of thirty-five or more children, and that these are children who come from the most deprived, disorganized and unstable homes and neighborhoods; we are told on a news broadcast that the "air pollution index" is "at a critical level," and we are aware that millions of children are breathing in and out in this tent of poisonous gases, but we go about our daily tasks. Then, one child gets stuck in a well in some small midwestern town, and the entire nation finds itself waiting, praying, thinking of little else, as TV cameras, radio announcers, the nation's press arrive at the scene to record this drama of life and death for us; we are both enthralled and horrified—and 150 million of us collectively sigh with relief if the child is rescued alive or go into mourning if the rescuers fail. We are informed that there are 5,000 tenements that are dangerous fire traps in which children live, but we are able to live with this knowledge until we hear about one family in which three out of five children perish in a tenement fire and the parents and two remaining children are homeless. Money pours in from people all over the country to help the family get a new start; people who would scream bloody murder at the thought of a tax increase for housing projects manage to find money, clothing, food, sometimes even a place for the family to stay.

Individual compassion and charity are wonderful, but

our problem is that as our communities become larger and our problems more and more serious and complex, we have to develop a capacity to imagine, to identify with *millions* as strongly and with as much mercy and tenderness as with one. Responsibility and involvement are such difficult qualities to nurture and reinforce in a mass society. We know, as perhaps no previous generation in all of human history has ever known, how deep this responsibility goes, and yet, at the same time, it has never been more difficult to involve oneself, to become committed, to take action as individuals.

We of the twentieth century are, I believe, in a state of shock; not the Judeo-Christian ethic, not the advancement of knowledge in the understanding of man, not the scientific revolution seem to have provided us with the capacity to solve the problems of man's inhumanity to man. The promising "age of reason" finds us living in a world in which have occurred the most terrible social atrocities ever conceived of. Part of that state of shock comes from what confronted us at the end of the Second World War, when we were faced with the unbelievable nightmare of what had taken place in the concentration camps. Nobody seemed to be responsible for anything that had happened! During the Nuremburg and subsequent trials of Nazi officials, we simply could not conceive of the fact that men and women who were parents themselves, who had been "loving fathers and mothers, devoted husbands and wives," could have participated in the horror of the death camps, where six million men, women and children had been liquidated by means that were too terrible to fully comprehend. Was it possible that "good family men" had planned and executed the "final solution" of the gas chambers? Was it possible that human beings who provided their own children with ten-

der, loving care could have participated in the inhuman out-
rages we learned about? It was not only possible—it had
happened. Men who went home to their own families at
night had in the course of a day's work smashed the bodies
of children against stone walls. Doctors who were fathers
themselves had been capable of pumping cement into the
wombs of women; fathers who sang lullabies to their children helped to shovel thousands of bodies into ovens; not
just a few insane murderers, but thousands upon thousands
of family members, who served, who knew and stood by,
who did not try to stop it. And when they were questioned,
they said, "We were obeying orders; we were not responsible. There was nothing we could do."

No story in human history has spoken more clearly to
the problem of personal responsibility. We had to face the
fact that it *was* possible for people who were tender and
kind and loving with their own families to be able to destroy the lives of millions of other families—and apparently
without feeling guilt or remorse. We found out, irrevoca-
bly and with utter horror, that being a good parent to one's
own child was never and in no way enough; until we were
all responsible for all the children of the world, no child
would ever be safe, no society could survive

Wars of the distant past seem like child's play compared
to the wars of the last fifty years. We find ourselves confronted with the *fact* of the wholesale murder of millions of
innocent children, of wars that have killed off millions in
civilian populations and the threat that any major war in
the future may, indeed, wipe out all human life as we know
it. We stand by, feeling helpless, anguished—how can this
go on, when we see ourselves, individually, as being civilized, intelligent moral people?

We are so frightened, so overwhelmed by the awful dangers of life in today's world that we cannot bear to let ourselves care. Confronted with one death, we are still capable of shock and guilt; when Kitty Genovese died, while more than thirty people heard her screams for help on a dark street in Queens, there *was* a deep and pervading social remorse, an awakening to the dangers we each face when we lose touch with one another. What remains far more difficult for all of us is facing up to the same dangers when we turn away from each other in large numbers.

A militant citizens' group is formed in a comfortable middle-class Christian suburb to fight with desperation against the possibility that three "token" middle-class Negro families might move into the neighborhood. The plans for a housing development for low-income families are dropped when violence erupts in a Jewish neighborhood as news of the project is made public; individual parents, who attend churches and temples, who believe themselves to be religious and therefore to have accepted the moral values of their faiths, scream wild and filthy epithets at government officials, hurl rocks and garbage at young children who want to enter their schools or play in their neighborhoods. Recently a New York newspaper reported that Governor Rockefeller had "spoken out bitterly" against community resistance to an addict-treatment center planned for one city area. He said, "They'd rather leave them on the street —mugging, robbing, stealing and murdering—than have them housed where they can be properly cared for." It seems that money which two years earlier had been allocated to two such rehabilitation centers still remained unused because of the refusal of one community after another to allow the building of such facilities in their own neighborhoods. The Governor added, "They say fine, take care of them, but don't do it in our neighborhood, we don't want them here." And perhaps somewhat helplessly and hopelessly he added, "We're going to do it—someday." Individually most people would never be able to do the things they are capable of doing in groups. Power *does* corrupt, in the sense that it gives us anonymity and makes us feel less responsible when we function in power groups, whether these groups be large and powerful unions, religious affiliations or political and industrial organizations.

It is all very well for us to feel individually that we are responsible parents, concerned about the welfare of our own children; but until we really understand that no child can be safe or well cared for until all children are, we are not "good" parents. Despite bigness, confusion, alienation from each other, a feeling of being helpless in the face of the magnitude of social institutions, we must begin to understand and accept the fact that the fundamental moral issue is no different today than it has ever been; *morality begins and ends with individual commitment*. In fact, the larger the issue, the more important it is that each person take responsibility for his own behavior—for behaving about broad social issues in *exactly the same way* as he does when confronted with a moral decision in his own family, involving his own children. It would be a sick society in which a father would save himself from a burning house, rather than try to save his trapped children even if, in so doing, he were to die himself. It is no less a sick society if the burning house be the whole world and the potential victims all children if any father hesitates to try to save any child—and the awful challenge of our times is that so many of us know this and do so very little about it.

There are thousands of issues that might be discussed in these terms; the examples that follow are simply those that seem to me to be particularly pertinent and pressing for today's parents, in our everyday living with our own children and all children. They seem to me to make it clear that we simply cannot protect our own children until we are able to take on the responsibility, *individually* for the social care of *all* children.

1. *We know that as individual parents we cannot protect our own children from an incessant and overpowering exposure to violence.* In 1964 the *Ladies' Home Journal* estimated that the average American child between the ages of five and fourteen witnesses the violent destruction of 13,000 human beings on television, mostly during the "children's hours" from four to nine P.M. Violence has become a familiar part of our everyday lives; whether it be wars or riots, or senseless, sick murders, as parents we know that our children live in a world in which we cannot protect them from daily exposure to the most unspeakable kinds of violence.

The New York *Post* (March 3, 1966) had the following item: "Morris L. Ernst, the lawyer, was criticizing the networks because of the crime shows. He began by stating that there are 2,000 more homicides each year on TV than in real life. 'I'm sure,' he added, 'that all of NBC's programming would be improved if each show were to be introduced with the billing; Dave Sarnoff Presents with Pride.' " Without having to stand up and be counted as an individual, corporate bigness and depersonalization make it possible for people to behave irresponsibly because they can do so without having to think of themselves as directly involved in a personal relationship with other human beings.

In a New England town of 300 people in the 1880's if a

printer released a newspaper or pamphlet containing violent or pornographic subject matter, he had to face the fact that his actions would precipitate an immediate and direct confrontation, asserting his personal responsibility. Today the publisher of sadistic violence, salacious and pornographic magazines or comic books prints millions of copies; he does not come face to face with any of his readers; he can easily rationalize what he is doing by saying, "Nobody has to buy this stuff—if parents don't want their kids to read it, let them stop them from buying it." In abdicating from being a social parent, such a publisher cannot really be a responsible parent to his own children.

It is possible today for a man who in his private life abhors violence, who teaches his own children to hate war and to view all crime as ugly and terrible, to be the manufacturer of toys which include make-believe lethal weapons and to feel no sense of personal guilt. Children want these toys, parents let them have them—why shouldn't he make a profit? If he does not, somebody else will. If he himself had to hand out each toy to each child, if he could be imaginative enough to see himself as a responsible parent to all the world's children, what would he do? How would he feel?

The "Notes and Comment" section of *The New Yorker* (November 13, 1965) reported:

> The following toys are in the toy department of the E. J. Korvette store at Forty-seventh Street and Fifth Avenue: (1) Special Forces Invasion Play Set (includes tanks, trucks, self-propelled guns, howitzers, landing craft), (2) Long-Range Bazooka for Jungle Guerrilla Warfare (includes harmless rockets, "exploding pillbox," and adjustable range site; shoots

thirty feet), (3) U-2 Spy Plane ("Takes secret photos automatically"), (4) Formex-7 Cast Your Own Military Company Set, (5) Battle Action Machine Gun Nest, (6) Iwo Jima Play Set, (7) U.S. Air Force Space Patrol Command (includes control center, orbital missiles and launchers, multi-firing equipment), (8) Bulldog Tank with 25-Man Combat Team, and (9) Battle Action Booby Trap Road ("Road explodes when truck strikes hidden mines").

I cannot believe that every one of the manufacturers of these delightful toys really believes that they are necessary or sound additions to children's play, or that they are likely to encourage attitudes that may eventually lead to the development of adult citizens committed to an eternal struggle for peaceful means of solving human problems. But since there is no direct confrontation with the families or the children involved, it is easy to say, "Somebody is going to supply these toys, anyway—it's not my problem." This way lies disaster; it means in effect that anybody can do anything, whether or not it fits in with the moral or ethical standards by which he may live personally.

In 1966 CBS Television announced it was going to show Alfred Hitchcock's horror movie *Psycho*. A few months later the network announced that the showing was called off. I have no idea what really went on behind the scenes—CBS stood to lose $800,000 in this reversed decision—but what I'd like to believe is that some top executive said to himself, "If *I* don't watch out for the kids—who will?" *

---

* My naive optimism was somewhat excessive; several months after writing this, I learned that *Psycho* had again been scheduled for television.

2. *We know that as individual parents we cannot control the experiences, attitudes and behavior of our own children in relation to the "sexual revolution."* Unless we each take our children and go to live in a cave somewhere, cutting off all contact with the outside world, our children are inevitably going to be exposed to attitudes and behavior that may not bear any relationship to our own values. This does not mean that there have not been certain assets and elements of progress in the fact that subjects which were once hidden behind locked doors are now being aired quite openly; that the hypocrisy of silence and the rigidity of Puritan morality have been largely abandoned; and that, in general, there now seems to be a growing ability to consider the human problems of sexuality more honestly. But with this increasing freedom and openness, our children are being constantly exposed to a degree of sexual titillation, a freedom of choice in selecting their own attitudes and behavior, unknown to children ever before.

However much we may value the more open acceptance of sexuality as a healthy and necessary part of human experience, we have paid a high price for our "enlightenment" during these early years of change and readjustment, as we try to find a new kind of balance in our thinking. In the 1920's and 1930's, when parents were first beginning to talk more openly about sex in the education of their children, they tended to separate sex information from human relationships; we gave facts, as though we were talking about how to put a radio together or what made an electric bulb light up.

An example of this was the "sex-educated" boy of five who, after being given graphic and specific information about the reproductive activities of adults, commented with great seriousness, "I know *what* they do, and I know *when* they do it—but I don't know *why* they do it"! As in any revolution, we went to the opposite extreme, from too much secrecy and social subterfuge to an attitude which suggested that the act of sex was in no way related to other than physical factors, to feelings and to a system of values. The forbidden, the hidden subject is now so open, so freely discussed, so blatantly exposed that it seems to have lost some of its most important attributes. Someone said recently that we have ruined the best "private enterprise" we ever had! As sex in the context of a meaningful private and personal relationship tended to be underemphasized we began to sense that we might have robbed our children of far more than whatever price may have been paid for the earlier conspiracy of silence.

Most of the parents I meet and talk with are greatly concerned about what is happening to their children. There are more and more early marriages due to pregnancy, marriages between young people in no way ready for the responsibilities of marriage—or even ready to choose each other for an enduring or responsible relationship. Young people who may not be at all ready emotionally are being catapulted into sexual experimentation because they feel it is "the thing to do."

Dr. Mary Calderone, Executive Director of the Sex Information and Education Council, was recently quoted in *Today's Child* (November 1966) as saying:

> We have done away with chaperones, supervision, rules, close family relations and privacy from the intrusions of the communication media. As a result we have left our children totally vulnerable to the on-

slaughts of commercial exploitation of sex, tabloid reporting of sordid sexual occurrences, wholly unsupervised after-school occupations and easy access to cars.
We adults are entirely responsible for the defenselessness of the adolescent today.

As individual parents we can, of course, try to communicate our own attitudes, beliefs and feelings to our children,
and at one time that might have been enough. It is not
enough anymore—we simply cannot supervise the activities, the experiences of our children, when inevitably so
much of their learning and growing takes place outside the
home. There is literally no way in which we as individuals
can keep our children sheltered from a pseudo-sophistication about the technical details of sexuality; by the time
they are twelve or thirteen years old they know more about
petting, birth control, perversions and "positions" than
most of their parents did when they got married. Like the
learning of any facts out of the context of mature understanding and sensitivity to the totality of what is involved,
they speak with pseudo-sophistication of matters about
which they cannot possibly know anything of relevance or
importance to mature sexual fulfillment. They see movies in
which the act of sex is explicit in every physical detail, but
they are too young and immature to understand the deeper
implications of the total interaction between the lovers;
they see magazines that exploit nudity, that titillate the
senses but exclude such deeply integral aspects of sex as
genuine passion and tenderness. Sex becomes a highly
touted commodity, divorced of its humanity. There is the
story told by one young mother, who with her husband
and two young sons worked for two years in the Peace

Corps in Africa; when they returned to the United States they visited the home of an aunt who had just had a baby, and they watched while she gave the baby a bottle. The older boy, eight, wanted to know why the mother did not feed the baby "from her breasts," and when his parents tried to explain, he asked very seriously, "Well, if they don't use their breasts for anything in this country, why do they show naked pictures of them all over?"

We find ourselves relatively helpless in any attempt to help plan or exercise reasonable controls regarding our teen-agers' social activities. One example of many such situations was the group of parents who discovered that after their children had left a teen-age club sponsored by their church and supervised by trained adults, many of the young people had gone to Greenwich Village, had purchased marijuana with no difficulty at all and had then gone to the apartment of some college-age students they had met casually, where they were either participants in or observers of an exhibitionistic "sex game." These were "nice kids" from "nice families"; if they had been growing up twenty-five to fifty years ago, chances of such an encounter would have been considerably less than is the case today, since such unsupervised activities were, to say the least, far more difficult to come by.

Many parents are concerned about the fact that the "new freedom" has tended more and more to lead to a dehumanization, a mechanization of sexuality. No matter how often we may reiterate to our own children that for us sexual relationships are most fulfilling and significant in relation to love and to a mature and responsible concern for another human being, we know perfectly well that they live in the world of Dr. Kinsey's questionnaires and Dr. Masters' di-

rect observations of intercourse, as described in his best-
seller, *Human Sexual Response.* I admit that I can find very
few scientists who share my abhorrence of the work of both
these researchers; I am still convinced that their point of
view about sexuality, as expressed in what I believe to be
the pseudo-scientific nature of their work, is more damaging to the future sexual fulfillment of our children than
were all Cotton Mather's warnings of hellfire and damna-
tion. We have been so busy dissecting sex for the past half-
century that this may well lead to a time when an orgasm
will be evoked by ringing a bell, a conditioned response,
like Pavlov's salivating dogs—without wasting any time on
such decadent notions as courtship, flirtation, affection or
falling in love! Instead of young people's being ignorant
about or frightened or ashamed of sex, they have become
ignorant and frightened and ashamed of love; they know
every minute physiological detail regarding sex, and if they
worry about anything, it is only that maybe they will not
be sexy enough, orgiastic enough, original enough in their
experimentation. Where the Victorian lady may have been
ashamed of the fact that she enjoyed sexual intercourse, her
granddaughter today is only ashamed if she does not enjoy
it "every time." The young Victorian husband, who may
have had some guilt about "demanding physical gratification" from his wife, has grandsons who only feel guilty if
they come home too tired and would prefer to drink a can
of beer in front of the TV set rather than rush off to bed
for more of that great new freedom. By concentrating so
much on the technique of sex, we have divorced it from
feelings; we have in our manuals and in our "objective research investigations" said to our kids, "Better a cold, selfish
lover with skill than a tender compassionate lover who

stumbles a bit." As individual parents we cannot say that we really believe that sex is an integral part of a deep and private human relationship and then, at the same time, as social parents, suggest that one can gain useful and important information about this subject by investigations that re-assert the mechanical, isolated, depersonalized aspects of the physical components of the experience. Our children know that respected scientists have set up laboratories in which men and women are observed during sexual intercourse in the same way that one would study rats or chimpanzees, as though there were no qualitative difference between a private sexual relationship of lovers and one in which microphones, thermometers, cardiographs and cameras are used for recording and observing reactions as though one were experimenting with mechanical electrical robots. I have often wondered, as I have read the statements of these scientists, if (1) they would be willing to have their own children serve as subjects, or (2) if they would be willing to have their own children involved in the research staff, or (3) would they be willing to reverse roles and be the participants themselves—and have their children know about this?

The large majority of people with whom I have argued this matter have ended by saying, "Well, you may have a point, but the research findings will make it all worthwhile." To me that sounds very much like "the ends justify the means"—a point of view that I do not think most of these same scientists would take in matters of social or political action. Whatever choice bits of information may be discovered, it seems to me that in the process we will have so alienated ourselves from passion and tenderness and love that no amount of physiological know-how will do us the slightest bit of good. The attempt to apply the scientific methods of physics to human sexuality will have fragmented it beyond repair. Information, honesty and candor may be admirable and might well have continued to be helpful if there were adequate interpretation of the wholeness of human experience.

Sex is something we *are*, not something we *do*, if we are all of a piece and entirely human. It is this aspect of freedom that has been left out—and which leads to the increasingly common observation among psychotherapists who work with young adults that sexual experimentation may go along swimmingly so long as it involves casual, superficial relationships; when these "free," informed, sophisticated young people fall in love, however, they tend frequently to become impotent and frigid. Advertisers, manufacturers and scientists have taught them *how* to do it, but not *why*.

During all these years of increasing freedom and supposed enlightenment, few people of prominence in the social sciences have come along with as comprehensive and influential a statement, point of view or program that has been in any way as effective as those of the salesmen or the scientists; no group has emerged with equal prominence to insist that we concern ourselves with the *quality* of a relationship, not merely its physical functions. Ministers preach and psychologists and sociologists lecture to the converted, and individual psychotherapists do what they can to repair the psychic damage, and politicians threaten to disenfranchise the out-of-wedlock baby, but where is the social parent, the individual who is able to be not only vocal and impassioned about asserting some values but who can also offer a sound program to protect all our children? We argue violently about including sex education in the school curriculum, at the same time that we know that our children can buy contraceptives in dispensing machines in thousands of gas stations; we deplore the psychological damage of pushing children into inappropriate sexual roles too early, at the same time that we know that every department store sells padded bras to eight- and nine-year-olds. The manufacturer of this equipment for the flat-chested social set must learn to conceive of himself as the father of all the little girls who are providing him with his affluence; the movie producer who provides seduction after seduction on film, who feels it is necessary to graphically present every perversion, every sordid or lurid sexual aberration on the screen in the name of art but in the game of making money, must come to see himself as the parent of every child who comes giggling nervously into his theater. The scientist who is busily poking a minute camera or microphone into some cooperative lady's vagina and then observes and records her every physiological change in the act of intercourse in the name of pure science must face up to the fact that he is the parent of every young person who knows what he is doing, and that he will share responsibility for the quality of sexual maturation and fulfillment—or lack of it—of every youngster who is thereby being assured that sex as a purely physical act has a validity all its own. The advertiser who capitalizes on the insecurities and uncertainties of our children's feelings about sexual inadequacy by exhorting them about the horrors of bad breath, body odor, acne and wrinkles, obesity and curly hair must know that every anxious, pimply-faced, plump, miserably self-conscious teen-ager whom he *terrifies* into purchasing all his junk preparations, as if they would provide masculine virility or feminine attractiveness, is his own child, desperately searching for his own sexual identity.

Without compassion, without tenderness, without a deep
and private personal involvement, sex may become as boring as cleaning one's teeth! Come to think of it, exposure to
a mechanistic view of sex may solve the population explosion; it just won't be worth the bother. Until every adult,
consciously behaving like a social parent, begins to take responsibility for guiding all young people toward an all-
embracing human view of sexuality in the context of relationships, none of us can be fully successful in providing
this kind of orientation for any of our children.

3. *No individual parent can fight the horrors and hazards
that have accompanied the rapid increase in urban living.* As
I sit writing, looking out at part of the New York skyline, I
know that during the past three years of observing this particular view I have watched the deadly pall of smoke increase to such an extent that where three years ago I saw
some of the most exquisite sunrises, there is not a single day
any longer, no matter how cloudless the sky, when the view
is not made ugly and evil by a veil of polluted air. Rachel
Carson was only too painfully right when she wrote, "The
human being is the only animal that fouls its own nest."

What parent wants his child's lungs filled with the pollu-
tants of furnaces, cars and factories? What parent can comfortably accept the process by which our cities become increasingly ugly, barren, dangerous places in which our
children live and grow? We choke ourselves off from sky
and earth, we cut down our trees, we destroy all space for
play, we build more office buildings and highways, we let
millions of cars pour into our cities every day, we encroach
on every wooded area left in our suburbs—and as individual parents, or even as groups of parents, we feel helpless
and impotent to change the tide. Until every individual
feels personally responsible for the careful planning and the

preservation of natural resources, the inexorable destruction will go on.

Speaking at a conference of the Play Schools Association in New York in October 1965, on "A World of Change," the British economist, Barbara Ward (Lady Jackson) stated:

> The rapid growth of urbanization . . . is a problem which seems almost beyond [man's] capacity to deal with creatively. . . . [Cities] are not particularly attractive places in which to live . . . whether you are thinking of Rio de Janeiro, which has four million people and is increasing by 5,000 a week, or of greater Tokyo, which has twenty million; New York comes briskly up behind with twenty million by 1980. London may spread over the whole south of England in the next twenty years. . . . With industry you bring men together in enormous numbers to produce the goods . . . this is the origin of the modern city. It is hardly surprising that the moment anyone has a little bit of income . . . he heads for the suburbs as fast as he can. The trend is to go out and out and out—in search of what you ultimately do not get. . . . The decay of the city based upon a disagreeable industrial structure and the flight outward makes for an uncertain urban structure. . . . The people on the outskirts are unwilling to contribute to the reconstruction of the inside because they feel it is no longer their job. The community itself begins to decay. . . . Cities are worth living in if you work eighty hours a week (as in the past); but if you have to live in them while working twenty-five hours a week, you have an enormous

amount of time. And time in this kind of settlement is intolerable. . . . What comes of this? The worst of all social attitudes; failure of competence and failure of self-respect, deep emotional deprivation of every sort, and finally anger which is just the other side of apathy. It is a world-wide phenomenon—the highly technological society with all its emphasis on consumer goods and consumer satisfactions, creating centers in the cities where people cannot enjoy its benefits.

One example of the mixed blessings and curses of modern society is the automobile. We have gained remarkable mobility—and we may be paying for it with our lives. In Los Angeles, even after years of very careful and responsible research proved that car exhaust was causing the highest percentage of the smog problem, automobile companies tried as hard as they could to avoid accepting responsibility and providing the safeguards that were necessary. They hired their own researchers and attempted for several years to disprove the fact of the automobile's considerable responsibility for the smog. Only when the outrage of the voting public reached the proportions necessary for getting protective legislation passed did the car manufacturers begin to accept defeat, but they are still trying to squirm out of responsibility. This is another example of the problem of low visibility in a mass society; if, from the beginning, each manufacturer had thought to himself, "I am the father of every child who is breathing in car exhausts," could he hold out? If there had been that sense of immediate and personal involvement, what father would want his own children to know that when Ralph Nader brought the nation's attention to the physical dangers in the present construction of cars, he and his associates had hired a private detective to try to discredit Mr. Nader's judgments? If every automobile manufacturer could see every individual child killed or maimed in accidents due to poor design, how long would it take to redesign cars for greater safety?

Without that sense of personal responsibility, protection of any of our children is impossible. Only when a city is close to destruction, only when the financial risk becomes too great, is action likely to be taken. In Pittsburgh, after the Second World War, when industry was expanding rapidly, the pollution of the air had reached such a point that industrial leaders found that they could not entice families to move there to work in the new plants. Then, and only then—when a city was poisoning itself out of existence—were the means found for a massive clean-the-air campaign. If, 150 years ago, in a small town, a single blacksmith's shop had produced fumes lethal enough to envelop his own neighborhood, he would have been forced to accept a sense of personal culpability for creating a health hazard for his own and everyone's children as they walked to and from school. That was easy; one's deeds were seen and felt with immediacy, a high visibility. It will take a completely new kind of imagination and sense of social responsibility for a Con Edison official, located in a sprawling city, with his own children safely installed in a neighboring suburb, to understand that he is responsible for the air breathed by all children—and that if he does not accept this burden, his own suburban hideaway will soon be unsafe.

Similarly, in a small town with one or two schools parents knew very quickly if they had to spend a little more money for better teachers; they felt the impact of any deficiency in curriculum or discipline; they knew that if they did not repair the school roof, it might fall in on their own children's heads, or if an epidemic occurred because the town stream was polluted, their own children might die; and so it was easier to enlist community responsibility. Today, in our big cities, inhabited so extensively by the poor who must be near their places of work, often newcomers uprooted from other less urban environments who fill the unskilled jobs, where the problems and needs grow greater every day, it is exceedingly difficult to get people to care enough to really commit themselves and their resources to even protecting themselves from future disaster. Commuters, who need the city to work in, the wealthy who also suffer inevitably from increasing crime rates, increasing rates of mental illness, fires, dirt, violence, poor means of transportation, the dangers of increasing numbers of unemployable people of discontented, warped human lives— people who will inhabit this earth with their own growing children—are outraged by the prospect of having to pay for the social and educational services that might remove city blight; the goal is too removed, too impersonal, too indirect.

In a series of articles in *The New Yorker*, which later appeared as a book, *Our Children are Dying* (Viking, 1966), Nat Hentoff described the work and the philosophy of an outstanding and dedicated man, Dr. Elliott Shapiro, principal of Public School 119 in Harlem. The book tells of the pervasive and overwhelming problems of the children and their families, of the teachers who were trying against unbelievable odds to help relieve the agonies of psychological and social deprivation. Dr. Shapiro emerges as a creative, inventive, compassionate human being, deeply committed to his work, courageously struggling against city blight and bureaucratic red tape in order to provide remarkable innovations in education; one is left with little doubt that this kind of person, in an important and responsible position of authority over the lives of youngsters, might very well be able to help the most socially deprived of our children to become self-respecting, self-fulfilling human beings, as well as responsible and useful citizens. At about the time of the publication of this report on an outstanding school program, Dr. Shapiro was offered a job in Rochester, N. Y. —an opportunity for research, demonstration and training of others—that reflected an appreciation of his great gifts. But Dr. Shapiro insisted that before accepting this appointment, those who had requested his services must first obtain a statement from the New York City Board of Education that the city system was willing to see him leave. Such an inquiry was made, and Rochester was informed that the New York Board of Education had "nothing special in mind for Dr. Shapiro." Rather than applauding and encouraging talent and dedication, we are almost relieved to see it slip away.

There are always some very special, idealistic, creative, dedicated people who devote their lives to trying to bring the world a little closer to their own special inner vision of what it might be like, and it is a heartbreaking experience when one sees such people working to the limit of their strength and vitality to solve problems of city life, constantly badgered and burdened by lack of funds. I recently visited a large industrial city in which some years ago there had been serious race rioting. Since that time, with less money than we spend in one week in the war in Vietnam, imaginative and exciting programs had been initiated to solve some of the awful problems of the poor and deprived in this city.

The social workers, teachers, psychologists and others involved in these programs were talented and committed—in-
spiringly so. At one point I sat in on a meeting of some of
the people involved in this city's anti-poverty program
when the chairman was called out suddenly by an emergency meeting of the City Council. When he came back, he
announced that 30 per cent of the funds needed for the following year's projects had been withdrawn. The dedication, the willingness to invent and to make do, the individual investment of time and talent and hope and the excellent
results of two years of intensive work, with very little
money to begin with, were now so conveniently dismissed
that it was possible that the whole program might collapse.
This is a typical example of the "un-parenting" that is part
of urban life. Despite the obvious and crying need for programs that can help to prevent some of the worst results of
the dying city, the wherewithal was gone; the city would
go on paying for prisons, policemen, firemen, courts—all
the services needed to counteract the failures in a community—but it was necessary to accept the fact that it was not
yet possible to get enough people so concerned that they
would invest in preventive-treatment programs.

The inevitable bigness and anonymity of modern life has
given low visibility to charity—to compassion for those
who suffer. It was so much easier to take a Christmas basket
to a poor family or to collect warm clothing for families
caught in a flood or to help to rebuild a farm destroyed by
fire. Even when, as a nation, we want to express our concern for the distress of part of our population, the institutions developed to carry out such socially responsible and
caring services become so big that those involved often find
themselves beaten and bowed under the strain of red tape

and depersonalization. In essence, the anti-poverty program has, in the deepest and best sense, the qualities of charity and brotherhood; but the numbers involved are so tremendous, and the implementation of responsibility becomes, almost without anyone's wishing it, bogged down in problems of administration. Several years ago I received a letter from a friend who was directing one of the most inventive and promising of the anti-poverty programs in a midwestern city. His despair was typical of the kinds of problems involved in a mass society. He wrote:

> I have been overwhelmed by a devastating attack of a new disease known as "impersonalized bureaucracy." We are being bombarded by emergency calls from OEO [Office of Economic Opportunity] related to "immediately needed" figures, statements, papers and contracts, while we try to prepare our budget, revise our budget, cut our budget, rewrite our budget, etc. All this seems so devoid of human concern and feeling; here it is June 27th and we have not even been funded to continue after June 30th. The result of this attack on my sensibilities and humanity is that every new request for more statistics, papers, numbers, etc., finds me falling into a worse state of depression. What is so frightening is that the top officials relate to us solely in terms of budgets, costs and procedures. No one knows what we are doing, no one seems to care. No one has visited us . . . no one seems to care about the meaning of our work, only the effect of our work once this has been translated into statistics. . . . I get an all-pervading feeling of failure—until all the details are settled, and I am free to go back to the people and to

work with them—but by then I am too beaten to feel the joy or pleasure there might have been.

Until every adult is every child's parent, there will never be enough money or enough ways found for a more humanitarian approach to implementing programs that might save our cities. One example of the kind of person who can focus on this problem in such a way as to become this needed social parent is Barbara Ward. In the same speech mentioned earlier, she outlined some of the ways in which individually and collectively we could begin to come to terms with the problems of decaying cities. She compared the problems of the city to private homes and how we plan there. She said:

> In the home we make certain distinctions about functions of rooms and corridors; we do not deliver the groceries straight into the baby's crib. In hospitals we do not take the food trolleys right through the operating chamber, and we rarely have the recreation room next to the convalescent room. We sort out the functions. We have to sort out the functions of the city and the streams of traffic and re-create arterial systems that allow us to breathe . . . rest rooms, recreation rooms, rooms for family living, should have the security, the shape, pattern and sense of community which you expect if it were a house.

She went on to describe an "Education Park," which would be a place planned for children, including schools and safe playgrounds in one setting. She said that this kind of urban renewal is going to cost money and asked if constructive change is too costly, observing that "one good riot" costs more than to keep a good recreation program running for a generation. She said that we would develop a different perspective on cost if we were to consider the addicts, the delinquents, the crime, the enormous network of violence that has to be prevented as a result of sending into the world children who ultimately grow up with so little confidence and so little knowledge as to who they are and what they can do that they turn to violence. In an economy of such great wealth and growth as ours, we need to develop new attitudes toward what it is worth spending on:

> One of the problems of going to the moon is to make a capsule for the space man which will keep him alive in a difficult environment. Isn't it worth spending a small portion of that amount [needed for space travel] on creating a rather larger capsule for the child so he can live in the somewhat dangerous atmosphere of the modern city? Why do we accept as normal the infinite trouble, the infinite investment, the infinite care put into having people live and breathe on the moon and don't give a damn whether they live and breathe in the Bronx?

In one of the cities affected by the acute water shortage several years ago, the city fathers decided that it would not be possible to allow the park sprinklers to be used even in the worst of the summer's heat. There was a reaction of outrage on the part of some citizens, who pointed out that the rule against watering lawns and washing cars had been lifted in outlying suburban areas. After several days the announcement was made that the park sprinklers would be turned on, after all. And one member of the City Council in a TV interview commented, "I thought of how I would feel if my own child wasn't allowed to play in his wading pool in the back yard, while he watched me washing the car—and somehow the whole thing seemed indecent." That is the simple, direct kind of social parenting that is needed to restore our cities and save our city children.

4. *Individual parents find themselves totally unable to cope with the pressures on their children to buy merchandise that is useless and unnecessary.* Living as we do in an economy of abundance which depends on the built-in obsolescence of goods and on luxury buying, it was hardly surprising that children would become the most important market for the non-necessities, the junk products of such an economy. We have moved so far away from an economy of goods for survival that we are even made to feel unpatriotic by some of our national leaders if we do not purchase luxury goods beyond our means. There are those brave and rugged individualists who somehow manage, despite the pressures, to keep the old car running for ten years, and who will not buy a washing machine until they can pay for it in full—but this is a vanishing breed of adults; when it comes to children, they are almost invariably herd creatures, who want what "everyone else" has, and victims of incessant and savagely insatiable impulse buying. It is the nature of childhood to want anything that may provide some momentary pleasure or gratification; by the time they may have curbed some of these childish appetites, they are adolescents, and so beset by anxiety and confusion about what it takes to be grown up that they are easy prey for any promise that guarantees success in the struggle to grow up. In an affluent society in which parents themselves buy goods far beyond the necessities of life, manufacturers and advertisers know perfectly well that children can bring

enough pressure to bear on parents to buy anything—if they scream loud enough.

The New York Times Magazine (June 5, 1966) published an article by Charles and Bonnie Remsberg entitled "Wooing the 'Dimply, Pimply.'" This, they said, was the phrase used by a New York sales consultant to describe the promotional campaign aimed at the teen-age market.

> Aided by a growing stable of researchers, promotion artists, public relations experts, merchandising consultants, ad agency psychologists, and others who specialize in converting quirks of the teen-age psyche into cash receipts, our economy is mounting the biggest youth-kick ever. . . . The cult of teen-age worship is rapidly spreading from the traditional industries—phonograph records, movies and soda pop—into practically every other area of retailing. . . . "A businessman has to get interested in teen-agers when he sees the statistics, no matter what he's selling," observes Lester Rand, head of New York's Youth Research Institute.

The authors reported that there are more than twenty-five million young people in the United States between the ages of thirteen and nineteen, with more than $18 billion in earnings, gifts, allowances and family hand-outs. By 1970 there will be approximately thirty million, with disposable incomes totaling $30 billion. The article goes on to point out that manufacturers are well aware of the influence youngsters have on parent purchases as well, and many of their promotional campaigns are aimed at influencing kids to influence their parents.

What amazes me is that nobody quoted in this article is the least bit ashamed of what he is doing. These "ad agency psychologists" seem to have one major goal: to search out the insecurities, the hidden dreams, the vulnerability of children, so as to sell them more and more goods they do not need and that may even be bad for them, such as hormone skin creams, fake nails and hair bleaches and dyes.

We have time and we have money; we have food, clothing and shelter; the idea that continued economic growth depends on drowning ourselves in junk is puzzling to a non-economist like myself. It just does not seem to make sense that we must all become, and allow our children to become, mindless, insatiable, infantile consumers, when there seem to be so many things we *really* need to do as social parents in providing better homes and schools and hospitals and recreation centers and social services for all our children.

Two out of every five teen-agers have charge accounts; a $2.5 million dollar shopping center for teen-agers only has been built in California; the *New York Times* article mentioned earlier concludes: " 'If you haven't struck the shimmering, glimmering teen-age lode,' market consultant Bernice Fitz-Gibbon told 1,500 leading merchants meeting in New York, 'there must be something wrong with you!' "

Under this kind of pressure parents feel hopeless and impotent to stem the tide. A mother who feels a deep sense of outrage that her pre-pubertal daughter of ten should be concerned about looking like a woman in full bloom cannot endure her child's anxiety and genuine heartbreak if she should insist that it is too early for bras; how can a child of ten be asked to stand alone in a gym locker, the only one who still wears an undershirt? The father who knows that he is robbing his son of the pride and the pleasure in his own accomplishments when there is no personal effort or work in the acquisition of such expensive "toys" as cars, boats, private telephones and hi-fi sets finds himself fighting a war against the thousands of fathers who derive gratification and pleasure from satisfying every whim of their children, who may use things as a substitute for attention and affection, or for whom material possessions symbolize success and social prestige.

My husband and I found ourselves appalled, several years ago, to discover the amount of, and the frequency with which our teen-age daughter and her friends were using, mud packs, face masks and skin conditioners; here were these lovely, healthy, beautiful fifteen-year-old faces, with skin perfectly capable, in the first flush of youth, of keeping itself glowing with the help of a little soap and water—and they were behaving like narcissistic women of sixty or seventy, who cannot bear to grow old. "I don't know what to do to stop this," I started to say—firmly believing that there must be *something* one could do. My husband brought me back to reality quickly by saying, "Yes, there are two things you can do; you can send your daughter to a nunnery, or you can round up every single person who makes, advertises and sells this garbage and personally make them put it on the faces of their own children." If there will ever be an end to the demoralizing effects of too-much-too-soon and too-much-that's-no-good, it may well take that kind of action and the reappraisal it would inevitably bring.

5. *No parent alone can create a moral climate conducive to decent human relationships.* During the Eisenhower administration there was a scandal at West Point relating to cheating on examinations. Shortly after several young men had been very severely punished, the U-2 incident took place, during which at first President Eisenhower categorically denied that we had reconnaissance flights over Russia;

that is, until the evidence of the captured plane itself made it necessary to change the story. At this point a sociologist suggested that cheating on exams at West Point was good practice for the subterfuge, hypocrisy and downright lying that seemed to be a necessary part of maneuvering in politics and international affairs. We lecture our children on the immorality of bribes, of "special interest," of stealing and a hundred other offenses—and as soon as our children are old enough to read, they follow in the newspapers the shenanigans of a Bobby Baker, an Adam Clayton Powell or a Jimmy Hoffa, and they know that what we are really saying, in effect, is that such morals are not for *children!*

The greatest internal moral crisis this country has faced has been the problem of racial equality. The issue is not complicated at all—it is perfectly simple: a certain number of American citizens do not have the rights and privileges guaranteed by the Constitution of the United States. It is quite clear to the majority of the nation's adults (whether they admit it or not) that this situation should have been rectified long ago, and that whether it sits well with everyone or not, things must be changed. With TV in almost every home, our children have been witnesses to some of the most degrading scenes of inhumanity, of ignorant and outrageous demonstrations of immorality; fire hoses and dogs turned on children and old people; Negro children walking with dignity into a school, while white mothers scream and hurl rotten vegetables at them; the discovering of the bodies of three young American men, buried in a dam, for following the principles outlined in the Bill of Rights; a young white mother of five shot and killed for riding in a car with a Negro.

Our children know that some of the very social and reli-

gious institutions which supposedly are most concerned
with the guarding of morality have managed to move so
slowly on one moral issue after another, in order to do
things "safely," that they have lost their influence and cannot control the naked furies of the most ignorant and primi-
tive elements in our society. What we *hear* is, "We have to
move very slowly in order to change men's hearts"—but
what our children *learn* is, "It is possible to equivocate
about what is right and what is wrong, and let me, as your
adult leader, teach you how to do it."

Another moral issue which faces mankind is whether or
not we are willing to take responsibility for seeing to it that
our children and grandchildren have room in which to live.
The issue of the population explosion is so vast, the future
consequences so frightening, that one can hardly comprehend their full implications. Without a major war, a nuclear
holocaust, a great famine or plague, this planet will, in the
next few generations, provide standing room only for the
world's population. But long before that day the psychological stresses placed on human beings who are crowded
together, who are deprived of space, privacy and quiet, will
cause increasing eruptions of violence—a social savagery
that threatens all mankind. Individual concern, personal responsibility for one's own family alone, can never provide
answers to these problems. Social parenting demands a realistic concern, an acceptance of the universal necessity for
birth control, for legalized abortions and for effective programs to encourage family planning. While some speak pi-
ously of "destroying human life," I walk through the
streets of New York City, and I see such *hatred* of children! Weary teachers are screaming in playgrounds
mobbed by too many children, harassed and exhausted par-

ents are screaming out of tenement windows and passersby are screaming at "those damn young hoodlums." Typical of the "brilliant" solutions being devised to deal with the miserable, rejected, deprived and understandably hostile children of New York City was a radio news report of a Board of Education plan for a "Brat Patrol" in the school hallways, when a group of junior-high-school teachers went out on strike because of disciplinary problems in the schools. No one would be foolish enough to deny the real and present dangers in the schools, but it would be equally hard to deny the hatred of children expressed in this "solution." There are more children than anybody really wants; and from the fury and misery in the eyes of these children one knows that human life is being destroyed very thoroughly and very completely. But we insist on waiting until these children are born and old enough to feel, and then we reject their existence. What we desperately need is the social parent who can understand that the laws and legislation he accepts or opposes will directly affect the problem of whether or not human life may be utterly destroyed within a century or two.

Certainly the moral issues of war and peace affect the moral climate in which our children are growing up, and here, of course, the issues are anything but simple. It does seem to me, however, that no matter how complex and subtle these may be, it is immoral for adults to vilify those young people who, whether well advised or ill advised, suggest by their actions and their statements that there *must* be some better solutions to major problems of intertional relations than war. Next to "drop-out" and "underachiever," the most despised epithet for youth is "draft-card burner." It seems to me that the social parent is obliged to extend his sympathy, his compassion and his support of their right to act, whatever his own beliefs may be, to those young people who are wrestling with the most vital moral issue of our times: whether or not human beings can learn to live together in peace.

Dr. Spock is an excellent example of a man who has realized that becoming a father to all children, by providing medical advice on questions of child care, was not enough; to really help children grow well in their own families, it was necessary to help to make the world safe for all those individual children. Whether or not one agrees with his stand in heading SANE, his concern for peace in Vietnam and the need for test-ban treaties (I do), it is clear that he has accepted personal moral involvement and has truly taken responsibility for "fathering" the world's children in a decisive and meaningful way. The way he feels is the way we all have to learn to feel; that all of us, in any role or in any sphere of our personal, professional, business, public or private lives, must assume responsibility for protecting all children, according to our own personal views and values.

Social parenting involves the capacity to become involved and to make decisions—to take personal responsibility for others and for oneself. It is a quality that must become a more intrinsic part of our children's education, if we want them to become social parents. Dr. Alice Keliher in a recent issue of *Childhood Education* wrote: "Decision-making is a basic part of education for life in a democracy. It calls for practice. Through successful sharing of planning and carrying out decisions comes the essential attitude of *wanting* to be involved." An example of the failure to do this in education is a Westchester school in which the head of the guidance department called a white mother into the school to tell her that her tenth-grade daughter was "getting too involved" with a Negro boy classmate. The mother was told that Janice was "emotionally disturbed," that she was expressing her lack of self-confidence in a neurotic way and that the relationship must be discouraged. The frantic mother sought help outside the school, insisting that her daughter be seen by a psychiatrist, despite Janice's fury at all the adults involved. Fortunately for all, the psychiatrist reported that while it was true that Janice was shy and somewhat inept socially, she and her young friend were being wonderfully helpful to each other —confiding their uncertainties to each other, writing poetry about their problems which they shared with each other, and that in general "this was a tender and compassionate relationship, unlikely to cause any serious problems if the young people were given some respect for their feelings and good judgment." When the mother investigated further, she discovered that whenever a "mixed couple" was observed in this school, both were tested and interviewed by the school guidance personnel and were told that they were "acting out" in a neurotic way. There are, of course, all kinds of situations in which young people may need help in understanding their motivations for behavior that may be hurtful to them, but such a narrow-minded and arbitrary approach to a complex social issue, disregarding the necessary and inevitable changes in social relationships among all young people, deprive them of the opportunities to make decisions about their own involvement. Given a fair and respectful opportunity to make decisions in an atmosphere in which there can be free and honest discussion of the issues and the consequences of involvement, it is my impression that our young people have much they can teach us. If we want our children to grow up feeling a deep sense of commitment to the moral issues of their times, we have to back them up.

Several years ago in a Long Island suburb three high-school youngsters refused to participate in an air-raid drill on the grounds that they believed there could not be any real protection against atomic bombs and that it was dangerous to present any group of citizens with a false sense of safety or hope where none existed; it would be more fruitful to fight harder for nuclear test-ban treaties, and to solve international crises by peaceful means than to pretend we could be safe any other way. These young people were good students, popular with their classmates, getting along well at home—they were rebels *with* a cause. After being threatened with very serious retaliatory punishment, two of the three youngsters gave in; their parents had become terrified, they warned their children that further action might affect their chances of getting into good colleges, they went to school to placate the principal, they groveled and they insisted that their children beg for forgiveness, even though the parents themselves agreed with their children's stand. Only one set of parents took their daughter's side; they told Anne exactly what the difficulties and the price might be, and they said they would stand by her right to protest. When she became really terrified herself, they encouraged her not to give in. At one point, losing all control over his anger at this "defiance," the principal told Anne she might have to be sent to reform school; she was threatened with expulsion and warned that this might keep her out of college permanently. During a period of suspension, the principal forbade her teachers to supply her with her class or homework assignments. The parents were asked if this child had ever been to see a psychiatrist, and it was suggested that now might be a good time—since she was obviously unable to accept adult authority. The psychological pressures became so great that Anne herself began to feel that she must have been entirely in the wrong. Her parents kept insisting that her original protest had not in any way warranted the kind of threats and punishments she received. Her father fought the situation out; it eventually involved the entire school system in this community, the newspapers and the local government. One father, taking a stand, started other fathers thinking—and within a few weeks, a reaction began to set in. Anne was cleared of charges, reinstated, given a chance to make up her work; she has since entered an excellent college, without the slightest difficulty, despite continued active participation in social issues. One father could not do it alone; but by taking the first stand, he inspired others to share the responsibility and to move in a positive direction.

There are situations in which individual parents, even taking a stand themselves, cannot change the parenting in a community; but they have to take the stand anyway. An example occurred when a family were to move from a suburban community into a neighboring city and wanted to encourage a Negro family to buy their house in what had always been a white community. They notified various civil-rights organizations that they were about to move and that the house was available if they knew any families that might be interested in buying it. The three adolescent children in the family were tremendously involved in this project. They discussed it with pride with their friends, and for a while it seemed that the children would have the great gift of self-respect for doing something they believed was right. As it turned out, there were not enough "social parents" in the neighborhood to make this possible. Out of perhaps 150 families, five supported this action. The others were so vocal, so challenging and threatening, the climate became so frightening, that no Negro family with young children was willing to take the chance of moving in. The project was given up; ten parents lost out to 300 in trying to create a moral climate for children. And yet, despite their ultimate defeat, health is as contagious as disease, and sooner or later, those ten parents will still count in having at least started an inevitable course of change.

The indulgence, the over-permissiveness, which is destroying the moral fiber of so many kids is probably partly due to the guilt of individual parents about their failure to do anything to parent all children. If you lose the war, at least you think maybe you can win one small battle; you couldn't or didn't even try to get that public beach built— so you give your own children a motorboat; you didn't quite get to that meeting to protest about the lack of traffic lights near the school—so you buy your own child a car. I once stayed at a large New York hotel during a busy spring week end during which hundreds of college students traditionally came to the city. They had just taken over the hotel: they ran in packs, swarming through hallways, the dining rooms, the lobby. The noise was incredible, the vandalism hard to believe. They were disturbing to all the other guests all night long. Rooms were mobbed with drinking, shouting, singing kids. Couples were necking all over the place in the most blatant display of bad taste and exhibitionism. The hotel officials looked angry and uncomfortable—but they also behaved as though they were help-

less. The same has been true when things have begun to get
out of hand at the Newport Jazz festival, or on the Florida
or California beaches—until matters reach riot proportions,
and the police or National Guard have to be sent for. Long
before that, all adults, responsible for all children, should
have been planning: what was to be allowed, what was unsafe; alternative activities provided by a community for
spirited kids in ever-increasing numbers. We expect this of
individual families—but in the communities in which we all
live, we do not have that same sense of responsibility. We
do not provide the needed resources for control and man-
agement of young people too immature to control and
manage themselves.

It has seemed to me that these young people, full of defiance, with hot contempt in their eyes, are really asking us to
begin to act like parents; not angry policemen, but parents
who really care—who out of love and concern provide the
resources and rules that are needed by children. The message comes through loud and clear in a story told me by a
friend who was walking along a beach and saw, scrawled in
the sand, "Parents Do Not Exist." The more rebellious and
defiant they are, the more openly and flagrantly our young
people show their contempt for all authority, the more
clear it seems to me that they are begging us for meaning in
their lives, and for controls when they cannot create them
for themselves. The father of two teen-agers once said to
me, "You know, I have to re-learn it over and over again—I
don't know why it's so hard for our generation to believe
it: I guess we've been brain-washed—but every time I really get good and fed up and finally put my foot down
about something, these kids are so *relieved!* They calm
down, they become quite attractive and lovable—and you

have to really watch it, because the minute you get lazy or try to be genial and palsy—boy, off they go again, into the wild blue yonder!"

Young people today have made it quite clear that they are hungry for standards and that they are capable of being courageous and can act with integrity. In the face of endangering their own security, college students have protested against selective service rules which favor *them;* despite personal danger, great unhappiness and discomfort to their families, most of the peace demonstrators are not exhibitionistic rebels without a cause. The majority really know what hazards they are creating for themselves and others; and whether or not one can sympathize with their point of view, there is a kind of purity in their insistence on doing what they feel was right. They may sometimes be naive, even childish, but they are capable of a kind of personal commitment, far beyond what many of their parents would be willing to accept. I will never forget seeing in the films made in the aftermath of the floods in Florence the faces of the young people who came from all over the world to help save a rich and magnificent cultural heritage. They looked so alive, so at peace, as they worked around the clock for no other reward than to have participated in a noble enterprise.

There are beginning to be some hopeful signs that "social parenting" is at least beginning—that there is an increasing awareness of this necessity, for the safety and well-being of all children. This has happened in isolated places throughout the country with regard to certain special issues. It has always been true around disaster situations, so I am not speaking of those. A flood or a fire activates that "old-fashioned" pioneer, rural, small-town sense of group parenthood, in which everybody works to save everybody's children. I am thinking of the newer and more complicated issues of our modern life that require this same view but which have not traditionally evoked similar concern.

For example, there is a community in Pennsylvania where, whenever a child under the age of sixteen gets into trouble with the law, he is placed in custody of a juvenile officer who in turn "passes sentence." He has behind him a corps of volunteers who serve as "probation officers" or big brothers and sisters. Any child who steals a bicycle, or cosmetics from a department store, for example, rather than being committed to a detention home or reform school or just getting a warning, must be referred to the voluntary counseling service. The community realized that it was wrong to treat youngsters like adult criminals, but it was equally wrong to ignore their misdeeds. Adapted from a Swedish system, and started by a local minister, this project was first set up by a board of community leaders made up of police, clergy, businessmen, educators, social workers and the like. They then sought out suitable volunteers and started with about fifteen people who were "on call" for Saturday counseling sessions. Workshops were set up for these counselors, where they were given orientation and guidance by professional specialists in the community. The program starts when a child is apprehended. The juvenile officer meets with the child and his parents, and if he feels it appropriate, he refers the child to twelve one-hour counseling sessions. In actual practice the relationship may continue for a much longer period, or, if the relationship does not work out well, the child may be transferred to another counselor. It takes some time to convince the children that these sessions are not for the purpose of punishment but are motivated by a genuine wish to help the youngster with his problems. For many of the children this may be the first time that anyone has taken a genuine interest in them. The counselor often functions as a kind of substitute parent for children of poverty and neglect, from broken homes or large families where parents do not have the resources to serve as models to their children. A typical case was that of Mike, who was picked up for theft. He was living with his alcoholic father, who said he did not care what they did with Mike when he was caught. At first Mike was tough and defiant with the local businessman who became his counselor; but only five weeks later he went to the juvenile officer and asked if a counselor could be assigned to his younger brother, "to help him *before* he gets himself into trouble." In some cases the youngsters are expected to make amends immediately for what they have done, by replacing shrubbery, cleaning a defaced wall and so on. There has been a notable decrease in second offenders. Naturally there have been difficulties, mistakes and failures, but the results have been exceedingly promising. This does something good for all the children, including the children of the counselors themselves, who receive the precious gift of pride in what their parents are doing to help others.

Another example that seems small and simple at first glance but that has the same quality of concern and involvement, took place in a suburban town with a very dirty river. One woman decided that it was time to clean up the river, which had been used for a dumping ground for more than twenty years. She started a personal crusade to do something about this. Before she was finished, a whole town had turned out one morning to participate in the project. Fathers wearing hip boots borrowed from the local fire department dragged old refrigerators, rusty beer cans, old bed springs, tires, and machine parts, to the shores of the river; their sons and daughters carted the refuse of many years to town trucks, borrowed for the day. Campfire Girls served coffee and cupcakes they had baked themselves, and the Garden Club volunteered to landscape the river banks. How did one woman become a "community parent"? She started with her neighbors and friends, as well as church and civic women's groups, who put signs on their cars when they went shopping or to the railroad station to meet commuting husbands, announcing the clean-up campaign, so that everybody in the town knew about it. The high-school chorus wrote songs about the project and played them all over town from loudspeakers in cars. The clean-up day became an exciting community event, in which everyone wanted a part. "The idea is involvement," the lady who started the whole thing said. "The next time someone sees anybody throwing something in *our* river, they aren't going to sit by and watch!"

This kind of action does not have to happen in small towns only, where it has always been far easier to deal with the "high visibility" of a problem known to all. Neighborhoods can do the same thing—in three or four square blocks that can become "a town of concern and involvement." In a large city one woman realized that the reason she feared her Puerto Rican neighbors was that she did not understand what they were saying. One day she walked into a community center and said she wanted to know if a class could be set up for learning Spanish. This developed into an informal discussion group, led by Puerto Rican neighbors, volunteering to teach Spanish while also learning more English themselves. The program provided a meaningful sense of participation and prestige to the rejected minority group.

It is not the size of the communities in which we live nor the complexities of our problems that are any excuse for apathy or indifference. All it really takes is a beginning somewhere, as an individual, to respond with fervor, imagination and dedication to the immediate and pressing social needs of all our children. It will not be easy—it has not been the custom of the whole human race to take the initiative. It is far easier to live one's own life as pleasantly and comfortably as possible, hoping that no crisis will arise in which we will have to take a stand and be counted. But we simply cannot afford the luxury of uninvolvement any longer. Edward Albee's recent play *A Delicate Balance* seemed to me to be an eloquent statement of the challenge we face. He tells of a comfortable, suburban couple, Agnes and Tobias, who have their own internal family problems and who are faced suddenly by a visit from a couple who have been their friends for many years. Edna and Harry arrive unexpectedly and announce that they want to come and live with Agnes and Tobias "because we are afraid." The play deals with the question of whether or not we are required to respond to the needs of others; of how we react as individuals and family members to the human agonies, the loneliness, the desperate search for human warmth and compassion of those around us. Are we our brother's keeper? Can we afford to go on, isolated, separated from one another, nursing our private nightmares, or are we ready to begin to understand the ways in which we must be able to respond to the needs of others in order to give meaning to our own lives? It is "a delicate balance," indeed, and when Tobias finds that he cannot really offer succor, even to old friends, he nevertheless begs them to stay, saying, "I find my liking

you has limits, BUT THOSE ARE MY LIMITS! NOT YOURS!
. . . that's my poverty." We are left with the sense that
there is a "plague" alive in our world—a plague of terror,
of separateness, that makes us unable to reach out to others
and to share their suffering. Can we say, "Yes, I'll take your
plague, no matter what the cost"? Albee makes it clear that
this is our dilemma, the terrifying challenge of our times,
and as his hero cries in anguish about his limitations, we begin to realize that there is no alternative for civilized men
except to begin to take responsibility for each other's lives.
If we truly dare to be alive and human ourselves, we must
accept the commitment, however painful and terrifying, to
care about each other. In the play, Agnes tells her husband,
"Your house is not in order, sir," as they try to face the
question of involvement in the human distress that has invaded their lives. As individual parents, our houses cannot
be in order until we can overcome our limitations, our impoverishment of spirit and can accept the "plagues" of mankind and make them all our own.

Several years ago a TV news program showed a little
Negro girl weeping as she was being led into a forcibly in-
tegrated school amid the fury of the mob around her. A
reporter asked her, "Are you coming back tomorrow?" and
the weeping child said, "Yes, I have to." Until we can echo
that "Yes, I have to," no child anywhere will have the parenting he needs.

ELEVEN

"Let Me Be How I Grow": The Sacredness of Childhood

BECAUSE this book is essentially about how one grows up to be truly and deeply oneself, the line "let me be how I grow" has been a kind of background music all the way along. When I was about six years old, there was much discussion between my parents and the dentist about whether or not I needed to have orthodontia. It was a relatively new procedure in those prehistoric days, and they did not want to wait until adolescence, as I believe is usually done today. When I heard what was involved, I said with a good deal of feeling, "Why can't you let me *be how I grow?*" The orthodontist won out as far as my teeth were concerned—but all through the years of my childhood I sensed that my question had a deeper meaning than I could fully understand at the time. As an adult, I finally came to understand what I had been saying, and I have spent a good part of my adult life in exploring what it means to "be how I grow." I have learned that the closer I get to being myself, to finding my own way, to living out whatever is special and important to me, the more creative I become, the more understanding and compassionate toward others; the more I am contented and accepting of life, the more civilized I become.

Our intrinsic possibilities are there when we are born, they are there as we grow. To the degree that we permit a child to unfold himself, he can have the kind of deep sense of personal fulfillment that I am describing; the degree to which we arbitrarily manipulate nature will be the degree to which our children become puppets—twisted out of shape, never again quite the selves they were meant by nature to be. John Holt, in the November 1965 issue of *Redbook*, wrote:

> We can think of ourselves not as teachers but as gardeners. A gardener does not "grow" flowers; he tries to give them what he thinks will help them grow, and they grow by themselves. A child's mind, like a flower, is a living thing. We can't make it grow by sticking things onto it any more than we can make a flower grow by gluing on leaves and petals. All we can do is surround the growing mind with what it needs for growing, and have faith that it will take what it needs and will grow.

Our basic problem is that we have "conquered nature" in a scientific sense, and in so doing we have lost respect and reverence for that part of nature which we must never try to conquer—the living minds of living men. What is sacred about childhood is that it is the beginning, the essence of human life, the potential and the promise of individual uniqueness, which we cannot predict and which we therefore must not try to harness—for when we do, we restrict the possibilities. No one has understood this or said it better than Jean Jacques Rousseau, who had this reverence for nature and for "natural man"; and despite the sophistication of our technological age, our sense of power over nature, we need somehow to return to his understanding of childhood:

> Hold childhood in reverence and do not be in any hurry to judge it for good or ill. Give nature time to work before you take over her tasks, lest you interfere with her method. . . . Nature wants children to be children before they are men. If we deliberately depart from this order we shall get premature fruits which are neither ripe nor well flavored and which soon decay. We shall have youthful sages and grown-up children. Childhood has ways of seeing, thinking and feeling peculiar to itself; nothing can be more foolish than to substitute our ways for them.

How do we go about providing that "garden" in which a child has an opportunity to find himself, to do his own growing? We do it first of all by respecting *time*. Genuine individual growth simply cannot be rushed or forced. The unfolding of human personality cannot be arranged, it cannot be forced into a convenient or efficient time schedule. We need to watch and listen—waiting for the child to give us the cue that he needs some new challenge, some special enrichment. If we let him, *he* will bring his questions, *he* will demand to know.

Growing takes place best when we permit times for quiet and reflection, when we respect the fact that sometimes the best growing is going on when we can see it least. In the front of A. E. Hotchner's book *Papa Hemingway* (Random

House, 1966) he cites a quotation of Hemingway's which is the essential plea of the creative mind: "There are some things which cannot be learned quickly, and time, which is all we have, must be paid heavily for their acquiring. They are the very simplest things, and because it takes a man's life to know them the little new that each man gets from life is very costly and the only heritage he has to leave." The truly creative person has always understood this, and respected the quality of time. When we rush our children into clever performance of skills, when we organize their daily lives so that there is not a moment for inner contemplation, we decrease the possibility of genuine thought and individual growth. Typical of our modern children was the little boy who was studying the Ten Commandments in Sunday school and did not understand what the word "covet" meant. After the teacher had explained this to him, she suggested that he try to use it in a sentence. He did: "I go to school six days a week, I take violin lessons, I go to Scout meetings and I go to dancing school. I covet the kids who have time to do nothing."

Doing "nothing" is really doing something; it is having time for one's inner world of being. Christopher Robin understood this when he said, "What I like *doing* best is Nothing. . . . It means just going along, listening to all the things you can't hear, and not bothering." We have kept our children so busy with "useful" and "improving" activities, that we are in danger of raising a generation of young people who are terrified of silence, of being alone with their own thoughts; and yet, in every avenue of human progress —as much in the sciences as in the arts—lonely reflection is essential. A high-school English teacher recently asked a group of his students to write a composition, a fantasy of the worst possible thing they could imagine happening to them; he was startled and then horrified to discover that out of thirty-one compositions, fifteen of his students had described situations in which they were completely alone, in a room or on a desert island, with "nothing to do and nobody to talk to," without books, radio or TV.

A remarkable elementary-school principal, with a deep sensitivity to the needs of children, told me what he does when a teacher sends a child to his office because the child has been unruly in class and the teacher wants him reprimanded. "I'm very lucky," he said, "because our school faces on a wide river, where boats are making their way to the ocean. I ask the child to stand at the window for five or ten minutes and count the ships that pass. I ask this in such a way that the child feels he is really doing something that matters a great deal to me—and then I watch his face. In a short time, I see a kind of quiet peacefulness settle on him—and then I know we can sit down together and really talk about what is bothering him."

We need to have faith in time all through our lives; it is *never* too late to learn anything we want to know, do anything that we want to do. For many years my husband was engaged in a research project that involved his undertaking psychotherapy with terminal cancer patients. It was not at all unusual for a person with as little as three months to live, handicapped by severe illness and pain, to live more fully than ever before—to discover new things about himself, to do things he had always wanted to do but had never had the courage to try. In other cases, where patients lived for several years, they often changed jobs, came to understand themselves profoundly, had relationships with others that had never been possible before.

One patient said, "I know now that I'm intelligent, I have courage and my opinions are as good as anyone else's. Just knowing this has made a big difference in my life. I can see the good things I've given my children, not just the bad things." Another patient said, "You know, Doc, for the first time in my life I *like* myself!" A shy young girl admitted one day that she had been writing poetry for many years; she had never had enough confidence in herself to show it to anyone. When it turned out to be first-rate and worthy of publication, she said, "All I ever really wanted was to have the courage to call myself a poet—and now I can!" A brilliant research scientist had not been able to make any progress in his work for several years. One day he reported that he had begun to write an important theoretical article the night before. He said, "I felt that what I had to say was worth saying. I can't wait to get back to it." A thirty-nine-year-old woman who had never had a love relationship before told the therapist one Monday morning about her wonderful week end at the beach with a man she had met three months earlier. As they sat and watched the sun setting over the water she had felt as though "all those glorious colors were inside of me!" Each of these patients was dying; none lived more than one year after these incidents took place, and two died within four months. Perhaps it is my knowledge of these true events that makes me feel that there is something obscene, a kind of moral outrage, when psychologists or educators now talk about all important learning taking place in the first few years of life, and when they state that all is lost if we do not capture those brief moments.

Working for a short time on a project of the Manhattan Society for Mental Health that involved working with

Golden Age Clubs, I was constantly astounded and inspired by the degree to which people in their eighties, and even older, were learning new things, developing new talents, finding new areas of personal fulfillment. We simply do *not* learn everything we need to know in childhood—and even if we could, what a horror that would be! We can go on growing and experiencing and learning to feel more alive until the hour that we die. A psychologist recently told me about a patient he was seeing, a woman in her late fifties, who felt that her life had come to an abrupt and terrible ending when her husband left her after twenty-eight years of marriage. The therapist had tried to point out that what his patient was feeling was the loss of the way in which she had viewed herself all through her adult life, as somebody's wife or mother. He had said to her, "Now you have a chance to find out who *you* are, to be your own person, to explore what you want to be and to do." The patient was thoughtful for a moment and then said, "Just yesterday I was talking to one of the most remarkable people I've ever known in all my life; she's ninety-five years old, and she is more involved in living now than I ever was. All she said to me, as we passed each other in the hall, at a church meeting was, 'I didn't learn to swim until I was sixty.' I think I'm just beginning to understand what she meant."

A beautiful and touching French film, *The Shameless Old Lady,* tells the story of a woman who has spent seventy years doing what she had to do, taking care of her husband and home, raising her children, never questioning whether or not this was what she wanted to do with her life. Slowly but surely after her husband's death she begins to explore the world, to do the secret things she has always wanted to do; she takes a ride in a carriage, she spends whole days walking through department stores looking at expensive clothes, cosmetics, and new-fangled electrical equipment for homemakers. She refuses to live with her grown children; they are horrified at first and then philosophically accepting when she uses her small means and what little extra they can give her to befriend a young prostitute, to attend meetings of a small group of leftist intellectuals, to buy a car and go on a long holiday trip with her new friends and finally to help a young shoemaker buy a new store. If she cannot sleep at night, she gets out of bed and takes a walk along the harbor, which she loves; she eats when she is hungry and sleeps when she is tired; she looks and listens, smells and tastes and touches, with a renewed delight in the wonders of life. She has a special rapport with a young grandson who is trying very hard to find himself. He is not willing to settle for less than being himself: he struggles against working at a job he hates, marrying and settling down to a life of quiet desperation as his father did. For eighteen glorious months the "shameless old lady" is truly and deeply herself, and because she is, she is able to feel a deeper compassion for others, a greater unselfishness. Out of her own sense of final fulfillment when she dies, she leaves a package of photographs for her grandson; they are a kind of pictorial chronicle of the last year and a half of her life—gay pictures, funny pictures, scenes taken in sunshine and happiness, scenes of holiday good spirits, pictures of loving warmth with her new-found companions. They are a message to her grandson to continue the courageous struggle to find himself, a moving and inspiring testament to the fact that there is always time, so long as we live, to become more truly ourselves.

A respect for time, a removal of the sense of pressure for

accomplishment, bathes a young child in a warm glow in which he can expand. There is the old fable about a competition between the North Wind and the Sun to make a man take off his coat. The North Wind blew as hard as it could, and the man pulled his coat more tightly around him the colder and stronger the wind blew. The Sun with its slow gentle radiance warmed the man, and when he relaxed and felt warm and comfortable, he took the coat off by himself. The raising and educating of children follows exactly the same principle; the only way to encourage a child to open himself to his own possibilities and to the fullness of life is by surrounding him with a warm and gentle radiance.

He needs to feel that it is good to be young; that childhood has its own value and validity and that he does not have to try to be a grown-up until he's ready. There is the charming story of the five-year-old boy who was having dinner in a restaurant with his parents; the waiter treated him with great politeness, and although it was obvious that the boy could not read a word of it, the waiter handed him a menu and said, "And what would you care for this evening, sir?" The boy turned to his parents in wide-eyed wonder and in an awed whisper said, "He thinks I'm *real!*" Each child needs to know that he *is* real, that he is not merely becoming but already *is* a person. He needs to know that the child he is will be part of him for the rest of his life and that this inner companion is good. Unless he can be glad about being the child he is, he can never truly be glad to be the adult he will become. He needs to feel that he has a right to have fun, to play, to explore the world in his own way. He needs space and freedom for his own adventures in growing. In Sunday-school class the children were asked to write their own Ten Commandments, and one seven-year-old put at the head of his list, "Thou Shalt Have Fun!" He was right; the fun, the playfulness of childhood is a legacy that reaps rich rewards forever. One mother told me this story: Her son, a senior at college, came home one Christmas vacation in a state of great exhaustion. He was in a severe depression—worried about his mid-term exams, worried about graduating, worried about his chances of getting into graduate school, full of self-doubts, questioning everything he was doing with his life. She was frightened by his physical weariness and his sense of hopelessness and defeat and wondered if there were something special bothering him. Three of his college friends came to spend a long week end, and she discovered that they all seemed to be in the same mood: dull, humorless and lifeless. On Saturday night she and her husband went out to dinner and theater. When they came back, they found a wild party going on. For a moment they wondered if these twenty-year-olds had been drinking—they seemed so utterly different—gay, light-hearted, full of energy and good spirits. She told me, "Do you want to know what those intellectual grinds had been doing? They had been playing Monopoly and Pin-the-Tail-on-the-Donkey! The fatigue, the boredom, the feeling of defeat were all gone—and I realized that 'child's play' was as important as it ever had been for them!" Dr. Bruno Bettelheim, head of the Sonia Shankman Orthogenic School at the University of Chicago, put it another way when he said, "It is very difficult to cheat a gifted child out of making good use of his intellectual abilities, but it is very easy to cheat him of his childhood. . . . Enjoying childhood experiences to the full is the best preparation for becoming a mature adult."

Children of all ages need opportunities for simple pleasures, for doing what comes naturally, for being free from constant adult watchfulness and direction. One summer when my husband and I were planning a two-week vacation on Cape Cod, just as a sort of a joke I bought him an army-surplus inflatable life raft. It was big and unwieldy, but we had a marvelous time with it. When we saw some of the fancy and expensive motor boats and sailboats in the harbor, being used by many of the teen-age youngsters, we felt like idiots splashing about in our silly raft. But within a day of our arrival these sophisticates had abandoned their veritable yachts and wanted to play with us! Why? Because with a simple raft you can test your own ingenuity, you can feel a sense of challenge when the water gets rough or the tides strong. And you can laugh a lot!

Several years ago a mother told me mournfully that she and her husband had canceled their own vacation trip to Europe because their seventeen-year-old son wanted to go on a mountain-climbing trip with two friends, and they would be too nervous about being so far away. "He says we should go," she told me. "But suppose something went wrong? Suppose he needed us?" Her son was not a novice, he had gone mountain climbing under supervision before and he was a sensible and competent young person. But her reaction was typical of our tendency to over-supervise, to breathe down the necks of our children and not let them test their own strengths. We are caught in a vicious circle; our fears and discontents about our own lives make us distrustful of children and impatient with childhood; we feel guilty about our anger toward children, and this feeling makes us anxious and we become over-protective—we never want to let them out of our sight. The more we begin to be ourselves, the more we open ourselves to adventure and accept life with all its realistic hazards and challenges, the more we

will free our children to make their own discoveries. Our
children cannot grow in self-understanding and self-confidence, hemmed in as they are by so many restrictions and
safeguards. We have to leave them alone more; we have
to provide the time and the life-space in which they can
adventure on their own. They need un-organized time. But
there is a vast difference between *un*-organized and *dis*-
organized time; the first implies a planned setting in which
free exploration can take place; the second is a total abdica-
tion from planning and guidance. I am certainly not recom-
mending that second alternative. Obviously, a five-year-old
cannot use the same quality or quantity of freedom as a
twelve- or fifteen-year-old. We can provide the ingredients
for self-testing, and then we must permit our children to
make the most they can of these. It is the responsibility of
adults to create resources and opportunities—but once they
have done this, they really must have the courage to let
go.

Mrs. Jean Schick Grossman, a pioneer in the field of
parent education, has frequently asked parents and educators to complete these sentences: (1) "Out of my childhood I love to remember . . ." and (2) "Out of my childhood I hate to remember . . ." She has reported a very
interesting consistency in the responses; rather than writing
about stereotyped happy or unhappy moments, many of
the people "hated to remember" times when they were
treated in such a way as to feel *less* worthy as human beings,
and "loved to remember" experiences that made them feel
more truly themselves, more worthy of pride and dignity.
One young student teacher wrote:

Out of my childhood I hate to remember the time that
my parents bought my stool for me. I was about 12

years old, and one day I passed an antique shop and fell in love with a charming hand-carved old milking stool. I have no idea why it appealed to me so much, but I just felt I had to have it. I spoke to the storekeeper and arranged to give him a certain amount of money each week—almost every penny of my allowance. I begged my parents to give me jobs to do so I could earn more money. At first I didn't want to tell them what I was saving for—I wanted to keep it my own private secret—but they were so insistent that one day I showed the stool to my mother when we passed the store. I don't think I'd ever worked so hard for anything in my life—and I had it almost half paid for when my parents, wanting to make me happy, decided to surprise me for my birthday, paid the balance and gave it to me. I hated that stool . . . I felt cheated of a private victory.

Here was a situation in which parents were being genuinely thoughtful and kind—ordinarily one would expect this to be a happy experience for a child—but she felt diminished by it, made less of a person; she had challenged herself to achieve something on her own and had then been thwarted in her struggle for a feeling of autonomy and accomplishment.

One of the most important aspects of growth is an acceptance of the necessity, the inevitability of error and failure. Genuine growth is impossible unless we are willing to risk failure—and we *will* fail, many times. But the alternative is to never be truly alive at all. Despite the fact that every discovery, every invention, every work of art, has been created out of the inner courage, the capacity to accept the possibility of failure, we seem to be forcing our children into a position where failure is intolerable and to be avoided at all costs. As soon as a society places such a heavy value on marks, on test scores and on school grades, the message is loud and clear; failure is the enemy.

Similarly, children need our help in understanding that genuine commitment to living fully involves risk taking and danger. Openness to learning and experiencing can only occur where there is a willingness to live dangerously, to attempt the impossible, to ask questions that cannot be answered. A group of teachers in an in-service-training seminar were discussing the fact that it was very difficult to teach from a syllabus that restricted the subjects they might take up with their classes; teaching was becoming boring, it was harder to encourage children to really think for themselves. They all agreed that formal directives on what to teach were *safer;* in that way each teacher would know what had been covered the year before and what would be covered the following year—but it was also dull and unchallenging and often made it impossible to pick up on special interests and talents in a class. At the end of one of these sessions, after much discussion of the pros and cons, one teacher leaped out of her seat and said, "O. K., everybody, let's all go out and live dangerously!" Learning takes place in an encounter between people who want to know and are ready to find out. That process is more disorganized, more difficult, more hazardous—but it is the only way in which anything can really happen.

We need to help our children understand that we value risk taking more than success; we value commitment and involvement more than doing things "right" or safely. Several years ago a young niece of ours, who had gotten a Fulbright scholarship to teach English in an Italian school and who had looked forward to this experience with breathless excitement, stayed with us the night before her departure. She got "cold feet" during the evening and became very nervous and apprehensive. Suddenly she had realized how far she was going, that she would be gone for a whole year, that she would be completely on her own in a strange town in a foreign country. "I'm *scared!*" she wailed. "But of course," my husband said. "Anything that's worth doing at all *has* to be a little scary!"

When we repeated this story to an elementary-school teacher she said, "That gives me an idea; when school starts this fall, I'm going to tell my children learning is a scary business! I never said that to them before—and yet, all the years that I've been teaching, I've known that there was something holding back some of the most exciting children in my class, but I never could put it into words. The children who are most scared, are probably very often the ones who can learn the most—once somebody shares with them the danger of discovery, the necessity of facing learning with the courage to fail—often. You know, I think I'm even going to say that, in the beginning, when we start long division—I'm going to say that I'm very happy about *mistakes!*"

The ability to tolerate uncertainty and error, to accept the dangers of true adventure are prerequisites for self-discovery, the search for meaning and purpose in life. Such a struggle is never "safe"—we have to take chances; the moment when we can stand up and fight for our own individuality, when we have the courage to be ourselves and act according to our own values, is the moment when we truly come to life. In *Man and Superman* Bernard Shaw wrote:

"The reasonable man adapts himself to the world; the unreasonable one persists in trying to adapt the world to himself. Therefore all progress depends upon the unreasonable man."

I spoke in the first chapter of the overpowering effects of living in a society of such rapid change, such uncertainty about values, a world in which we feel lost in the crowd, where we feel we become ciphers in big institutions. There are also potential advantages in these aspects of modern life —if we dare to make the most of them. One of the greatest attributes of a complex and changing world is that it allows more room for differences; rather than having to regiment ourselves or our children to suit some institutional vision, we can insist that bigness can also actually allow for more variety. If we are courageous enough to begin to make some personal choices, we find that the very vagueness and uncertainty of social expectations and demands has given us room to discover what it is to be uniquely and wonderfully ourselves.

It is a tough challenge to find one's own answers—but it is possible; and as we become increasingly self-directed, we will begin to feel a new sense of significance. I do not think that it is any accident that at a time in human history when we feel most overwhelmed by technology, when we feel most uncertain about our capacity to become masters of our own destiny, there seems to be a great revival of interest in the story of Don Quixote, who symbolizes the idealist, the dreamer, the man who knows what he believes in, and who struggles against all kinds of odds in quest of *his own dream.* One of the most moving moments in the musical *Man of La Mancha* is when Don Quixote, in a testament of faith, sings "The Impossible Dream," in which he affirms the essential dignity of human life—the necessity for each man to struggle against impossible odds for the realization of an inner dream, an unreachable perfectibility, a personal vision, belonging only to oneself.

And yet, even as we begin to come to this view, we are still trying to find some blueprint, some way of manipulating the ways in which our children grow—ways in which we can predict what they will become. In our attempts over the past half-century to learn new and better ways to raise our children, we have tended to overlook or to underestimate the profound and precious qualities in each child that need to "be as they grow." Because we thought that we might discover some "good" or "perfect" ways to raise our children, we have often been frightened when our children, each so new and special, so truly unpredictable, do not fit our calculations or expectations, but instead persist in defying all our formulas!

I recently attended the birthday of a four-year-old girl. Grandma had brought Lauri a walking-talking doll, who proceeded to walk stiffly across the floor in front of an admiring audience, saying, "Hello, I love you, hello, I love you." Lauri's mother broke the silence by exclaiming, "Now *that's* what *I* call a perfect child!" She was joking of course—and yet I had the feeling that she was reflecting a feeling that is quite common among today's parents. Whatever most of us may be saying outwardly, the inward wish for children to behave like mechanical dolls seems to me to be very real and widespread. And, unfortunately, I am afraid that at least some of this discomfort with the reality of unpredictable, often mysterious and unsettling human children rests with those who have devoted their time and professional talents to the study and understanding of children. For the first time in history it seemed possible to create the perfect child; that this subtle promise has remained unfulfilled strikes many of us as a sign that we have failed in becoming perfect parents—rather than what seems to me a more rational alternative, that we should not have ever set such a goal in the first place.

Attitudes toward child raising have changed from decade to decade, reflecting whatever kinds of knowledge or insights we thought we had arrived at during a particular period. This has undoubtedly been true throughout history, but during the past fifty years these opinions and directives have had the prestige of "science"; we have therefore tended to forget that even in an age when we think we have discovered sound scientific methods for observation and evaluation, yesterday's theories still tend to be thrown on tomorrow's scrap heap.

As we have tried to explore human behavior, each succeeding school of psychological thought and research has tended to provide us with stereotyped methods of child raising and a rigid set of expectations, instead of simply opening up new *possibilities* and providing us with new guidelines of insight and understanding, to be evaluated, accepted and discarded in a general enrichment of our knowledge.

For example, psychiatry and psychoanalysis made us more aware of repression of unconscious feelings that needed to be understood and accepted—and so we valued the child who could "show his feelings." For a while we thought of the "well-adjusted child" as the one who got along well with other people; then we began to see that we sometimes paid too high a price for conformity, that we were discouraging worthwhile and exciting differences.

The heyday of "human engineering" is now upon us in full force, and we have felt confident that we could make our "learning machines" (our children) as streamlined, predictable and clever as our teaching machines. Today's concept of "the perfect child" has at its core the wish for a no-nonsense child, who grows up as quickly as possible, with or without his emotional quirks. Technological expertise has given us the image of the child who can be manipulated and controlled in such a way that he will read and write at two, solve calculus problems at ten and graduate from an Ivy League college at eighteen.

It would seem that each social era has provided the psychological research and findings that best suited our needs and expectations; that these are unrealistic, destructive and arbitrary seems borne out by the fact that we have certainly not produced a perfect child under any set of methods or theories. Parents seem to find themselves drowning in a sea of controversy, swaying somewhat drunkenly from one expert pronouncement to another, continuing to seek for some standardized goals where none are really possible or desirable.

Let us imagine a hypothetical child, Fred Smith, now attending junior high school, the living, breathing amalgamation of fifty years of psychological investigation. What would make him "the perfect child" in the eyes of his hopeful parents? That he should be healthy and athletic goes without saying; good nutrition and antibiotics allow no room in the "perfect child" concept for puny weaklings! He should be free from guilt about wrong-doing but, being loved and understood, he should prefer to be good. He should understand that people are not always responsible for their actions because of unconscious emotional needs and problems, but *he* should be able to do whatever is necessary for his future success. He should be able to express his fears and anxieties, but these must not affect his schoolwork. Understanding his natural feelings of hostility and rebellion, he should be able to handle these in socially acceptable ways. He should not be shy or a loner, but then again, he should not be too extroverted; popular and successful socially, but able to think his own thoughts—provided this does not involve daydreaming in class. He should be highly competitive in academic achievement and sports, but he should never cheat. He should be responsible and independent, but also content to be financially dependent on his parents until he is twenty-five or older. He should be intelligent, interesting, creative, socially mature—but never to the degree that he becomes rebellious enough about the imperfections in the world about him to look or act like a beatnik. He should, when requested reasonably and democratically to behave, do so, reasonably and democratically. Most of all, he should love his parents, so that they may feel properly rewarded for their child-raising techniques.

The Fred Smiths who live in our homes bear little or no resemblance to such paragons of psychological virtues. And this, as our children would say, is where we get hung up. As we have learned more and more, we seem to have less and less humility about what can and cannot be done in quest of human perfectibility. Despite our new knowledge, some Fred Smiths are shy, some are lone wolves, some are aggressively outgoing, some are usually happy and serene, while many others who are also in no way "sick" or "maladjusted" may be rebellious, insecure and moody. We are challenged to face the inevitable fact that "mental health" is not a concept that allows for inflexible classification. Slowly but surely there begins to emerge a growing awareness that however much we may think we know about human beings in general, we must not use this growing body of information as a way to manipulate, control or predict what will be essential or useful or good in the growth and development of any specific, unique individual person. If we have learned anything from the past, it ought to be that what is most precious about human beings is their refusal to be categorized and pigeonholed. We are each of us partly a product of our own interesting and entirely unique arrangement and assortment of genes and chromosomes, with all this implies about inborn constitutional differences; we are also the product of a myriad of combinations and possibilities of interactions with our environment, with all this implies about social change and our unique relationships with other people. Beyond all this, no school of psychological thought or investigation has yet come along that should allow us to dare to decide what "perfection" might be for any person or group. Without regard for any conception of "the perfect child," it is time we devoted our energies to creating a climate in which every growing person has the opportunity for fulfilling himself, whatever he may discover that self to be, an environment so rich in resources, challenges and opportunities that all formulas for self-realization disappear and each child is helped toward a sense of meaning and purpose in life, without regard to standardized or preconceived goals.

In the published report of the 1960 White House Conference on Children (Columbia University Press) there is a chapter by Eric Larrabee entitled "Childhood in Twentieth-Century America." In it, he gives examples of different kinds of child-raising methods and expectations since we first focused a scientific eye on the study of children. He finds that the more store we have set by a theory, the more disappointed we are when the results fall short of expectation; he comes to the conclusion that children have been victimized by our demands and expectations. We have invaded the world of childhood with our changing views, not always improving the lot of our children to say the least, and Larrabee's conclusion is that "a little inattention might do them a world of good."

That the winds of change are upon us is attested to by the election of Dr. Abraham Maslow, Chairman of the Psychology Department of Brandeis University, as President of the American Psychological Association. In his book *Toward a Psychology of Being* (Van Nostrand, 1962) he states:

> Every age but ours has had its model, its ideal. All these have been given up by our culture: the saint, the hero, the gentleman, the knight, the mystic. About all we have left is the well-adjusted man without problems, a very pale and doubtful substitute. Perhaps we shall soon be able to use as our guide and model the fully growing and self-fulfilling human being, the one whose inner nature expresses itself freely, rather than being warped, suppressed or denied.

Our notion of perfectibility must be replaced by the goal of spontaneity, self-realization and individual fulfillment. We ought to exult in the refusal of human beings to be labeled, packaged or standardized, however arduously and enthusiastically we may have been trying to accomplish this hopeless and fortunately impossible task! It may seem to some that in the process of self-discovery, of searching for a unique and special individuality, we may be encouraging a self-centered selfishness, an indifference to the needs and rights of others. Nothing could be farther from the truth. A college guidance counselor told me that in discussing future plans with one of his advisees—a brilliant young man who was very individualistic and who could not see why he had to take certain required subjects—he had said to him, "You know, as long as men are not living alone but in groups, they have to give up some of their individuality." The student had replied, "No, I think you're wrong—*behavior* has to be governed, but not my individuality."

It is misleading to believe that nurturing and reinforcing one's individuality means that we do so at the expense of others. The individual who feels most free to be himself is actually the best member of the group—for what he demands for himself, he also feels obliged to encourage and foster in others. A group of mothers were discussing the question of how to find a balance between defending one's own rights and needs and also behaving responsibly in meeting the needs of others. One mother said it succinctly for all when she observed, "I don't feel that anything is taken away from me by my family—quite the contrary. My individuality grows the more I try to encourage my husband and children to be individuals themselves. The more each of us becomes special and different, the more we give to each other."

The sum and substance of what I have been saying is that what children need from grown-ups is an affirmation of the significance of childhood—and there is only one way to give them this: by a genuine acceptance of the child *within ourselves*, the qualities that make us each special and different, the qualities in us that we were born-to-become. If we really want our children to be themselves and to be glad about it, we must first understand and accept our own uniqueness.

The conspiracy against childhood is really a conspiracy against ourselves. We cannot help our children to discover and nurture their inner selves unless we are able first of all to do this as adults, as parents and as teachers—as persons. It is a strange irony that at the same time that we seem so inclined to mechanize our children, to hasten them into adulthood, we are discovering how dangerous and destructive it can be for adults to become alienated from their own childhood. In the psychotherapeutic treatment of unhappy adults, a primary goal is to encourage a process of de-intellectualization, an attempt to help the individual re-find and re-explore the child within himself—the feeling, creative, growing person he once was. When we lose our way as adults, it is not because we are not smart, not because we do not know enough facts, not because we cannot be "successful" in terms of getting into college or making money; it is that we have somewhere along the line lost touch with who and what we were to begin with.

Maurice Sendak, who writes the most wonderful and imaginative stories for children, was asked by Nat Hentoff (in a profile of him in *The New Yorker*) what it was that seemed to make it possible for him to communicate so sensitively with the needs and feelings of childhood. He said, "Reaching the kids is important, but secondary. First, always, I have to reach and keep hold of the child in me." This is not only true for the creative artist who wants to communicate with children. It is true for all of us if we are to engage in a continuing search for what is unique in ourselves—a search for personal identity that can in turn give us a sense of meaning and purpose in our lives. We have no alternative! No one, nothing in our society, is going to provide us with ready-made answers to the questions, "What do I believe in? What gives my life significance?" The old answers just do not work in a world of such rapid change and complexity as ours. If there is one central problem of our times it is that so many people lead lives of quiet despair —a feeling of inner discontent, a sense of emptiness—because they have been unable to discover their own new meaning, their own sense of values.

The January 1966 issue of *Redbook* carried a story by Anne Taylor, a young housewife and mother who wrote, "I don't know where to look for me." There was nothing very remarkable or unusual about her life as she described it: she had the typical concerns about child raising, about being a working mother, about financial worries and adjusting to the early years of marriage. But what she really seemed to be writing about was a kind of lonely uncertainty about the meaning and purpose of her life; she felt somehow lost and alienated from herself. The fact that this was an accurate reflection of much of modern living, was borne out by the fact that *Redbook* received over 7,000 letters in response to this article; it had hit a nerve. The thread that ran through almost all of these letters was an awareness that we are struggling with a problem that was all but unknown in our grandparents' time: a search for personal identity, a need to find new meaning and significance in our lives.

Most of us grew up laden by "shoulds"—claims and expectations that were unreal, inflexible, unsuited to the adult world in which we now find ourselves. If we behaved in the "right way" we *should* be rewarded; material comforts for which our parents and grandparents worked so hard to make possible *should* make us happy; if we learned the right methods, our children *should* be well adjusted, our marriages *should* bring contentment and fulfillment. We hear some echo from the past, a voice which tells us, "You *should* do this, you *must* do that"; and because these voices reflect the parental demands and social pressures of our childhood rather than our own urgent cry to be ourselves and to be free, we remain uncertain, discontented, knowing somewhere deep within ourselves that we are existing, not living.

In searching for oneself one must get rid of the "shoulds" of life. We are truly free only when we begin to look for our own new answers, when we try to find our own individual way. The most important unfinished quest for each of us is in finding new dimensions within ourselves.

We are just beginning to learn that in order to search for our own identity in a world that offers us such a variety of possibilities we need to look for what is most alive within ourselves. The challenge of having to make so many free choices is that it demands a kind of self-knowledge never before needed. How can we decide what to do with our lives until we know who we are? We need to become intensely aware of the inner companion with whom we live. When we do not know where to look for ourselves, we may really be saying that somewhere along the line we sold out, we rejected some deep and significant part of ourselves. We listened to other voices, not our own.

A recent Italian film, *Juliet of the Spirits*, seemed to me to embody the modern struggle to find meaning in one's life. In the film Juliet is a young wife who finds that her husband has been unfaithful to her. At first glance it would appear that she has surely been wronged and that her despair is quite understandable, but as we learn more about her, we begin to realize that she is a parasitic plant living off another human being because there is not enough of *her* to make a whole person. As a child she was made to feel that the only way she could gain love and approval was by denying her natural, spontaneous feelings, her exuberant warm delight in the world. A beautiful and unapproachable mother had made her feel ugly, unworthy and inadequate; two beautiful, self-assured and flamboyant sisters had made her feel that she was a nobody; a puritanical, "hellfire-and-brimstone" school, with teachers who were afraid of life themselves, had terrified her into abject submission—a total denial of her own sensuality, her humor, her creativity. The only person who had tried to encourage her to be herself, to accept all of life joyfully and freely, was her grandfather; and he deserted her finally, out of his own need to escape the antiseptic, rigid, punitive world in which she was being raised. In school and at home she was taught that "good little girls" submerge and deny what is most lifelike and special about themselves, and that one is rewarded eventually for being good by having "a nice life." We begin to realize that Juliet's despair is not because her husband may leave her, but because if he did, she would feel utterly abandoned. She would be alone—but not with her real self. She is bedeviled by frightening fantasies, representing all the parts of herself that she has been afraid to acknowledge all her life. She only begins to feel deeply alive when, desperate to know where to look for herself, she has the courage to accept and love the poor, frightened child within herself, the self she has feared and despised, the self she has treated with contempt—the self that was always trying too hard to please others, rather than herself.

She loses her fear of being alone when she ceases to reject

the qualities in her deepest self, when she no longer distorts that self to please others, when, in finding her own inner companion, she begins to sense the riches of her inner world —riches that can nurture and sustain her.

A Spanish guest of her husband's tells her, "In my country we have a proverb that says, 'I am my own roof, my own window, my own hearth. My words are my food, my thoughts are my drink. Thus I am happy.' " Juliet's moment of personal triumph comes when she embraces the self she always needed to be and in so doing becomes "her own hearth." The author of *Juliet of the Spirits*, Federico Fellini, in talking about the film, said, "To demand from others a fidelity to ourselves is monstrous; it is an anti-religious thought. The only true fidelity is to oneself and to one's own destiny, absolutely respecting each one's individuality . . . . Juliet, alone, at the end of the film, should mean the discovery of individuality."

Like Juliet, we are often afraid to begin the search for our inner selves, because we feel that we will dislike what we find. When we are little children we see ourselves through the eyes of the adults around us, and we interpret their expressions of annoyance, anger, disapproval, and disappointment as being the full measure of our worth. We need to remember that children, in their helpless uncertainty, punish themselves more severely than do their parents and convict themselves of crimes they have never really committed. As adults we can look back at ourselves with new compassion and understanding; we can recognize how vulnerable we were, how desperate for parental approval; we can see at last the shimmering sensitivity of the young child who never wanted to be bad but only full of life and loved.

In the ordinary experiences of life one can do a great deal

to search for the young and hopeful and tender part of one-self. It is not by accident, for example, that stories of young lovers almost invariably describe them going on picnics, running along the seaside barefoot, visiting a zoo, bicycling or eating ice-cream cones on a roller coaster. When we begin to fall in love, we know instinctively that somehow we find our truest selves in the playful games of childhood. One way of getting close to one's inner life is to do young things; rolling in the grass in springtime, finger painting with a child; lustily singing rounds on a car trip, stuffing oneself with hot dogs and popcorn at a ball game or drive-in movie. This is why doing things spontaneously, without too much planning, living outdoors in the country when-ever one can, watching the changing seasons, making things with one's hands, enjoying silences on a starry night, walk-ing in the rain, all seem to mean so much in the search for self; they are reminiscent of childhood, a time of innocence and wonder and a deep yearning for life.

Another technique for discovering who and what one is is to say to oneself, "If I wanted to give myself a present, what would I give? Suppose it was for a friend and I wanted to give something that would have very special meaning?" One woman who asked herself this question went out and bought a painting; another gave herself a membership in an amateur theater group; a third built her-self a miniature hothouse, where she could grow exotic flowers. Whatever a person does to reawaken a sense of de-light in the world around him helps him to find what it means to be the special person he is, what makes him differ-ent from anyone else in the world.

This personal search for the child within oneself is noth-ing more nor less than the affirmation of what is most precious in human life. As we start out on this quest ourselves, we begin to open up new possibilities for our children. Out of our sense of glory in being alive and ourselves we free our children to discover who they are and what they may become.

The healthy capacity of each growing person to struggle to find his own meaning is really what we are after. We cannot do this by cramming facts into our children's heads; we cannot do it by turning away in despair and abdicating from our responsibilities as adults, leaving our children to their own devices. We need to use all the rich resources of knowledge at our disposal to create a climate in which children can be nourished intellectually, but where they can also feel free to nourish themselves, through their own feelings and experiences—where intellect combines with emotion in order to engage our children in a quest for greater humanity.

I had the privilege recently of seeing a book of poetry written by Melissa M. Cruser, sixteen-year-old daughter of a friend. This was a private publication, consisting of one copy, produced by the author herself. She is, it seems to me, a shining example of what we must strive for in our children and in ourselves: she is curious, alert, adventurous; she is open to new ideas, she can learn those facts and skills that will enrich her life experience. She is uniquely herself, at home with her feelings and at home in the world of people. She dedicated her book of quite excellent poems as follows: "To my parents for providing the raw material and my teachers for what they have done to it and ESPECIALLY TO ME for not paying any attention." The final poem in her book was:

PRAYER

Because I love Mankind, one single hope
Forever lies uppermost within my mind:
That this cruel-careless Child we call Humanity
Will someday grow to manhood, and be kind.

Reading List

THE following list of suggested reading is in no way an attempt to cover the vast amount of material now available in such fields as child psychology and educational philosophy. It is simply a list of books that I have found interesting and provocative, and that have influenced my own thinking in the past few years. They cover a wide range and offer stimuli for making one's own judgments. I have included my own earlier book, since I think it provides background for many of the ideas I have expressed in this one. The books that are starred are ones that seem to me to be particularly pertinent to the subjects I have discussed and that I have found especially meaningful.

Association for Childhood Education, *Don't Push Me!* 3615 Wisconsin Avenue, N. W., Washington, D.C. 20016, 75¢.

Bruner, Jerome, *The Process of Education.* Harvard, 1960.

* Chess, Stella, Alexander Thomas and Herbert Birch, *Your Child Is a Person.* Viking, 1965.

Dexter, Lewis Anthony, *The Tyranny of Schooling.* Basic Books, 1964.

Erikson, Erik H. *Childhood and Society.* Norton, 1963.

* Erikson, Erik H., ed., *Youth, Change and Challenge.* Basic Books, 1963.

* Friedenberg, Edgar Z., *Coming of Age in America: Growth and Acquiescence.* Random House, 1965.

Fromm, Erich, *The Sane Society.* Holt, 1955.

Gans, Roma, *Common Sense in Teaching Reading.* Bobbs-Merrill, 1963.

Getzels, Jacob, and Philip Jackson, *Creativity and Intelligence.* John Wiley, 1962.

Goodlard, John, and Robert Anderson, *The Non-Graded Elementary School.* Harcourt, Brace, 1963.

* Goodman, Paul, *Compulsory Mis-education.* Horizon, 1964.

Goodman, Paul, *Growing Up Absurd: Problems of Youth in the Organized Society.* Random House, 1960.

Gross, Martin L., *The Brain Watchers.* Random House, 1962.
* Grupp, M. Michael, *The American Classroom: The End of Excellence and the Birth of Mediocrity.* The Ethical Platform, May 29, 1966. 2 West 64th Street, New York, N. Y. 10023, 25¢.
Hentoff, Nat, *Our Children are Dying.* Viking, 1966.
Hoffman, Banesh, *The Tyranny of Testing.* Crowell-Collier, 1962.
* Holt, John, *How Children Fail.* Pitman, 1964.
Hymes, James, *Effective Home-School Relations.* Prentice-Hall, 1953.
Hymes, James, *Understanding Your Child.* Prentice-Hall, 1952.
Jourard, Sidney M., *The Transparent Self.* Van Nostrand, 1964.
LeShan, Eda J., *How to Survive Parenthood.* Random House, 1965.
* Maslow, Abraham, *Toward a Psychology of Being.* Van Nostrand, 1962.
Mayer, Martin, *The Schools.* Harper, 1961.
Neill, A. S., *Summerhill: A Radical Approach to Child Rearing* (Foreword by Erich Fromm). Hart, 1966.
Read, Katherine H., *The Nursery School: A Human Relationship Laboratory.* Saunders, 1960.
* Redl, Fritz, *When We Deal with Children.* Basic Books, 1966.
Riesman, David, *Abundance for What?* Doubleday, 1964.
Riessman, Frank, *The Culturally Deprived Child.* Harper, 1962.
Rudolph, Marguerita, and Dorothy Cohen, *Kindergarten: A Year of Learning.* Appleton, 1964.
Torrance, Paul E., *Guiding Creative Talent.* Prentice-Hall, 1962.
* Wickes, Frances, *The Inner World of Childhood* (Revised ed.). Appleton-Century, 1930.
* Wickes, Frances, *The Inner World of Choice,* Harper, 1963.

Index

Abortion, 310
Achievement, 73; academic, 99, 128; over-, 159-160, 245; under-, 135-164, 169, 181, 197, 201, 231, 311; uniformity in, 181
Adjustment, 205; emotional, 72; mal-, 206; social, 72
Adler, Felix, 71
Administrators, school, 3, 17, 20
Adolescence, 289, 305
Advertising, 10, 49, 294, 306-308
Aeschylus, 248
Albee, Edward, 322-323
American Humanist Asso., 269
American Montessori Society, 79, 81
American Psychiatric Asso., 206
American Psychological Asso., 167, 177
Ames, Louise Bates, 164

Anger, 10, 64, 72, 88, 113-114, 119 ff, 126, 129, 297, 334
Antibiotics, 32, 72, 342
Anxiety, 72, 85, 100, 116, 124, 159, 191, 343
Apathy, 205, 297, 322
Aristotle, 83
Asbell, Bernard, 265-267
Asso. for Family Living, 141, 155-156
Asso. for Higher Education, 225
Athletics, 12, 36, 93-94
Atomic age, 17, 68, 146, 314
Austill, Allen, 220-221
Automation, 5, 191, 199-200, 262-263, 268
Automobiles, 72, 125, 297-298
Autonomy, 228, 336

Bain, Winifred E., 6-7
Baker, Bobby, 309

Barclay, Dorothy, 224
Barnard College, Columbia University, 202
Bed-wetting, 120
Beethoven, Ludwig van, 155
Behavior, 206; during testing sessions, 192; evaluation of, 170, 195; responsibility for personal, 283
Behaviorism, 27, 241, 341, 346
Bettelheim, Bruno, 333
Bill of Rights, 309
Biology, 273
Birth, 68, 126, 139; control, 289, 310
Biting, 92-93, 113
Black, Hillel, 176
Boards of Education, 22. See also under individual names
Books: on child care, 58; comic, 285; on education, 58; text-, 147
Boredom, 93, 252
Bower, Eli, 117, 143
Bowers, William J., 169
Bowles, Frank H., 225
Brandeis University, 206
Brussel, Eleanor, 91
Bureau of Child Guidance, 275

Calderone, Mary, 288-289
California, 307, 317
California State Dept. of Education, 108
Camps, 93-94
Carlyle, Thomas, 61
Carson, Rachel, 295

CBS. See Columbia Broadcasting System
Cheating, 142-143, 216, 343; in examinations, 25, 169, 308-309
Child Study Asso., 117
Childhood Education, 6-7, 312
Churchill, Winston, 31, 155
Ciardi, John, 175, 219
Cisqua School, Mount Kisco, N.Y., 91
Citizenship, responsibilities of, 22
Civics, 25
Civil rights, 315
Clark, Marguerite, 213
Climate, social, 41
Cole, Larry, 274-275
College Discovery Program, N.Y. City, 231
Colleges, 134 ff, 154, 181, 224-226; difficulties of admission to, 13-14, 21, 90, 92, 123, 217; Ivy League, 11, 136, 201, 212 ff, 342; junior, 28; pressures on entrance to, 21, 49, 97, 138, 185, 200-201, 208, 226, 243; small, 218, 234
Columbia Broadcasting System (CBS), 286
Columbia University, 28, 169. See also Barnard College and Teachers College
Communication, 103-104, 179, 220, 347; between generations, 23-24, 44, 65, 88, 118; mechanized, 33; verbal, 59-60, 76, 118

Communism, 72
Competition, 141, 185; problems of, 119
Computers, 18, 29, 33, 47, 50, 62, 68, 145-146, 184, 244-245
Conformity, 6, 67, 158, 196, 205, 240, 341; age of, 239
Constipation, 59
Contemporary Issues, 207
Contraceptives, 294
Coordination, 187-188
Copland, Aaron, 249
Counselors, 99, 232, 319-320; guidance, 3, 12, 33, 162, 172, 179, 181-185, 191, 195-196, 206, 313, 346; high school, 181, 265; teacher, 273
Creative Playthings, 104-105
Creativity, 68, 83, 87, 90, 157-158, 249, 255-256, 277, 325, 327
Crime, 25, 299, 304
Cruser, Melissa M., 353-354

Da Vinci, Leonardo, 55
Dale, Edgar, 155-156
Dartmouth College, 155
Darwin, Charles, 156
Death, 69, 125, 129
Dehumanization, 220
Democracy, 72
Denmark, 276
Dennis, Patrick, 237
Depression, economic, 96
Devine, Margaret, 229-230
Dewey, John, 20, 71, 85, 254
Divorce, 24, 115, 269
Doman, Glen, 51, 55

Doman-Delacato Reading Development Program, 51
Domination, maternal, 121, 187
Douvan, Elizabeth M., 224
Dress, 10, 65
Dressel, Paul, 21, 177
Drop-outs, 5, 25, 197-236, 311; college, 197, 204, 207-212, 224, 226; high school, 198, 224
Drugs, 4, 30, 282; psychedelic, 243. *See also* LSD *and under other individual names*

Esty, George, 143
Ethics, 22 ff, 269
Euripides, 248
Examinations, 29, 168

Failure, school, 4, 5, 30, 337. *See also* Fear of Failure
Family, 129, 189; life, 24-25, 35, 130
Fantasy, importance of, 107, 114
Farber, M. A., 253-254
Fascism, 72
Fatigue, 64
Faubus, Orville, 26
Fear, 63 ff, 72, 78, 88, 100, 116, 119 ff, 124, 129, 141, 322, 334, 338, 340; of the dark, 120; of failure, 19, 166, 238; of school, 19
Fellini, Federico, 351
Fischer, John, 22
Fitz-Gibbon, Bernice, 307
Fleming, Alexander, 55
Florence, Italy, 318

Florida, 317
Florida State University, 195
Food, 64-65, 307
Ford Foundation, 225
Free Universities, 236
Freedman, Mervin, 217-218
Freud, Anna, 71, 118
Freud, Sigmund, 55, 71, 78, 117-
    118, 241
Friedan, Betty, 243
Frigidity, 293
Frost, Robert, 156
Frustration, 64, 116, 277; in
    idealism, 206

Galileo, 83
Genetics, 147
Genovese, Kitty, 282
Gesell Institute, 164
Glassboro State College, N.J.,
    109
Golden Age clubs, 330
Goodman, Paul, 234-236, 263,
    276
Grading, 143, 154, 166 ff, 176-
    178, 234-235
Greenhut, Martin, 275
Greenwich Village, N.Y. City,
    290
Gross, Ronald, 15, 50
Grosse Point, Mich., 109
Grossman, Jean Schick, 335-336
Growth, 63, 68, 73, 94, 124, 326,
    336; age periods of, 102; appe-
    tite for, 62-63, 84; child's total,
    131, 134; emotional, 56, 102;
    industrial, 129; intellectual, 63,

Growth (continued)
    80; mechanistic concepts of,
    70; physical, 102, 116; rates of,
    152, 195; social, 102; stages of,
    39
Guilt, 122, 124, 140, 316, 334;
    parental, 194

Hair, loss, of, 4, 16
Harbor General Hospital, Los
    Angeles, Calif., 108
Harlem Youth Opportunities
    Unlimited (Haryou), 229
Harper's Magazine, 234-236
Harvard University, 14, 45, 58,
    90-91, 155, 177, 201
Haryou. See Harlem Youth
    Opportunities Unlimited
Haskell, Henry, 87
Haslam, Mary, 109-110
Hatred, 66, 119, 124-125
Hausner, Gideon, 31
Head Start Project, 98-100, 229,
    261
Health, mental, 67, 95-96, 205,
    343-344; clinics for, 222-223,
    267
Hechinger, Fred M., 225
Hefferman, Helen, 108
Hemingway, Ernest, 326-327
Hentoff, Nat, 299, 347
Heroin, 25
Hersey, John, 244-246
Hitchcock, Alfred, 286
Hoffa, James, 309
Holt, John, 19, 60-61, 144, 325
Homework, 5, 10-11, 138, 140,

Homework (*continued*)
150-152, 159, 163, 180, 193,
250, 259, 264-266, 272
Homosexuality, 25
Hostility, 85-119, 343
Hotchner, A. E., 326-327
Hoving, Thomas, 251-252
Hoyt, Donald P., 178
Hume, David, 155
Hunt, J. McV., 174
Hunter Elementary School,
N.Y. City, 91
Hymes, James L., 5-6
Hynd, Allan, 183-184

Identity: loss of, 38-39; personal,
131
Illingsworth, Cynthia, 155
Illingsworth, Ronald, 155
Illness, 64, 126, 129, 206; mental,
223, 299
Imagination, 66, 72, 87
Immaturity, 187, 203
Impotence, 293
Indians, American, 100
Individuality, 78, 346
Indulgence, 10
Industrialization, 32, 35, 98, 129
Infants, 45-48, 59-68, 80; care of,
47, 67
Insecurity, 187, 307, 343
Institute for Achievement of
Human Potential, Philadel-
phia, Pa., 51
Institute of Personality Assess-
ment and Research, 158
Integration, 26, 282-283

Iowa, State University of, 17,
141
I.Q.'s, 27, 92, 105 ff, 133, 137,
157, 165-196, 245, 273
Irwin, Elizabeth, 71
Isaacs, Susan, 71, 118

Jacques, Louis, 108-109
Jealousy, 64, 66, 88, 129
Jefferson, Thomas, 236
Jenkins, Gladys Gardner, 141-
143
Jersey City (N.J.) State Teach-
ers College, 17
Jews, 282
Job Corps Training Program,
199, 231-232, 273
Jourard, Sidney, 195
*Journal of the American Asso.
of University Women*, 217-
218
Jubilee, 79
Jung, Carl, 241
Juvenile delinquency, 27, 181,
261, 278, 304, 319-320

Kaplan Fund, J. M., 275
Karplus, Robert, 15
Kaufman, Bel, 175
Keliher, Alice, 252, 312
Kennedy, John F., 201
Kiernan, Owen B., 201
Kilpatrick, William Heard, 71
Kindergarten. *See* Schools,
kindergarten
Kinsey, Alfred C., 290

Ladies' Home Journal, 284

Lambert, Clara, 117 fn., 128-131

Language, 60, 104, 118, 123, 191; development of, 60

Lanham Act, 96

Larrabee, Eric, 344-345

LEAP. *See* Lower East Side Action Program, N.Y. City

Learning, 53-55, 59-66, 75-77, 83, 99, 102, 106, 116, 123-124, 138, 152, 160, 168, 207, 221, 228, 235 ff, 252, 337; capacity for, 18, 106; early accelerated, 51, 56, 128; evaluation of, 146; first-hand, 5-6, 55, 66, 81; infantile, 60-61, 64, 98; mechanistic concepts of, 70; personal-exploration in, 95; preschool, 55-56, 71, 88-89, 97-98, 110, 123 ff; schedules of accelerated, 181; uniformity in, 181

Leary, Timothy, 243

Leisure, 22, 34-35, 327; increased time for, 264

Leonard, George B., 167-168

Lesbianism, 25

Lincoln Center for the Performing Arts, N.Y. City, 247

Little Rock, Ark., 26

London, England, 296

Look, 167-168

Los Angeles, Calif., 297

Love, 47, 63-66, 83, 88, 119, 124, 277, 291-292, 317, 351-352; parental insistence on, 36

Lower East Side Action Project (LEAP), N.Y. City, 274-276

LSD, 27, 207, 243, 246, 250

McComb, Miss., 203

McGinley, Phyllis, 166

MacKinnon, Donald W., 158

Manhattan Society for Mental Health, 329-330

Marijuana, 11, 25, 213

Marriage, 24-25, 36, 69, 269, 349; early, 288; inter-, 27

Maslow, Abraham, 206, 345

Materialism, 247

Mathematics, 5, 11, 23, 154, 191, 342

Mather, Cotton, 291

Maturation, 89, 95, 99, 195, 223, 237; emotional, 83, 99; sexual, 294; social, 99, 343

Maturity, 30, 53, 66-67, 93, 137, 259, 333

Mead, Margaret, 176

Mechanization, 32-35, 45-48, 63, 69, 70, 292, 295, 347

Melby, Ernest, 164

Menninger Foundation, 107

Mexicans, 100

Michelangelo, 67

Michigan State University, 152, 164, 176, 224

Migration, 35

Millay, Edna St. Vincent, 67, 175

Miller, Arthur, 241-242

Milliken, Henry O., Jr., 91

Mills College, Oakland, Calif., 229
Milton, Ohmer, 167, 177-178
Minnesota Optometric Asso., 108
Minority groups, 100, 322
Mobilization for Youth, N.Y. City, 266
Montaigne, 254
Montessori, Maria, 70-72, 75, 79-84, 87-88
Montessori Method, 70-89
Moore, Omar Khayyam, 50, 104
Morality, 22-23, 26-28, 310, 314; present-day, 309; Puritan, 258; sexual, 219
Motion pictures, 72, 130, 286, 289, 294, 306, 330, 349-351
Motivation, 136, 142, 254, 313; toward communication, 60; for learning, 53-55, 82-83, 227
Mozart, 155
Murphy, Lois, 107
Mussolini, Benito, 82

Nader, Ralph, 297-298
National Broadcasting Co. (NBC), 284
National Commission for a Sane Nuclear Policy (SANE), 312
National Education Asso., 22
National Institute of Mental Health, 117, 143
National Science Foundation, 28, 241
Nazism, 280

NBC. *See* National Broadcasting Co.
Negroes, 26-27, 100-101, 146, 228-229, 261-262, 282, 309, 315-316, 323
Neighborhood Youth Corps, East Harlem, N.Y., 228
Neuroses, 8, 191, 206, 313
New Jersey State Education and Health depts., 143-144
New School Bulletin, The, 220-221
New York City, 34, 91, 251, 266, 275-276, 290, 295-296
New York City Board of Higher Education, 224, 275, 300, 311
New York School for Nursery Years, 91
New York State Education Dept., 193, 261
New York World's Fair (1964-1965), 68
New Yorker, The, 59, 143-144, 181, 202, 204-205, 285-286, 299, 347
Newport (R.I.) Jazz Festival, 317
Newton, Isaac, 55, 155
Nightmares, 120
Nonconformity, 204-205, 340
Norman Foundation, Aaron, 275
Nuclear test-ban treaties, 312, 314
Nuclear weapons, 28
Nursery Education Journal, 157-158

Nurses: pediatric, 3; school, 192

Obedience, 87
OEO. *See* Office of Economic Opportunity, U.S.
Office of Economic Opportunity (OEO), U.S., 267-268, 302
Olson, Willard C., 152-153
Over-protectiveness, parental, 206, 334
Oyle, Irving, 275

Pain, 64, 116
Parent Teacher Asso. (PTA), 151, 193
Parents Magazine, 60, 87-88
Pavlov, 291
Peace, 312; demonstrations, 318
Peace Corps, 204, 223-224, 227, 260, 289-290
Pediatricians, 3
Pediatrics, 45
Pengilly Country School, New Rochelle, N.Y., 109-110
Penicillin, 146
Pennsylvania, 319
Perception, development of sense, 81
Permissiveness, 10-11, 48, 85, 316
Perversion, 289, 294
Pervin, Lawrence A., 208
Piaget, Jean, 71-72
Picasso, Pablo, 154
Pinson, Penelope, 87-88
Pittsburg, Pa., 298

Plato, 55
Play, 6, 88, 95, 105, 110, 118-122, 125-131, 333; child-parent, 130; equipment, 74; imaginative, 78; nursery-school, 96, 112 ff, 128; programs, 76; shared, 116, 133; as therapy, 71, 118, 122, 127
Play Schools Asso., 5-6, 117 fn, 128, 296
Playgrounds, 303
Pollution: air, 32, 43, 279, 295 ff; water, 32, 68, 299
Population explosion, 21, 32, 69, 98, 129, 269, 279, 295, 310
Pornography, 285
Post, N.Y., 26, 101-102, 228-229, 274-276, 284
Potentials, 155; arbitrary notions of, 139; human, 52, 196, 200, 202
Poverty, 71, 99, 100, 228-229, 269, 279, 320; programs for anti-, 98, 200, 228, 256, 267, 301-302
Powell, Adam Clayton, 309
Pratt, Caroline, 71
Pregnancy, unmarried, 25, 213, 288, 293
Pressure, 6-7, 142, 237-238, 253, 256, 305, 307, 349; academic, 26, 90, 97, 135, 143, 151, 169, 195, 243; for accelerated mental development, 100; toward early maturation, 66, 73-74, 78, 89, 104, 109-110, 131, 242; parental, 10, 13-16, 37-39, 48-

Pressure (*continued*)
51, 93, 163; psychological, 315;
toward standardized achievement patterns, 73, 92, 201-202.
See also Colleges, pressures on
entrance to
Princeton University, 208, 229
Programs: academic, 136, 153;
civic, 303; experimental, 272;
recreational, 304; training, 56,
145, 200. *See also* Play programs *and* Poverty programs
for anti-, *and* Reading readiness
Promiscuity, 30
Psychiatrists, 3, 38, 82, 117, 166-
167, 179, 212, 313, 315
Psychiatry, 4, 67, 94, 96, 118-
119, 160, 276, 341; research in,
71, 120, 128; revolution in, 36
Psychoanalysis, 71, 341
Psychologists, 3, 18, 45, 50, 56,
80, 95, 97, 104 ff, 117, 128, 159,
170, 179-180, 183 ff, 192, 195,
208, 241-242, 301, 306-307,
329-330
Psychology, 30, 41, 71, 94-95,
109, 128, 132, 160, 184, 273,
341 ff
Psychotherapists, 293
Psychotherapy, 67, 118-119, 172,
214, 347
PTA. *See* Parent Teacher Asso.
PTA Magazine, The, 144
Public School 119, Harlem,
N.Y. City, 299
Puerto Ricans, 100, 229, 274, 321

Radio, 4, 17, 72, 130, 146-147,
279
Rambusch, Nancy McCormick,
79-81
Rand, Lester, 306
Reading, 14, 104, 164; age-group,
108-109; difficulties, 159; early-
age, 14, 30, 49-52, 55, 58, 62,
65, 67, 80, 87, 107-108, 122,
150; learning speed in, 60, 62,
100
Redbook, 60, 265-267, 325, 348
Redl, Fritz, 278
Remsberg, Bonnie, 306
Remsberg, Charles, 306
Report cards, 176, 178
Repression, 78, 124
Research: child development,
95, 109, 118; laboratories, 242;
scientific, 150, 219. *See also*
Psychiatry, research in
Riessman, Frank, 156-157, 172
Rio de Janeiro, 296
Rioting, 303-304; race, 300
Rochester, N.Y., 300
Rockefeller, Nelson, 282-283
Rome, Italy, 71
Roosevelt, Franklin D., 201
Rousseau, Jean Jacques, 106,
326
Rugg, Harold, 71
Rutgers University, 50, 104

Salley, Ruth E., 224
SANE. *See* National Commission for a Sane Nuclear Policy

Sarah Lawrence College, Bronx-
    ville, N.Y., 166
Sarnoff, David, 284
Saturday Review, 85, 219, 241-
    242
Schools, 98, 195; college-prepar-
    atory, 21; crowded, 98; ele-
    mentary, 30, 90, 97, 134, 138,
    143-144, 164, 271; experimen-
    tal, 20-21, 28; graduate, 137,
    150, 158, 167-168, 221, 234,
    270; high, 25-28, 90, 134, 137-
    138, 153, 199, 230, 243, 258;
    kindergarten, 6, 15, 52, 92,
    103, 108-109, 143, 185, 189 ff;
    Montessori, 70, 73-76, 79-81,
    84-88, 93, 122; nursery, 38, 70,
    74-79, 82 ff, 90-117, 122, 128,
    131, 134, 150, 185 ff, 200, 223,
    267; private, 21, 91, 96; public,
    20-21, 97; suburban, 3; sum-
    mer, 161
Science, 5, 11, 16, 18, 23-25, 28 ff,
    36, 45, 69, 221, 240 ff, 272-273,
    294, 325, 341, 345; progress in,
    55, 73, 103-104, 146 ff, 219;
    revolution in, 18, 97, 280; so-
    cial, 104, 272, 293
Scientists, 55, 240, 252-255, 292-
    294
Seeley, John R., 268-269
Selective service, 318
Self-care, 22, 83
Self-control, 88, 133
Self-discipline, 26, 134, 239, 254
Self-expression, 85, 95, 133

Self-fulfillment, 84, 95, 99, 344-
    345
Self-knowledge, 26, 29, 78, 90,
    94, 102, 116, 127, 134, 269, 335,
    339, 349, 352-353
Sendak, Maurice, 347
Sex, 269, 287-291, 293- 295; edu-
    cation, 293; experimentation,
    288; intercourse in, 291 ff;
    orgies, 4; techniques, 291
Sex Information and Education
    Council, 288
Shankman Orthogenic School,
    Sonia, 333
Shapiro, Elliott, 299-300
Shaw, George Bernard, 338-339
Shepard, Martin, 275-276
Shuster, George N., 104
Shyness, 112, 179
Skinner, B. F., 45-46
Smith, Nila Banton, 109
Social workers, 3, 148, 179, 210,
    240, 267, 301, 319
Sociology, 24-25, 83, 191, 269,
    293
Socrates, 220, 250-251
Sophocles, 248
Space, 112, 115; age, 103, 250;
    research, 24, 240-241; travel,
    72, 148, 240, 304
Specialization, age of, 147, 256-
    257
Speech: as communication, 59;
    development, 44; learning of,
    59-62; problems, 187-188
Spock, Benjamin, 312
Standardization, 170, 198, 344

Stanford University, 217

Status seeking, 29, 37, 263

Stealing, 4, 28

Stevenson, Adlai, 154

Students: disadvantaged, 97, 99; gifted, 30, 56-57, 148, 171, 185, 239; late-starter, 153; mentally retarded, 169, 171; retarded, 155; slow, 153, 157, 185, 187

Suchman, J. Richard, 253-254

Suicide, 213; child, 4

Tape recorders, 4, 10

Taylor, Anne, 348

Taylor, Harold, 166

Teachers, 3, 8, 17, 20-21, 75-76, 84, 88, 98-99, 132-133, 138, 145, 150, 168, 176, 194, 219, 232 ff, 250, 254, 262, 269-271, 298 ff, 310-311; certification of, 97, 223; Montessori, 73, 76, 84-85; nursery school, 95, 97; special service, 262; strikes of, 311; training of, 144-145, 150, 337; volunteer, 161-162

Teachers College, Columbia University, 22, 103

Teaching, 8, 23, 26, 83, 149, 168, 235, 267, 271-272, 337-338; experimentation in, 272; lecture-method in, 168; machines, 14, 17-18, 25-26, 29, 68, 69, 138, 141, 145, 244, 274, 342; teams, 30, 138, 144-145; television, 5, 221

Technocracy, 40

Technology, 16-18, 24-25, 29-32, 34, 45, 47, 52, 68, 69, 97, 103, 128, 149, 184, 193, 219, 221, 248-250, 274, 297, 326, 342

Teen-agers, 10, 34, 260, 268, 290, 294, 306-308, 334

Television, 4, 10, 17, 72, 126, 130, 140, 146-147, 231, 242, 279, 284 ff, 304, 305, 309, 323. See also Teaching, television

Tension, 4, 15-16, 93, 159

Tests, 5, 138-140, 166-196, 192 ff, 200, 234, 250, 262, 274, 337; achievement, 138, 174; aptitude, 138, 174; Binet, 169; group intelligence, 173-174; multiple-choice, 167; personality assessment, 174-175; psychological, 92, 275; Rorschach Ink Blot, 175; Simon, 169. See also I.Q.'s

Therapists, 195

Therapy, group, 222

Thompson, Inc., Francis, 68

Times, The N.Y., 14-15, 27, 31, 50, 79-80, 91, 103-104, 145-146, 176, 224-225, 253-254, 306-307

Today's Child, 17-18, 87, 108-109, 288-289

Toilet training, 47-48, 51, 59

Tokyo, Japan, 296

Tolchin, Martin, 15

Torrance, E. Paul, 158

Toys, 4, 10, 65, 124; age-group, 105; lethal-weapon, 285-286; Montessori, 71, 87

Tranquilizers, 15, 143

Truancy, 25, 181, 268, 275-276
Tuchman, Barbara, 31
Tutors: special, 11, 161, 266;
   volunteer, 231, 265

U.S. Army, 199
U.S. Constitution, 309
U.S. Military Academy, West
   Point, N.Y., 308-309
University of California, 15, 108,
   157, 205, 219-220
University of Chicago, 240-242,
   333
University of Illinois, 253
University of Iowa. *See* Iowa,
   State University of
University of Maryland, 5, 220
University of Tennessee, 167,
   177
University of Virginia, 236
Urbanization, 32, 98, 295-296,
   299, 301, 303
Ustinov, Peter, 156
U-2 incident, 308

Vandalism, 316
Veatch, Jeanette, 17-18
Vietnamese War, 300, 312
Violence, 25, 120, 284-286, 299,
   304
VISTA. *See* Volunteers in Serv-
   ice to America
Vocabulary, 65, 104
Vocational planning, 30
Vocational training, 5, 199-200,
   226

Volunteers in Service to America (VISTA), 204, 227, 260

Wakin, Edward, 85
Wann, Kenneth D., 103
War, 9, 31, 72, 281, 285, 311
Ward, Barbara, 295-296, 303-
   304
Watson, John B., 47
Wechsler, James A., 274-276
Werner, Emmy E., 157-158
West Point. *See* U.S. Military
   Academy
Wheelis, Allen, 38-39
Wheelock College, Boston,
   Mass., 87
Whitby School, Conn., 79
White House Conference on
   Children (1960), 344
Wirtz, Willard, 198-199
Woman's Day, 183
World War, First, 30-31, 72, 79
World War, Second, 30-31, 71,
   72, 96, 218, 221, 227, 280, 298
Writing, 14, 67, 104, 164; diffi-
   culties, 159; learning speed in,
   88, 100; pre-school, 53, 87

Yale University, 58, 90, 176
York University, Toronto,
   Canada, 269
Youth Research Institute, N.Y.
   City, 306

Zike, Kenneth, 108
Zinsser, William K., 247

EDA J. LESHAN

A New Yorker by birth, Eda J. LeShan received her Bachelor's degree in Early Childhood Education from Teacher's College at Columbia University and a Master's degree in Child Psychology from Clark University. She has worked closely with children as a nursery-school teacher and director, a child welfare worker, and a diagnostician and play therapist in child-guidance clinics. She has also worked with parents as a Parent Educator at the Association for Family Living in Chicago, the Great Neck (N.Y.) Department of Adult Education and the United Parents' Association. In 1956 she was appointed Director of Mental Health Education for the Guidance Center of New Rochelle, N. Y., and, 1961, to the Manhattan Society for Mental Health. Mrs. LeShan's articles appear frequently in *Redbook*, *The New York Times Magazine*, *Parents' Magazine* and *P.T.A. Magazine*. She is the author of *How to Survive Parenthood* (1965), *The Only Child* (1960) and *You and Your Adopted Child* (1958). Currently a parent consultant at the Pengilly School in New Rochelle, Mrs. LeShan lives in New York City with her husband and teen-age daughter.